ADVENTURES WITH AUTHORS

ADVENTURES
WITH
AUTHORS

BY THE LATE
S.C.ROBERTS

CAMBRIDGE
AT THE UNIVERSITY PRESS
1966

Published by the Syndics of the Cambridge University Press
Bentley House, 200 Euston Road, London, N.W. 1
American Branch: 32 East 57th Street, New York, N.Y. 10022

Printed in Great Britain
at the University Printing House, Cambridge
(Brooke Crutchley, University Printer)

To

G.V.C.

*In memory of old times
and in gratitude for the
Index*

CONTENTS

I

Chapter 1

UNDERGRADUATE

It began with Andrew Lang. From him came the first authentic thrill, the thrill experienced by those who, for better or for worse, derive their principal pleasures from books and bookish men.

Adventures among Books was published in the spring of 1905, just at the time when I had finally decided to range myself on the classical side and to toy no longer with the higher mathematics. In January I had got as far as being a candidate for a mathematical scholarship at Corpus, but one term's concentration on mathematical work had shown very clearly my failure to advance beyond the elementary stages. As my form-master truly said, what I was doing was not mathematics, but just 'algebraical substitution'.

Homer was not the least of the attractions of classical reading and of course we had to learn something about Homeric criticism. In *Adventures among Books* I came upon an essay entitled 'The Paradise of Poets':

At their feet I beheld, in a vast and gloomy hall, many an honest critic, many an erudite commentator, an army of reviewers. Some were condemned to roll logs up insuperable heights, whence they descended thundering to the plain. Others were set to impositions, and I particularly observed that the Homeric commentato s were obliged to write out the *Iliad* and *Odyssey* in their complete shape and were always driven by fiends to the task when they prayed for the bare charity of being permitted to leave out the 'interpolations'.

As editor of the *Brighton College Magazine*, I had to produce some kind of 'middle' article for the summer term issue and Lang's essay gave me an idea. This I embodied in a short piece to which I gave the title 'Heat and Homer'. The setting was different, but the theme was similar. Drawing a bow at a venture,

Undergraduate

I addressed a copy of the *Magazine* to Andrew Lang. I didn't dare to hope for a reply and none came. But towards the end of October I received something more than an acknowledgement:

Thanks for your interesting magazine...As to Homer, I do not know whether you possess my 'Homer and the Epic' which is certainly a whole hogger and I shall be pleased to send it if you do not.

The critics, except Monro, are neither sportsmen, nor capable of literature, nor familiar with other early national poetry, nor anthropologists, nor clearly consistent. It is as easy to prove by their discrepancies that there are several distinct Jebbs and Leafs as that there are several Homers.

For me it was tremendous. Here was Andrew Lang, not patronising my crude little schoolboy effort, but writing as one man of letters to another. And the next day he was writing again:

I have asked Messrs Longmans to send you the book on Homer. I gather that your sympathies are not with the disintegrators. Mine never were, since Jowett made me read Wolf, who clearly knew nothing about the early use of writing. I once lectured at Bradfield on Homer and the ground man said freely that he would rather hear my ideas on bowling. If you are going to Oxford, I have still two or three friends there, whose acquaintance I shall be happy to introduce you to, if you care for it.

In reply, I explained that I was destined for Cambridge, but I cannot have written convincingly:

I think Oxford [the next letter began] is the likelier place for you. Literaryness goes a long way there...I should think my old college, Merton (of which I was a *socius*) is an easy place to get a scholarship at, and a beautiful old place to live in. If you take a shot at it, please let me know. My own college was Balliol and 'exhibitions' were to be got by agreeable journalistic effusions, without much philology. But perhaps now things are different...

When I wrote in December to tell him that I had been awarded an exhibition at Pembroke, I received a prompt message of congratulation—and advice:

I am much pleased to hear of your success, and hope it is the first wicket down of a lot. The antique beauties of Merton are its attraction.

I hope Pembroke has not been rebuilt by Waterhouse...I have only one word of advice, but that is of gold. Keep all your receipts of tradesmen's bills.

I never met Andrew Lang, but I corresponded with him, at intervals, up to the time of his death in 1912. I always enjoyed his casual commentary on cricket or dons or archaeology or literature in general. When, in my first year, I sent him some trivial verses he wrote: 'Why are all the poets Cambridge men except Shelley and me?' and added in a postscript: 'Cambridge Third Eleven could beat Oxford.'*

The reason for my choice of Pembroke was simple enough. Having no Cambridge connections, I consulted my house-master (a Clare man). He suggested Pembroke as my first choice and I took his advice. Had I known anything about the reputations of Cambridge colleges at that time, I might have demurred. For, to the world outside, Pembroke was primarily famous for its supremacy in games. I was keen enough on games, especially on cricket, but had no talent for playing them and at school I was frequently depressed by my incompetence. At Pembroke any such feeling vanished overnight.

Years later, someone questioned me about my time at Pembroke as an undergraduate. As I was no good at games, I must, he thought, have been very miserable. I assured him that his inference was ridiculous and his sympathy misplaced. No one thought the worse of me because I did not qualify for the Hawks Club. Certainly there were many distinguished athletes in the college and to them came a greater measure of publicity than to the scholars. The Pass Degree was then a substantial fact of academic life and of the eighty-odd freshmen of my year just under half were Pass men. Of the forty-five Honours men, fourteen gained first classes in their triposes.

For myself, I was a very callow and a very happy freshman. I studied *The Fresher's Don't* (a small brochure which explained

---

* Cambridge won in 1907, but not so easily as Lang expected. Oxford, after leading by 33 runs on the first innings, were beaten by 5 wickets.

what was and what was not 'done' in the University) and I bought my 'Fresher's Delights' (college and university arms) to hang over the mantelpiece. I had a cosy set of attic rooms in Old Court over the front gate of the College. There was no gas or electric light, but an oil lamp, when properly trimmed, served me very well. There were no bathrooms, but under my bed was a saucer bath which my bedmaker obligingly filled with warm water every morning. I shared to the full Samuel Butler's feeling: 'How can any boy fail to feel an ecstasy of pleasure on first finding himself in rooms which he knows for the next few years are to be his castle?' In short, I was quite unashamedly conventional. I knew little about Cambridge and most of what I knew came from books. One that I had recently read was A. C. Benson's *From a College Window* and one paragraph in it had caught my attention:

I wish that...throngs of young men would feel impelled to come in and talk to me easily and simply...In vain do I purchase choice brands of cigars and cigarettes and load my side-table with the best Scotch whisky. Not even with that solace will the vagrant under-graduate consent to be douched under the stream of my suggestive conversation.

For a moment I wondered whether to submit to the douche myself, but saner counsels prevailed and, instead, I attended a course of four open lectures on 'The Development of English Prose' which Benson gave at Magdalene in my first term. It was a series of thumb-nail sketches of prose-writers from Wyclif to the nineteenth century. From my notes I see that in one of his rare asides Benson ventured the remark that 'the recently inaugurated British Academy studies everything but litera-ture'. But what really pleased me was the *mise en scène*—the candle-lit hall; the massive figure of the lecturer in his high-backed chair; the soft, persuasive, slightly breathless pronounce-ments on the great figures of English literature. It all accorded with my romantic notions of college life and college dignitaries.

The same was true of the Master of my own college, Arthur

James Mason. He was a canon of Canterbury and seemed to me to look exactly as a Master ought to look. He was not tall, but he had immense dignity. His courtesy was punctilious and he always raised his hat when you passed him walking through one of the college courts. He gave breakfast parties to undergraduates and the fact that their duration (8.10 to 8.45) was clearly stated on the card of invitation sprang from his belief that every young man should be at work by 9 o'clock. He had married late and his wife (granddaughter of Edward Blore, architect of the Pitt Press) charmed us all. In his earlier days Mason had won a great reputation as scholar and preacher. He had a strong, resonant voice and preserved the short 'a' with tremendous effect. In one of his earliest sermons in chapel he had told his hearers that he desired to be their 'păstor' rather than their 'măster' and I well remember that at the end of one Easter Term he adumbrated his notion of the ideal Pembroke man: 'I would not have you, my sons, be mere scholastic pedants, nor yet languid dilettanti, nor even burly, but senseless athletes.'

The teaching of classics was almost entirely on a college, or intercollegiate, basis. As freshmen we went to Henry Jackson's introductory course on Greek philosophy and occasionally sat under H. J. Edwards at Peterhouse or W. H. S. Jones at St Catharine's. But it was on our own three classical dons that we relied.

W. S. Hadley, who was Tutor of the college, was a good lecturer. As he went through a play of Euripides, he would interpret certain passages with translations which were as elegant as they were faithful. He entertained parties of undergraduates at most agreeable dinners in his house on the Barton Road and always gave the impression of being at leisure. In fact, he was an extremely hard worker.

J. C. Lawson was a puzzling character. His conversation was completely matter-of-fact and did not tempt one to intimacy. There was little sparkle in his lectures until an opportunity came for him to relate the religious beliefs of ancient Greece to those of

5

the Greek islands of today. Such an occasion arose in my first term when he lectured on the *Eumenides*, the play chosen for performance in that year. Lawson lived for some years in the notoriously haunted Abbey House off the Newmarket Road and could occasionally be induced to talk about it. He would tell you about the ghostly nun who tramped along the passage and through his bedroom as if he were telling you about the man who came to inspect the gas-meter.

Leonard Whibley was my tutor as well as my teacher. At first I was rather afraid of him. He pounced upon my mistakes in syntax and ruthlessly deleted the purple patches in my essays. But, as will appear later, I owe more to him than I can properly express.

To an ingenuous freshman, the senior college servants are, or used to be, at least as impressive as the dons. In my rooms over the front gate I was very near to Stoakley, the head porter, and in my first year was much in awe of him. With his grey side-whiskers and his steely look, he seemed a more formidable arbiter of behaviour than any tutor. He could remember the college as a much smaller society and I suspect that he did not wholly approve of its expansion; but he was, of course, intensely loyal to Pembroke and correspondingly scornful of the habits of neighbouring foundations. He died before I had reached the stage of easy gossip with him, but a story which I heard many years later is a good illustration of his Olympian outlook. Comber, a Fellow of the college of whom I shall have more to say, was chatting to Stoakley on the day following a Foundress' Feast.

'Well,' he said, 'it was nice to see some old friends last night.'

'Yes,' said Stoakley, 'and do you know, sir, that as Mr — [naming an impecunious country vicar] was leaving, he put half-a-crown into my hand. Well, you know, sir, half-a-crown to him is like a sovereign to you or me.'

But there was nothing remote or formidable about the manager of the kitchen and buttery—Arthur Chapman. 'Chappie', as he was known to many generations of Pembroke men, was the supreme extravert. His father had been college baker and the college was the centre of his life. He had a twinkling eye and a rich 'Cambridge-Cockney' accent. From his room in the buttery, he controlled his staff and directed the feeding of the college. At any time he might be interrupted by an old member of the college with whom, over a glass of sherry or a tankard of beer, he would recall incidents and escapades of years ago. In the evening he would don his frock-coat and supervise the service of dinner in hall, ready always to explain college customs to freshmen or to exchange jokes with the seniors. Nothing pleased him better than to help an undergraduate who was planning a little dinner-party:

'Got ladies comin'? Well, I should start with a white soup.'

'What sort of soup?'

'Why not have a crème d'orge à la Frankfort?'

After some explanation of the soup's constituents, one passed on to later courses—to 'noisette Monica', also explained in detail, and to a choice of savouries, on one of which, I remember, 'you split your olive and have your pimento showin''. It was all very graphic and instructive.

But to return to academic instruction, the old Classical Tripos, Part I, was a degree course and we had no university examination to face until the end of our third year. In the years between we had intercollegiate examinations ('Mays') which had no official significance in the university, but could lead to variations in scholarship awards. There was one institution in Pembroke which made one feel as if one were back at school: every Saturday morning, from 8.30 to 10.0, all classical men were required to do a paper of unseen translation in the Old Library. For many it was followed, rather than preceded, by breakfast.

There were four classical freshmen of my year with whom I gradually became intimate: E. W. Mead, who, after some years spent in the Chinese Consular Service, returned to a Readership in the University of Manchester and died prematurely in 1941; F. A. Wallis (brother of my first wife), who also served as a consul

7

in China; P. R. (afterwards Sir Patrick) Laird, who became Secretary of Agriculture for Scotland; and B. C. Roberts, afterwards Bishop of Singapore and general secretary of the S.P.G., who died suddenly in 1957. 'B. C.' was not related to me, but it was natural that each of us should be known by his initials. Until recently, indeed, there were many old friends in Cambridge who were quite ignorant of my Christian names.

Another good friend of my own year at Pembroke was Geoffrey Keynes, son of Dr J. N. Keynes (Registrary of the University) and younger brother of Maynard. One of the earliest Sunday lunches that I remember was at 6 Harvey Road, a house which I was destined to know for nearly fifty years. Unlike me, Geoffrey naturally had a wide knowledge of Cambridge and was in close touch with the intelligentsia of Trinity and King's. I suppose that, if I had known more, I should have joined some university societies—the Union and, perhaps, the A.D.C. As it was, the college sufficed for me, both in work and play. I had barely risen to 2nd XI standards at school, so when the captain of the boat club came up to my rooms and suggested, with some firmness, that I should row, I obediently agreed. Being at that time a light weight, I was made a cox and had a lucky first year, steering the third boat to four bumps in the Lents and the second boat to two bumps in the Mays—not a particularly notable record, but it led to a surprising sequel many years later.

On the first Saturday of the Michaelmas Term all freshmen were invited to attend a meeting of the college debating society (P.C.D.S.). The President, wearing evening dress with a Pembroke ribbon across his shirt-front, was preceded by a mace-bearer, known as the Additional Member, and followed by the other officers of the society. After the reading of the minutes, a senior member called the attention of the President to the presence of strangers in the house. The President thanked him and instructed the Additional Member to eject the said strangers. The Additional Member having encountered some opposition, the President called upon the whole house to assist. After a few

8

minutes of turbulence the last freshman was expelled and the door slammed. Thereupon, having recovered his breath, some old hand proposed that the gentlemen of the first year be elected *en bloc* to the society; the freshmen were recalled by the Additional Member and the senior scholar returned thanks. The senior bachelor in college was J. K. Mozley. He was an ex-President of the Union as well as of the P.C.D.S. and I thought he was the finest speaker I had ever heard. A passionate Liberal, he had a natural gift of rhetoric, but it was not empty rhetoric; the thread of the argument was never broken.

A smaller discussion society in Pembroke was 'The Martlets', to which I was elected in my second term. At the end of the term Hilaire Belloc came to address the 'distinguished stranger's' meeting. I listened intently to his paper entitled 'The Writing of History' or something of the kind; but what I remember most vividly was the generous measure of beer that was brought in for his refreshment.

But not all our evenings were spent in debates and discussions. Early novels about Cambridge life frequently refer to billiard saloons in Chesterton as one of the more sinister influences to which undergraduates were exposed. But we did not have to go so far as Chesterton. In Mill Lane, on part of the site of the present lecture-rooms, John Porter kept two billiard-tables. He was a charming character—very polite, but very firm in his maintenance of good behaviour and decent language. He charged by the hour, but left the time-keeping to his wife. 'Mrs Porter,' he would call out at the end of the game, 'how long have the gentlemen been?' John was a true fenlander. Aeroplanes at that time were, of course, a novelty. 'Ever been up in an aeroplane, John?' asked B. C. Roberts one evening. 'Oh, no, sir. As a matter of fact, if I go up to the top of Madingley Hill, I feel a bit queer, sir.' Mill Lane was temptingly near and we went as much for the fun of gossiping with John as for the pleasure of a hundred up.

At the end of my first year B. C. and I were urged to come up for the Long Vacation and were advised to read with W. T.

Lendrum (afterwards Vesey) of Caius. Lendrum was an Irishman, a fine scholar and a notable horseman who hunted with the Cottesmore. His dapper figure was in marked contrast to that of the normal don and he received us with old-fashioned formality. 'What do you wish to read, gentlemen?' he asked. Eventually we decided upon a book of Thucydides, but I think it was his choice rather than ours.

Lendrum's scholarship was exacting and the notes he dictated were detailed and precise. 'Ah, well, take a little note upon it. The Athenians (A, T, H, full stop)...Stop a minute, Mr B. Roberts. Mr S. Roberts hasn't got it down, he hasn't got it down.' Altogether, Mr S. Roberts, whose interests were literary rather than syntactical, did not appear to advantage under Lendrum's instruction.

Cambridge in August can be very sultry and I did not enjoy it, but the one pleasant feature of coming up for the Long was that one got to know some of the senior men in college—Geoffrey Clayton, for instance, who was destined to be archbishop of Cape Town and A. A. Seaton, later a Fellow of the college, who was killed in France in 1915.

In the following year Edgar Mead, 'Pug' Laird, B. C. and I decided to organise our own vacation reading. We found a lonely farm-house south of Bude and contrived to do a good deal of work. One of our few distractions was a meet of the local otter-hounds. We did not see an otter, but every time we emerged from the streams on to the main road, the local brewer, with whom we had made friends, was there with a barrel of beer in his pony-cart. It was a day of blazing sunshine and I don't think I have ever drunk so much beer in a single day.

From my second term onwards I was a fairly regular contributor to *The Granta* (then a kind of undergraduate *Punch*) and a few of my light verses were embalmed in F. A. Rice's *The Book of the Granta* (1924). My first editor was C. E. Raven, whom I afterwards knew well, but I do not think we met as undergraduates. He was succeeded by Raglan Somerset ('the heavy villain from Queens''), whom I used frequently to meet in Mozley's rooms in Pembroke. Mozley was elected to a fellowship in the course of my first year and on Saturday nights, after meetings of the P.C.D.S., we frequently went up to his rooms over the cloister and talked until the small hours—politics, theology, college gossip, Yorkshire cricket. He was the first don with whom I felt able to talk on level terms, though not until years later did I call him by his Christian name. Raglan Somerset and Kenneth Mozley were close friends. They both loved argument and shared some curious tastes. Once they astonished us by bicycling back to Cambridge after an evening in London and a late supper at Pinoli's.

A later editor of *The Granta* was Harold Wright. Always delicate, he came up to Pembroke at the age of twenty-five. Fatherly and persuasive, he had a deep sense of fun which humanised his political and economic theories and made him equally suitable for the presidency of the Union and the editor-ship of *The Granta*. I wrote a good deal for him and occasionally he made me his dramatic critic. The Greek play in 1909 was *The Wasps* on which I wrote some verses commemorating Dennis Robertson as Philocleon, Jim Butler as Bdelycleon, and Miles Malleson as Sosias. I suppose this was one of Malleson's very early appearances on the stage—but not his earliest. He and I played together in *The Cyclops* at Brighton College in 1903.

In my second year I was made a junior officer of the P.C.D.S. and later succeeded F. P. (afterwards Sir Percival) Robinson as President. Normally, our debates were not of high quality, but they were preceded by three-quarters of an hour of 'private business', most of which was devoted to baiting the President—a most valuable education in chairmanship. Once a year we had a visitor's evening, when well-known Union speakers like Arnold McNair, Norman Birkett, Jim Butler and his cousin Geoffrey appreciably raised the standard of debate. On one such evening I had an anxious moment. Geoffrey Butler, speaking very fluently, suddenly stopped. There was a dead silence and, thinking the speaker might be ill, I hastily reached for a glass of water. Then, to my relief, Geoffrey went on quite easily with his speech. Afterwards I asked someone what had been the matter. 'Oh, don't you know?' was the reply, 'Geoffrey always learns his speeches by heart. He'd just forgotten his lines for the moment.'

The distinguished visitor to the Martlets in my second year was H. G. Wells. Geoffrey Keynes had become President and myself Secretary and we were both invited to the lunch which Whibley gave for the visitor. The other guests were Arthur Hutchinson and A. E. Shipley, to whom Whibley remarked that for a scientist he was a very human fellow. Wells's paper (on Socialism) was rather disappointing. It was the period of *A Modern Utopia*, but his talk lacked the spark and stimulus of his writing.

About the same time I was busy as editor of *The Pem*, a typical college magazine of the lighter sort. At times its scurrility had endangered its continuance, but in 1908 it was a medium of mild satire on the habits of dons and undergraduates. It was a slight affair, but it taught me two things: first, that an editor must be prepared to fill gaps with compositions of his own; secondly, that the financial stability of any magazine depends upon its advertisement revenue. My co-editor was Edgar Mead and, between us, we persuaded neighbouring tradesmen into advertisements which paid for the cost of printing.

Fortified by a memorable dinner given by Whibley to his pupils, we took the Classical Tripos in 1909 and were then free to indulge in any May Week festivities that we might choose. The May Races presented a spectacle very different from that of today. There were two races only—the first division at 4.30 and the second at 5.30. College supporters thronged the tow-path, but the proper course for a party of visitors to follow was to embark in a boat or punt at Silver Street about 2.30, paddle gently down to Ditton Corner or just short of it, moor the boat, and unload the spirit-stove and other concomitants of a picnic tea. After the first race, the younger members of the party made a perilous voyage by 'grind' to the fair on the opposite bank. After the second race, boats and punts pushed out simultaneously and frequently formed a solid jam from bank to bank. The long journey home was enlivened by the traditional practice of rudder-snatching. There were, perhaps, a few motor-cars in Ditton paddock—but they were regarded as an alien feature, justified only by the age or infirmity of their occupants.

After the college ball in the following week I went to stay with 'B. C.' at his father's rectory in the tiny village of Gosbeck in Suffolk. While we were there, the village postmistress came to the rectory with a telegram—we both had firsts in the Tripos, though rather humble ones. We received our degrees from our own Master, who was Vice-Chancellor 1908-10, and it may be worth noting that there were then three degree congregations— one for ordinary degrees; one for first classes in the Tripos; and one for seconds and thirds in the Tripos. University regulations prescribed dark clothes for the ceremony and one Pembroke man, F. P. Robinson, went to the Praelector (J. C. Lawson) and explained that he had no dark clothes except his evening dress suit. 'Well, wear that', said Lawson, 'and tell your friends to do the same.' So the Pembroke graduands of 1909, or most of them, appeared in the Senate House in evening dress and very soon the other colleges literally followed suit.

1909 was the year of the centenary celebrations of the birth of Charles Darwin and, on the day following the last degree congregation, the Vice-Chancellor presided at a dinner to the many delegates. The dinner was followed by a garden-party in Pembroke to which Mason, with characteristic thoughtfulness, invited the newly made Bachelors of Arts. Distinguished guests from all over the world trooped into the garden and I recall the tall sombre figure of A. J. Balfour surrounded by the brilliant medley of foreign academical robes. About midnight at the college gate a famous Pembroke figure of the past, the Rev E. J. Heriz-Smith, was reciting part of Calverley's *ABC* ('A is an Angel of blushing eighteen, B is the Ball where the Angel was seen...') for the benefit of a party of ladies whose cab was late in arriving.

During my last year at school my form-master asked me what I intended to do after I had come down from Cambridge. 'I don't know, sir', I replied. 'Then', he said, 'I can tell you what you will do. You will become a schoolmaster.' Up to a point, he turned out to be right. My father talked a lot about the civil service, but I wasn't enthusiastic. What I wanted more than anything was to stay in Cambridge. I knew that there was no chance of a fellowship, but at least I had a good case for a fourth year. I was quite happy in the prospect of schoolmastering and, if it came to that, it was obviously an advantage to be able to teach something besides Greek and Latin. So I decided to read for Part II of the History Tripos.

I enjoyed my fourth year enormously. About twenty B.A.s, including several of my best friends, came up and Edgar Mead and I were neighbours in Little St Mary's Lane. There was no room for us in Hall, so we had a dinner of slightly better quality in the Old Library. In contrast to the conditions of today, it is worth noting that very few, if any, of us were engaged in 're-search'. Most of us were taking a second part of a tripos or preparing for some other examination. Only one, I think, had his eye upon a fellowship. I got to know more people both in Pembroke and other colleges. In particular, I saw more of F. W. Thompson. He was a year senior to me in Pembroke and in later years, when he became librarian at Chatsworth, his friendship meant a great deal to me.

I also decided, after all, to join the Union. It was the year in which Theodore Roosevelt, after receiving an honorary degree from the University, was also made an honorary member of the Union. Norman Birkett, as Vice-President, proposed the election with the felicity for which he afterwards became famous. Refer-ring to Roosevelt's passion for big-game hunting, he expressed a fear that the lion which figured in the heraldry of his own college might be in some danger. I had made a maiden speech in the

Michaelmas Term and at the end of the May Term Geoffrey Butler was good enough to ask me to speak 'on the paper' at the retiring president's debate.

In college I gradually saw a little more of the dons with whom I was not directly concerned in my work. E. H. Minns, librarian of the college, learned in Slavonic, palaeographic and many other departments of scholarship, was always friendly except on one occasion when he severely, and rightly, admonished me for temporarily removing a standard work from the library. I also had occasional meetings with E. G. Browne, the famous Persian scholar. Unfortunately for me, he had married just before I came up and so I missed the famous evenings in his rooms which older Pembroke men have commemorated. But he was still interested in the Martlets and willing to advise about distinguished visitors. 'You might ask So-and-so,' he would say, 'he's in Parliament, but he's not a bad fellow. I ran into him the other day in the lobby of the House of Commons. "What are you doing here?" he asked. "Intriguing, of course," I replied, "trying to put some sense into that man Edward Grey about Russia."'

I also heard Browne speak at the inaugural meeting of a university society, the Heretics, to which I had been invited as a guest by F. C. Thompson, a classical scholar of Trinity and an old schoolfellow. He was, I think, the first secretary of the society, but the real founder of it was C. K. Ogden. There were several distinguished speakers at the first meeting, among them Browne and McTaggart, the Trinity philosopher. The subject was eugenics, against which Browne declaimed with characteristic fluency; McTaggart at one point protesting: 'Oh, you can base anything upon anything, if you're only illogical enough.'

Those of us who were reading history in Pembroke were under the care of Hadley. By modern standards of faculty organisation, he might have been regarded as an amateur, since he had taken nothing but the Classical Tripos and had not written any substantial books; but he was a fine teacher and widely read, especially in the Napoleonic period. Outside the college two courses were stimulating: J. R. Tanner's lectures on constitutional history were enjoyable, primarily because he clearly enjoyed them himself and there was always spice in his description of Tudor and Stuart politics. It was as though Thomas Fuller had suddenly been fortified by accurate scholarship. The other was Lowes Dickinson's course on political theory. I had been fascinated by *A Modern Symposium* and looked forward eagerly to sitting under its author. In some degree I was disappointed. The lectures had little of literary grace or charm. They were not, of course, meant to be literary exercises; they were meant to stimulate thought and argument about the theory and practice of politics—and they succeeded. At the beginning Dickinson assured us that he was concerned simply to expound theories and not to applaud or condemn them; but his sympathies and antipathies were soon apparent. I did a few essays for him, but I never knew him well. In fact I do not think I met him again until I arranged for the publication of his Memoir of McTaggart in 1931.

I also wrote some essays when I attended a revision course under the auspices of H. M. Gwatkin. Gwatkin was a man to whom a narrow specialisation could not be imputed. As a background to his Chair of Ecclesiastical History, he had taken firsts in Mathematics, Classics, Moral Sciences and Theology; he was also an acknowledged authority on the *radulae* (tongues) of snails. He was deaf and very short-sighted and a defective palate caused him to make a whistling sound whenever he pronounced a sibilant. At first, he was a bit difficult to follow; but when one got used to his extraordinary delivery it was a delight to listen to him. 'Now then,' he would begin, 'before a man attempt to answer an examination paper, it is above all things necessary that he first read the questions'—a warning which was not so otiose as it sounded.

I got my first in History, Part II, and like to think that it was of better quality than my I.3 in Classics. But at that time the History classes were not divided and I shall never know. So my fourth year, valuable as well as enjoyable, came to an end.

Undergraduate

Fifty years ago young men with literary tastes wanted to be journalists; today they all want to be publishers or B.B.C. producers. Certainly I hankered after Fleet Street, and W. L. E. Parsons, with whom I stayed more than once at the College Mission in Walworth, gave me an introduction to a Pembroke contemporary of his—J. B. Atkins. Jack Atkins was at that time assistant editor of *The Spectator* and I called upon him at the old office of the paper in Wellington Street. I thought then, and often thought afterwards, that he was the best-looking and the best-hearted man I had ever met. He was immediately sympathetic and gave me what encouragement he could. It was the beginning of a friendship which endured until his death in 1954. I also had an introduction to A. S. M. Hutchinson, who was then assistant editor of the old *Daily Graphic*. He had already written *Once Aboard the Lugger*, but it was before the days of *If Winter Comes*. He advised me to read Addison; it was a good Johnsonian precept, but not what I had hoped for.

My father was still anxious to see me in the civil service. At that time the competitive examination covered the Indian as well as the Home Civil Service and only those who were high in the list could expect to be offered a place in one of the home ministries. I had no desire to go to India and I knew that my chances of a high place were remote. So I went down and took a temporary post at my old school at Brighton, my father consoling himself by entering my name for a post in what was then the Board of Education.

While I was at Brighton and greatly enjoying the work, Leonard Whibley wrote to me to say that he had put my name forward for the post of Assistant Secretary at the University Press. I had then little idea of what went on at the Press, beyond the printing of examination papers and the publication of school books in the Pitt Press series. But the job was concerned with books and was in Cambridge—that was good enough for me.

I believe Whibley had one or two of the Press Syndics to lunch and gave them some of his best hock. In any event, my name was put on a short list and I was summoned to an interview with a committee with which I was to become familiar over a long period—the Business Sub-syndicate. Whibley gave me all the advice that he could. 'For God's sake', he said, 'try and make yourself look a bit older.' I did my best and presumably made a fairly good impression on the Sub-syndicate, for shortly afterwards I was summoned before the Syndics of the Press in full meeting. It was an impressive gathering with the stately, ambassadorial figure of A. W. Ward in the chair. As always on such occasions, the questions asked were as tentative as the replies. One that was pressed more than others was: Had I any experience of accounts? My reply that I had edited a college magazine and had been treasurer of the College Mission did not, I fear, sound very impressive.

My competitors were W. L. Hicks, a slightly older man from Liverpool with some business experience, and C. F. Taylor, who was afterwards a housemaster at Clifton for many years. Later in the afternoon I met Arthur Hutchinson, at that time a Press Syndic and afterwards Master of Pembroke, in Old Court. Kindly and regretfully he told me that Hicks had been appointed.

It was a heavy blow, for it seemed to mean bidding a long farewell to Cambridge. So I went home and sifted a number of communications from Gabbitas and Thring, who were obligingly sending me particulars of vacancies in many kinds of schools. I applied for one or two, but without success and eventually I took a post (at £80 per annum plus board and lodging) at a coaching establishment kept by A. V. Adams (an old Sidney man) in Freiburg-im-Breisgau. I went fully equipped with notebooks dealing with Roman history and Greek philosophy and was informed on arrival that I should, for the most part, be required to teach geography and précis-writing. It was quite hard work, but Freiburg was a lovely place to live in. I picked up what German I could and, on production of my B.A. certificate and of a modest fee, I became a member of the university and listened to a sermon to freshmen delivered by the Rector, wearing a gold

chain about his neck. I had no time to attend lectures, but I met
one or two Englishmen doing research work—among them was
G. E. K. Braunholtz, later Professor of Philology at Oxford. There
was a good theatre, at which drama and opera were alternately
played, and some really old-fashioned music-halls in which you
sat at a small table and drank your beer in comfort. But from the
middle of November onwards all eyes were on the Feldberg, or
rather upon the weather report from it, and when the report was
'Ski-bahn gut' we looked forward to Saturday, when the 1 o'clock
train took us up the Höllental, through Himmelreich to Hinter-
zarten. There we alighted on the snow and toiled up the long
slope to the Feldberger Hof. If the weather was good, we could
refresh ourselves with a drink on the verandah of the hotel and
watch the sunset glow on the distant Alps. After dinner we skied
about in the moonlight and on the Sunday afternoon we came
down the winding paths between the tall and silent pines to meet
the train at Himmelreich.

When I came home for Christmas, I found that I had been
asked to wait upon the Chief Inspector of the Board of Education
(E. G. A. Holmes). My dear old father had gone up to London
himself to explain my absence and by the time that I presented
myself in January 1911, Mr (afterwards Sir) Hubert Orange had
succeeded to the Chief Inspectorate. He talked to me very kindly
and I went back to Freiburg for my second term. In the middle
of it I received a letter which determined my future. It was from
M. R. James, who had succeeded Sir Adolphus Ward as chairman
of the Press Syndics. He wrote on 6 February 1911:

The Press Syndicate...have been revising some of their arrangements; they have thought it desirable in the interests of the London
business to add to the permanent staff there; and they have invited
Mr W. L. Hicks...to remain attached to the London business...The
secretarial post to which he was appointed is therefore still unfilled and
I am authorized by the Syndicate to offer it to you...The stipend
offered is at the rate of £200 for the present year, which period will
also be one of probation. After the end of 1911 the stipend will rise

to £250 and subsequently by annual increments of £25 until the sum of £700 is reached...I do not attempt to describe the duties of the post: they are, I think, sufficiently known to you. I will only venture to remind you that in our view it is essential that if you decide to accept the post (as I hope you will) you should do so with the intention of making it the main occupation of your life.

Almost immediately after this came a letter inviting me to be interviewed by the President of the Board of Education (Walter Runciman). But I had no doubts about my choice. In May 1911 I returned to Cambridge for good.

Chapter 2

PUBLISHING AND SOLDIERING

When I entered upon my work at the Press, the small one-storey building allotted to the Secretary contained three rooms: the Syndicate Room, which served also as a library of current publications; the Secretary's room; and a small room for the Secretary's Clerk.

As Assistant Secretary, I was given a chair and a desk in the Syndicate Room, but when there was a Syndicate or Sub-syndicate meeting, I had to gather up my papers and move out. The full Syndicate met, and still meets, on alternate Fridays in term-time and I was fascinated by the assembly of learning round the table—not that I attended meetings, but at the tea-interval I was bidden to share the strong brew prepared by William Keetch, the caretaker. Syndics' teas had a long tradition behind them and a receipt for tea (and coffee) served in 1815 was preserved in the Syndicate Room. Keetch, who lived to work in the Press for seventy years, took the service of tea very seriously. At a Sub-syndicate meeting tea-cups of normal size were provided; at a full meeting the Syndics were consoled with large breakfast-cups.

The Vice-Chancellor's deputy as Chairman of the Syndics was M. R. James, Provost of King's; but Sir Adolphus Ward, who had presided over my interview a year before, was still a member and a keen member, in spite of increasing deafness. By far the most powerful Syndic (though no casual visitor would have suspected it) was Hugh Anderson, Fellow and afterwards Master of Caius. Monty James never prided himself on financial acumen and insisted on Anderson taking command of the Business Sub-syndicate.

One of the few faces I recognised was that of Henry Jackson;

another classical Syndic whom I came to know well in later years was Peter Giles, recently elected Master of Emmanuel. Mathematics was represented by E. W. Hobson, Sadleirian Professor, and by the Rev J. B. Lock, Bursar of Caius and author of a once famous *Arithmetic*. Hobson was a remarkable figure: tall and gaunt, with a long neck and a continuously worried expression, he recalled one of those prehistoric creations in which E. T. Reed was at that time so prolific. In particular, Hobson's moustache fascinated me—every bristle of it seemed to point in a different direction and so to contribute to the inquiring bizarrerie of the whole figure.

Other Syndics were W. R. Sorley, the moral philosopher who remained a Syndic until his death in 1935; V. H. Stanton, Professor of Divinity and three who were destined to be heads of houses—Arthur Hutchinson (Pembroke), Henry Bond, (Trinity Hall) and A. C. Seward (Downing). But the most venerable Syndic was Aldis Wright, with whom I had an alarming encounter one day when I happened to be alone in the secretarial office. There was a knock at the door and there entered a figure that might have stepped straight out of the pages of Thackeray—snow-white side-whiskers, frock coat, silk hat. 'What's this that I've been sent?' he inquired peremptorily, holding up a book in his hand. I explained that I was but newly arrived and that I knew very little about anything.

'Who gave authority for the Revised Version to be printed in verses?' he asked.

Again I pleaded the ignorance of a newcomer and offered to make inquiries. I rushed into the printing-office and one of the senior clerks assured me that the book had been produced with the full authority of the Syndics. I hastened to pass on this information; but I made no impression.

'I shall write to *The Times*', said Aldis Wright. To this I did not venture to reply.

In 1911 the University Printer was John Clay, who shortly after my arrival arranged for me to be shown round the composing and machine rooms, the foundry and other departments. Normally I did not see much of him; on the other hand, I quickly got to know the staff of the counting-house, at the head of which stood Alfred Mason—a little man with a neat white beard who combined a strictly Victorian integrity with a frankly tyrannical exercise of power. He had an immense respect for the University, for the colleges, and for the Press as institutions; this respect did not necessarily extend to persons. One morning he came to the Secretary's office with a title-sheet requiring final approval. Reluctantly, as I was alone in the office, he turned to me.

'Do you understand imprints?' he asked.

'Yes, I think so, Mr Mason.'

'Thinking won't do, young man. You've got to learn.'

Some time later I heard of his response to a tentative inquiry about the competence of the new Assistant Secretary. 'Very clever man, they tell me...I've still to see it.'

His criticism was not confined to the young and ignorant. One day I happened to be speaking to him just after he had spent some time with Henry Jackson:

'There he goes,' he said, as he watched the venerable figure crossing the courtyard, 'and not the only learned fool who's wasted my time this morning.'

Or again, about A. E. Shipley: 'Too thick, too thick here' (bringing his hand up to his neck). 'No wife, no garden. What can you expect?'

To me personally he grew more avuncular. When he heard that I was engaged to be married, he brought me a prospectus of the Cambridge Building Society, calling my particular attention to the board of directors. 'All 5-figure men', he said. It was the Victorian hall-mark.

My closest contacts, naturally, were with my two seniors. R. T. Wright, formerly Fellow of Christ's and a prominent figure in University politics, had been Secretary to the Syndics (the first full-time Secretary) since 1892. A genial bearded figure, he treated me with great kindness, but, as he was due to retire at the end of the year, it was natural that I should receive more instruction from his successor-elect, A. R. Waller. Waller was a hard-headed Yorkshireman with a stubborn sense of business and a wide knowledge of English literature. He was not a Cambridge man, but had been brought into the Press as a man of letters who had had varied experience (in particular, with Duckworth and Dent) of the facts of a publisher's life. His sponsor had been Sir Adolphus Ward and, having been given the degree of honorary M.A., he became a member of Peterhouse. It was from him that I had my first introduction to the making and marketing of books. 'You'll find plenty of variety in this job,' he said to me one day, 'I've just initialled the title-sheets of two books—one called "The Vitality of Platonism" and the other "A Treatise on Epidemic Diarrhoea".'

Apart from day-to-day routine, the most controversial item on the Syndics' agenda in 1911 was the *Encyclopaedia Britannica*. In the previous year publication of the eleventh edition had been undertaken on a commission basis. No one disputed the quality of the work, but in the University and elsewhere there was caustic criticism of the method by which the set of volumes was marketed. The booksellers naturally resented the invitation to the purchaser to sign on the dotted line and to send the order form direct to the publisher; academic critics deplored that 'the University Press had consented to act as agents for the sale of a work prepared for the market by an American Syndicate in Bloomsbury'. The villain, or hero, of the piece was Horace E. Hooper. He had first approached Oxford, but after deliberation the Delegates declined the offer. Hooper was disappointed, but not daunted. 'They think I was trying to bribe them. I offered them too much. You go to Cambridge now—and offer them just half', he said to one of his editors.*

Hooper was a remarkable man who combined dynamic salesmanship with a genuine and devotional faith in the new edition of the *Encyclopaedia* as the greatest book in the world. On one of

* See H. Kogan, *The Great E.B.* (Chicago, 1958), for the full story.

24

his visits to confer with the Syndics I just caught a glimpse of his piercing eyes beneath bushy black eyebrows. It was part of the Cambridge contract that all advertisements were to be approved on behalf of the Syndics, but the circumstances made it impossible to exercise any effective censorship. Hooper did, however, withdraw one particular advertisement at the personal request of M. R. James, whom he profoundly admired and respected. It is difficult to conceive any community of taste between Hooper and Monty James. But Monty had read many of the articles in proof and was convinced that the *Encyclopaedia* was a good book. To Hooper it was more than a book—it was his Bible. And what more suitable publisher could there be than the Press of a great university?

During my first weeks I was given a variety of small jobs appropriate to the industrious apprentice—indexing minute-books, sorting miscellaneous correspondence, filing agreements with authors and such like. But at least I was in charge of one manuscript—*The Thunderweapon in Religion and Folklore*, by C. Blinkenberg. It was a translation from the Danish and had already been accepted for publication, but the English idiom was imperfect and I revised it as carefully as I could. It was the first of many such revisions entrusted to me in the course of thirty years; and, looking back, I am astonished at the hetero-geneity of the collection. It includes a *Life of Sir Albert Markham*, *The Muslim Creed*, *Cattle and Beef Production*, *The Photian Schism* and *What is Life?*

It was fortunate, perhaps, that I knew little about the subject-matter of these books. Knowing that I was not tampering with the substance of their work, the authors accepted my modifications of style without complaint and sometimes, indeed, with exagger-ated gratitude. When *The Thunderweapon* was finished, I was given another MS.—*The Problem of Evil in Plotinus* by B. A. G. Fuller. I was not concerned with the main body of the argument, but with the translation of the many quotations from Plotinus. I was not really familiar enough with the One and the Many and my versions were not as good as they ought to have been. In fact, they were severely criticised by A. E. Taylor in *Mind*. But they led to a happy friendship with Fuller. He stayed with me in Cambridge in the summer of 1914, and I had a day with him in Cincinnati in 1925.

A. C. Benson's appointment as a Syndic at the end of 1911 was of particular interest to me. In his diary he wrote: 'I have been put on the Press Syndicate, the centre of all Cambridge jobbery. It will mean much work, but I like to be included. I don't suppose I shall effect anything. But it means that I have after eight years a really recognised position here. Very unexpected...' Whether he found as much jobbery as he expected, I do not know. He certainly got on well with Waller, to whom a year or so later he confided that he wanted to make an experiment. If he published an essay anonymously, or pseudonymously, would anyone take any notice of it? Waller did not commit himself, but arranged for the essay to be printed as an elegant quarto on hand-made paper by Turnbull and Spears of Edinburgh and to be published by Chapman and Hall. The essay (*Herb Moly and Heartsease* by Sintram) was published at 1*s*. In *Escape and Other Essays* (1915) Benson reprinted it and told its story: 'I had sent it to papers for review and I even had some copies sent to literary friends of my own. The result was a quite enchanting humiliation. One paper reviewed it kindly in a little paragraph...only one of my friends even acknowledged it.'

The editor of whom I saw most at this time was F. H. H. Guillemard. He was general editor of the *Cambridge County Geographies*, a series which, incidentally, was a good example of the inevitable failure of an attempt to write for the schoolboy and the 'general reader' at the same time. But there were some good books in the series and Guillemard was a careful editor. What worried him was the collection of illustrations for each volume. These had to be obtained from various sources and gradually I found myself responsible for procuring prints and photographs ('on appro. for repro.') and, sometimes, for making diagrams. It was extremely valuable experience, quite apart from the pleasure of working with Guillemard.

Himself one of Nature's aristocrats, he was frequently puzzled by the background of some of the contributors to the series. Many of them used post-cards, a form of communication which he deplored.

'The fella's written to me on a post-card,' he would say to me in his plaintive, purring voice, 'and do you see where he lives? He lives at *Ealing*! Now fancy a fella living at *Ealing...*' It was something outside Guillemard's sociological experience. Not that his experience was narrow. After reading science at Caius, he went to St Bartholomew's at the time when Robert Bridges was house physician. He qualified, but never practised, as a doctor. In the 'seventies he had trekked across parts of Central and South Africa and liked to tell how Kruger, on his way to England to protest against the annexation of the Transvaal, had once been constrained to pledge the Queen's health in a Bloemfontein bar. His first book, *The Cruise of the Marchesa to Kamschatka and New Guinea*, was published in 1886; two years later he was appointed university lecturer in Geography, but there is no record of the delivery of a lecture. As a naturalist, he travelled far and wide and one of his later works was *The Ornithology of Cyprus*, a subject later pursued by an old Pembroke friend of mine, David Bannerman. All this was far behind Guillemard when I first met him in 1911. He then lived, and continued to live until his death in 1933, at the Old Mill House at the corner of Trumpington Road and Long Road. There was no gas or electric light in the house and even in the daytime the low-ceilinged rooms were darkened by an assembly of treasures from all parts of the world. He had a good collection of early water-colours and the house was perfectly administered by three maids. They wore the long black dresses, caps and aprons of the period and their combined length of service totalled more than 100 years. Annie, the parlourmaid, did more than minister to the pleasures of the table. If Guillemard mislaid a set of proofs, they were frequently recovered by 'the faithful Annie'. One day, when he told me that a missing packet had been retrieved, I queried 'the faithful Annie?' 'No,' he replied, 'the equally faithful Martha.'

Sunday evening dinners at the Old Mill House were memorable. It was usually a party of three or four, and George Wherry (surgeon and Charles Lamb enthusiast) was frequently one of them. Food, wine, glass and silver were exquisite and each guest was provided with a hot-water plate. Occasionally, when we had work to do on the *Geographies*, Guillemard would invite me to dine alone with him. 'I've got some proof returned by that horrible fella who will make his corrections with a *thick pen*...', he would murmur to me. It was late before we went up to his study and I would bicycle home about 1.30. Guillemard normally went to bed at 2.0 and breakfasted at 10.0.

His own handwriting was beautifully neat. It was not often that he had occasion to write to me. When he did so, he liked to affect an elaborate Eastern style:

Salaam aleikum! Roberts Effendi: May you live 1000 years and may no Suffragette come nigh your dwelling! Touching this card of the infidel...I have written to the dog and charged him to hold his peace.

Another son of Shaitan...maketh plaint that certain writings of his...purposed to supplant that which he had written aforetime, have not been made thus to supplant them. I have told this infidel that, Inshallah, they should appear in the next roll of parchments known to the Christians as 'page-proofs'...

In the literature of travel Guillemard was widely read. 'I suppose you've read *Arabia Deserta*?' I said to him once. 'My dear fella,' he retorted, 'do I ever read anything else?' He enjoyed the Victorian novelists, but if I tackled him about contemporary fiction I drew blank—except, curiously, for W. J. Locke.

One of the many attractions he held for me was his early knowledge of Pembroke. Having come up in 1871, he could remember the college as it was before Waterhouse's destructions and additions. His uncle, W. H. Guillemard, Vicar of Little St Mary's, had been a Fellow of the college and under John Power

(Master 1870–80) the old Lodge had been an open house to him in his undergraduate years. In the new Lodge, built by Waterhouse in 1873, he once met George Eliot and there in 1874 he was present at the notable meeting of the two discoverers of Neptune—Adams and Leverrier. As Adams had a cleft palate and as neither could speak the other's language, they had to be content with 'bowing and grimacing'.*

Guillemard was a loyal Caius man, but he retained a particular affection for Pembroke and it gave him great pleasure when in the 1920s he was invited to join the High Table. He lived to be eighty-one and until his last year was remarkably fit. On Sunday he regularly bicycled to Morning Prayer at St Botolph's and would then lunch in college or with a friend. When, one Sunday, I met him coming out of church and invited him to lunch, he replied:

'That's very kind of you, my dear fella, but I can only eat pap.'

'What's wrong?' I asked.

'Well,' he replied, 'it's a most extraordinary thing, but I'm in the hands of the dentist. D'you know, until I was 75, I'd never had any trouble with my teeth.' He spoke with the air of a man with a grievance.

The County Geographies were not the only books for which it was my business to collect illustrations. The demand for well-chosen pictures in schoolbooks was insistent and the work led me into many pleasant byways in the University Library and the print-room of the British Museum. It also led to a suggestion that I should compile a *Picture Book of British History*. It was eventually completed in three volumes and amiable reviewers helped it towards a modest success. Later, I realised that I had chosen the wrong kind of format. It was a large quarto and looked more like an album than a book. However, the first volume, published just before the First World War, provoked a long letter from Flinders Petrie. It was highly critical, but I was astonished

* I glean this from *The Years that the Locusts have eaten*, a typescript which Guillemard left to the University Library.

that an eminent scholar should take so much trouble over a schoolbook.

Meanwhile, I had been given full dining rights at Pembroke in the summer of 1911. Mason was still Master. I did not meet him very often at dinner, but I have a clear recollection of him at the college ball in that year—a distinguished figure in court dress. About midnight he gave his arm to Mrs Searle (widow of C. E. Searle, Master 1880–1902) and escorted her to supper, for those were the days when stately chaperons sat in a row on each side of the Hall.

In the Michaelmas Term of the same year Mason fulfilled his promise of reading a paper to the Martlets. The meeting, held in Lawrence Tanner's rooms (now the Senior Parlour) in Ivy Court, was a crowded one. The Master explained that he had not, in fact, written a paper, but that he proposed to read some sonnets of his own on Pembroke and Pembroke personalities. It was a memorable evening. Mason recited his sonnets in his most distinctive manner, adding appropriate glosses on occasion. Many of the lines seemed specially designed for his manner of delivery —this, for instance, on Denny Abbey:

> On every side the yellow roses wave;
> The elms are drench'd in sunshine. Barn and hall
> By fine-traced window or round arch recall
> The refectory, cloister, transept, nave.
> Alas! I cannot kiss our Lady's grave.

Or this on the Hall:

> The College grew. Money for Gray's sake given,
> Pitt helping, mounted up to build. At last
> A Quaker saint, as architect call'd in,
> Hall, library, and half the house—just Heaven!
> From the foundations Mary laid did blast.
> What is the punishment when good men sin?

Later, the sonnets were printed for private distribution and their fame spread beyond the walls of Pembroke. One who particularly relished them was Monty James. At the tea-interval at meetings of the Press Syndicate I would hear him mutter in my ear: 'Alǎs, I cannot kiss our Lady's grave.'

Another convivial occasion was the dinner in 1912 to celebrate the fiftieth anniversary of the P.C.D.S. (the college debating society). H. Barrs Davies, as President, was in the chair with the Master as the chief guest. The vice-chair was taken by the Rev J. C. Rust,* who had been President in 1863. There was a good gathering of ex-Presidents including several Fellows of the college. Among the junior officers were Humfrey Grose-Hodge (afterwards headmaster of Bedford) and Aubrey Attwater of whom I shall have more to say. When Mason was called upon to propose the motion 'That after 50 years of life this society is unrepentant', his linguistic frivolity astonished us. 'This motion', he began, 'would require not only fortitude, but fiftitude or sixtitude...' Later in the year he resigned the Mastership in order to give his whole time to Canterbury and was succeeded by Hadley.

The resident fellows were ten in number and of some of them I have already written. The Dean, when I came up, was the Rev. J. F. Bethune-Baker, but at the end of my first term he had been succeeded by H. C. O. Lanchester (afterwards Rector of Framlingham). Years afterwards I gathered that there had been a heresy-hunt. Baker was a leading Modernist and a man of great intellectual power. Equally powerful was his sarcasm; he was the vinegar, it was said, in the salad of a college meeting.

One of the best-known figures in the college was H. G. Comber. He had been elected primarily with a view to his taking over the finances of the college and he served as Treasurer for many years, but he was best known as the patron of all forms of athletic exercise in the University. Consequently he was credited with a concentration of interest upon 'blues'. Years afterwards I realised how partial and imperfect this assessment was.

* Vicar of Soham for fifty-three years; he once preached a sermon in Esperanto in Great St Mary's Church.

Mathematical teaching was in the hands of George Birtwistle, a former Senior Wrangler, but the only Natural Sciences don was Arthur Hutchinson, later Professor of Mineralogy and Master of the College. In 1912 J. T. Spittle, who had taken firsts both in Natural and Mechanical Sciences, was elected to a fellowship and became one of my closest friends. Another good friend, V. C. Pennell, was elected in 1914 to take charge of medical studies.

Outside the college I gradually got to know other people in the University, among them Charles Sayle and A. T. Bartholomew of the University Library. Theo Bartholomew and I were both frequenters of the Union. In those days there was no provision (except in Caius) of lunch in college and the Union dining-room offered an admirable meal for 1s. 6d. Its library was also most useful and the Union, indeed, provided the amenities of a club for those graduate members of the University who were not Fellows of a college. The 'non-Fellows' of those days, of course, were a small, and uncomplaining, party.

Soon after my return to Cambridge I found that the Heretics, whose inaugural meeting I had attended, had flourished and expanded. I was never a member, but I noted the announcement of an open meeting in the Guildhall. It was to be addressed by Bernard Shaw and Shaw did what he was expected to do—he amused and he shocked. England, he said, needed a new religion of its own, based on a recognition that the Universe was driven by a force—the Life Force. Nevertheless he frequently referred to God. When question-time came, a lady (whom I identified with reasonable certainty as Jane Harrison) protested against the use of the word God, 'with all its deplorable associations'. Shaw's defence was that he could find nothing better—the 'Life Force' didn't please people.

Some months later the Heretics held another open meeting, at which G. K. Chesterton (whose *Napoleon of Notting Hill* is still one of my favourite books) was invited to reply to Shaw. The large room of the Guildhall was crowded and Chesterton, perspiring freely, had some difficulty in deciphering his notes, which, he said, he had made in the cab. It was a rambling discourse, but I remember his saying: 'I understand that when my friend Mr Shaw was speaking here, some poor, blind old atheist got up and protested about the use of the word God...' Jane Harrison, I observed, was sitting in the front row.

But it was in dealing with questioners, that Chesterton was at his best. One earnest seeker after truth posed a question; Chesterton posed one in return. 'Do you', he asked, 'believe in your own existence?' The questioner paused and then said 'I have an intuition that I exist.' 'Cherish it', said Chesterton.

At the end of my first year at the Press my appointment was confirmed and I reflected that I should before long be expected to proceed to the degree of M.A. I also reflected upon some means of raising the required fee—at that time £18. I knew that a number of freshmen came up before having passed the Little-Go and I asked J. C. Lawson, who succeeded Hadley as Tutor of Pembroke, whether he could give me any such to coach. 'How many do you want?' he asked laconically. So I took two for instruction in the set books in Greek and Latin. One was fairly stupid; the other was brighter, but spent most of his time at Newmarket. I was fully satisfied when they both got through—4th class. Each paid a fee of nine guineas, so my M.A. degree was assured.

After my first marriage to Irene, daughter of A. J. Wallis, Fellow of Corpus, in April 1913, I spent six months working at the publishing house of the Press in Fetter Lane. We obtained two spacious rooms in Oxford Gardens at a remarkably low price and enjoyed what was for us the novelty of London life. Hansoms had not yet entirely disappeared and, when we saw one and could afford the fare, we made a point of hailing it.

The office of the Press was just south of the Record Office and behind it some of the old buildings of Clifford's Inn remained. There Emery Walker still worked and occasionally I had to consult him or his partner, Wilfred Merton, about the reproduction of drawings or portraits for some of our books. C. F. Clay, our London manager, introduced me to some London publishers and inside the house I learnt something of the technique of binding, advertising, and marketing.

From the point of view of sales, the Press business was clearly divided into two parts—'cloth' and 'leather'. 'Leather' denoted Bibles and Prayer-books; 'cloth' covered all other publications of the Syndics.

These two departments raised quite different problems of marketing. Except for the distinction between the Authorised and the Revised Version, the 'leather' travellers had no textual variety to offer and accordingly much ingenuity was devoted to novelty in binding styles. Thus did I get a first inkling of the problems underlying the typography of the Bible; years later they were brilliantly tackled by my colleagues.

It was a pleasant six months. I got to love Fleet Street and in the evenings we enjoyed the theatre, generally from seats in the pit. Two performances, in particular, I recall; the first night of *Androcles and the Lion* and the stir made by Ellen Terry's entry to the stalls; and the adorable acting of Wish Wynne in *The Great Adventure*.

But it was even more pleasant, in October, to return to the Press at Cambridge. There I found that an additional Assistant Secretary had been appointed—G. V. Carey. I knew his name, of course, as that of a Rugger Blue, but although we had taken the same tripos in 1909, we had never met. Very quickly we established a friendship which has grown with the years. Apart from anything else, it was a joy to have a man of my own age working alongside me and especially one who could share an appreciation of the many curious characters whom we encountered among the staff, and the clients, of the Press. One of Gordon's first jobs was to index the *Fragments* of Sophocles—a solid enough foundation for his later reputation as 'the prince of indexers'.

In July 1914, I had an interesting week in Germany. Leipzig has long been famous for its book-fairs and the 1914 fair was on an exceptionally grand and international scale. In what was called the Street of Nations, the British Pavilion, a quiet grey building designed to look like a college library and effectively contrasting with the bizarre murals of Austria and the golden pinnacles of Russia, contained a room devoted to the work of the Oxford and Cambridge Presses. I was especially pleased with the enthusiasm shown for E. H. Minns's recently published *Scythians and Greeks*. 'Ach, ze book of Minns!', said one reverential admirer. It was as if he were talking of the Book of Kells. In the Hotel Hauffe I met for the first time E. P. Goldschmidt, who had been up at Trinity just before me. He was later to become a famous book-seller, and after bookish talk we turned to the political situation. It was before, but not long before, Sarajevo; and Goldschmidt spoke, naturally enough, from the Austrian point of view. Austria, he said, was beginning to lose patience with the Serbs. 'They are to us', he added, 'what the Irish are to you.' But neither of us had any expectation that in a few weeks Europe would be a battle-field.

In August, Cambridge quickly assumed its military respon-sibilities. A committee to deal with applications for commissions was immediately set up in Corpus and, in Pembroke, Comber, who had earlier been a Major in the O.T.C. established a school of instruction for prospective, or newly commissioned, officers. 'Comber's Irregulars' were in origin a purely private enterprise, but in December the War Office recognised their value and put the school on an official footing and the Old Library became the headquarters not only of this school, but of the O.T.C. as a whole.

At the Press our numbers were quickly reduced. Many of the members of the printing staff were mobilised with the Cambridge-shires and others enlisted; Gordon Carey was commissioned in the Rifle Brigade. For myself, I reflected that, having been obliged to leave the school Cadet Corps as a result of some temporary weakness in my back, I was entirely lacking in military training of any kind. So, in October, I joined the O.T.C. and paraded in Pembroke every afternoon in the old grey uniform in company with hundreds of undergraduates. Other seniors (some of them very senior) joined and in the Lent Term of 1915 there were enough to form an M.A. Platoon. We were an odd assembly of professors and all sorts. Sir Harry Stephen, who was O.C. platoon, had some difficulty at first in determining the proper form of address. 'Gentlemen,' he would say as we assembled on parade, '...er...Masters...er...Squad!' Quiller-Couch, one of the professorial members, wrote in the *Cambridge Review* of 'the mud on the road to the Rifle Butts where the M.A. warriors of the C.U.O.T.C. drill and improve their waists, though they may never serve their country'.

In fact, the younger members (including P. H. Winfield, J. A. Venn and myself) took commissions and in October I was posted to a Territorial battalion of the Suffolks stationed at Cromer.

We were comfortably billeted at the Cliftonville Hotel and, to my satisfaction, I was soon on very good terms with the Commanding Officer, R. (afterwards Sir Robert) Eaton White of Boulge Hall, Woodbridge. He was, in the first place, typical of the country gentleman who naturally assumes command of local Territorials. He could talk to his men in their own dialect and took great pride in his Suffolk punches. More than that, he was well-read and his mind was not closed. As I was a little older than most of his subalterns, he used to encourage me to develop many arguments with which he personally disagreed. Above all, he had a delicious humour, especially in relation to King's Regulations and to military orthodoxy in general.

For the first few months, life was very pleasant at Cromer. Our job was the defence of the coast. In the event of invasion, our orders were, broadly speaking, to die on the beach—which we certainly should have done. The only invaders we saw were in the air. One afternoon, as we sat over tea after parade, a mess-orderly knocked at the door, stood to attention and said 'Zeppelin overhead, sir'. It was the first of several. The Zeppelins commonly followed the line of the Great Eastern Railway from King's Lynn to London and dropped bombs where they thought fit. As we were armed only with Japanese rifles, there was not much that we could do. Our normal duty was to keep the troops in good training and to supply watchful pickets at such points as Cromer pier and East Runton gap at night. Soon after my joining the battalion, I was placed in temporary command of a company and so became a mounted officer; and, for the only time in my life rode, in a very modest way, to hounds. The North Norfolk Harriers were still in action and welcomed us on Saturday afternoons.

On Friday mornings, the C.O. liked to deploy his battalion and obtained leave to use the park at Felbrigg for an exercise. Thus I became familiar with the exterior of a house which I was to know well in later years. Spy-mania was still prevalent. One evening, a sergeant and I squeezed ourselves into a lavatory in the Cromer Club to watch for suspected light signals; our vigil was quite abortive.

We were moved from Cromer in the spring of 1916 and thereafter were stationed at various places in Norfolk—Holt, Sheringham, Salthouse, Sidestrand and Weybourne. I forget the precise sequence, but I remember two incidents at Salthouse. Our camp was near the main road and between the road and the beach was a marsh. At the Rocket House on the beach we always had a strong picket, with an officer in command. One night, when I was on duty there, we had the Zeppelin warning and could see the machine very clearly. The noise of the engine grew so loud that, to our inexperienced ears, it seemed directly overhead. Then we heard the explosion of a bomb; it killed a cow at Weybourne.

We had a tidy little camp at Salthouse, with a square plot of grass in the middle, reserved for guard-mounting parade and similar ceremonies.

After lunch one day the Adjutant came into the ante-room and said: 'There's a prisoner in the guard-room who says he's Father Bernard Vaughan. Could any of you identify him?' At that time Father Bernard Vaughan's face was a familiar one in the illustrated weeklies, so I went with the Adjutant and the second-in-command to the Orderly Room. The prisoner was marched in by our Provost-Sergeant, a tough old Reservist, who proceeded to tell his story. Sitting in the village inn, he had heard the prisoner making inquiries about the fortifications on the beach, the number of troops stationed in the neighbourhood, and similar matters. Suspicious of these inquiries, he had thought it his duty to make an arrest. The prisoner's explanation was simple: staying at an hotel in Cromer he had set out for a walk and gone farther than he intended; finding himself at lunch-time in Salthouse, he had sought refreshment at the inn; not being very warmly welcomed, he had tried to make himself agreeable by chatting on topics of local interest.

From my recollection of photographs in the papers, I had no doubt about the prisoner's identity, so when I was invited to put questions to him, I thought I would give him an easy one.

'Father Bernard Vaughan,' I said, 'I know you preach at the Catholic Church at Worthing sometimes. Perhaps you would just tell me the name of the priest in charge?'

'Yes, of course I know him, but...but I can't for the life of me remember his name.' The poor man was greatly upset, but he quickly rallied. 'I'll tell you what,' he said, 'I know the Digbys at Worthing.' I also knew the Digbys and was entirely satisfied. At this point, the C.O. came into the Orderly Room, his eyes twinkling. After putting a few more questions and ringing up the Cromer hotel for verification, he told the prisoner that he left the court without a stain on his character—'or at least no fresh ones', he added. The prisoner bowed, and, leaving the Orderly Room, began to walk across the grass plot sacred to officers. 'Keep off the grass!' was the Provost-Sergeant's parting shot.

'Really, you know, the old man behaved very well,' said the Colonel that evening, 'I shall ask him to dine in the Mess on Saturday.' The invitation was accepted. There happened to be a concert in the canteen that evening and, after dinner, our guest came to it with alacrity. He also made an entertaining speech. 'I, too, have been in the guard room', he concluded.

In the early days Eaton White had hoped that we should be sent abroad as a battalion, but it soon became clear that, although the routine of coast defence remained, our main job was that of training. A bunch of men would be drafted out, and a bunch of recruits would take their place. Personally I enjoyed the barrack-square much more than the tactical exercise, since I had no 'eye for country'. Like every subaltern, I was sent on various courses and was for a time in charge of a Brigade Lewis gun school, with headquarters at the Sheringham Golf club-house. Mention of the Brigade reminds me that I occasionally met Venn and Winfield, who had been posted to the Cambridgeshires. Winfield was frequently briefed for the defence at courts martial. After a time, it was said, he was no longer so employed—he was too successful in securing acquittals.

Eventually, in July 1917, I was drafted, along with R. S. J. Rands, to France. We crossed to Boulogne and spent the first night (five to a tent) in Ostrohove camp on top of the hill. It struck me as odd that the only place at which we could get a meal was the Salvation Army hut, outside which two notices were posted: 'God so loved the world...' (John iii. 16) and 'Dinner 1/-'. On the following morning I was delighted to have a chance of calling upon Comber, now Intelligence officer at Boulogne, very busy but very cordial.

My period of service abroad was very short, very fortunate and quite undistinguished. My first piece of luck was in being posted to my own regiment—the 4th Suffolks. I joined them at La Panne, on the Belgian coast and after a few days of luxury at the Hotel Terlinck, we moved up towards Nieuport. We were not in the line, but we came in for plenty of shelling. Returning one night after throwing up a breastwork somewhere west of Nieuport, we were badly caught at a 'Suicide Corner' and had several casualties, including one officer killed. On return to camp, I made what I thought was rather an impressive report. It was received without comment and I began to realise that what was to me a new and exciting experience was for the seasoned campaigner

39

part of the day's, or night's, routine. It was the same with the minor duties of a subaltern. The old hands knew just what to expect when censoring letters; but I rubbed my eyes when I read a letter beginning: 'My lovely steak-and-onion-faced darling Alice...'

After a period of duty on the Yser Canal, we moved to billets near St Omer, whence later we marched through Cassel, Steenvoorde and Meteren into what is officially known as the Battle of Polygon Wood; but the names that I remember best are Clapham Junction and Stirling Castle, the latter being Brigade headquarters. From those headquarters in the afternoon of 25 September an urgent order was received for a party, in charge of an officer, to carry Stokes mortars to the 1st Middlesex, who were hard pressed by a German counter-attack. I was the officer detailed. The enemy shelling, as recorded in the regimental history, 'reached a pitch of great intensity', but somehow we got through. In my innocence, I expected a word of thanks. But when I presented myself to the Middlesex C.O. and told him what I had brought, he looked at me in dismay. 'Don't bring them here,' he said, 'they'll only be something more to blow up.' On the way back, one of my men was killed outright; another was hit as we approached a trench held by the Worcestershires and we were able to get a stretcher and carry him in. At this point I quote again from the regimental history: 'Shortly after midnight [i.e. 25/26 September] the battalion took up a line from Glencorse Wood to Fitzclarence farm. Gradually the situation grew worse. The moon had gone, the shelling became more persistent, and a thick mist arose.' The 'line' that we took up was a single straight trench, without traverses, into which we were jammed like sardines. There we sat until daylight, when the advance company moved forward. Our own company-commander went out to reconnoitre and came back wounded. I gave him some chocolate and did not see him again. Later in the day, as another subaltern and I were 'consolidating' a large shell-hole, I was hit. Without any heroic pretensions I thought, honestly, that it was a slight affair; but my right leg was broken. In the lorry-journey to

Poperinghe I did not feel too good, but my luck held. I looked up at the M.O. who was examining me and saw John Ryle, whom I had known well at school. He was infinitely kind and arranged for me to go into the operating theatre at once. The next morning he sent a personal telegram to my wife and saw me into the train for Etaples. There, in the Liverpool Merchants' Hospital, I had further experience of the kindness of old friends. One afternoon, a Red Cross officer entered the ward and paced up and down, obviously looking for someone. 'Oh, there you are, old boy', he said when he finally espied me. It was David Bannerman. I stared at him. 'But how in the world did you know I was here?' I asked. 'Oh, the Old Man, of course. He sent me to find you.' Comber had, no doubt, seen my name in the casualty list and it was characteristic of him that he had taken the trouble to trace me.

After about a week, I received the welcome news that I was one of a convoy for home. Again my luck held. I was one of the few stretcher cases and the M.O. at Calais affixed a label to me and said 'I'm marking you for Lady Carnarvon's Hospital. They like good surgical cases there.' So, about 1 a.m., I was carried up the stairs of a house in Bryanston Square. I woke to find a digni-fied butler bearing my breakfast tray. 'Good morning', I said. 'Good morning to *you*, sir.' Behind him was a footman, who asked not whether I would like a paper, but which morning papers I would like. It was the beginning of a delectable month. Lady Carnarvon was active and friendly and her staff was entirely civilian—and Irish; so there were few dull moments. The surgeon in charge, for instance, when he took you downstairs for an X-Ray examination would turn a number of switches on and off with an experimental air and then turn round and say: 'The whole place will probably blow up. You don't mind, do you?' Apart from one setback caused by an experiment with a new-fangled splint, my wound healed steadily and by Christmas I was able to go to my parents' home in Worthing with nominal attachment to a convalescent home for daily massage. I was still on crutches and, spending most of my time in an armchair, I

grew tired of novel-reading. Writing to Waller at Cambridge, I
asked him whether he could send me any proofs to read. He
replied by asking whether I could pursue the notion I had once
had about a book on Johnson. This surprised even more than it
delighted me. In the first years of my marriage I had read the
greater part of Boswell aloud to my wife, and at the end reflected
that many potential readers were probably deterred by the length
of the work. So I had tentatively suggested to Waller a little
book which might serve as a Boswell for Beginners. 'No,' he had
said quite firmly, 'you must not mutilate a classic.' And now here
he was, encouraging the suggestion. I sent at once for a second-
hand set of the Birkbeck Hill edition and was happily employed
for the next two months on what I chose to call *The Story of Dr
Johnson*. About the end of March I went before a medical board
which passed me fit for home service. Anxious to avoid the
tedium of a regimental depot, I qualified, after a course at Berk-
hamsted, as an instructor in an Officer Cadet Battalion and was
fortunate in being posted to No. 2 O.C.B. which had its headquarters at Peterhouse and Pembroke. It was pleasant to be at
home and I was not too pleased when, late in July, I was detailed
for an Anti-Gas course at Crowborough. There, on the last night
of the course (it was 1 August—Minden Day) I was engaged in
a gas exercise on Crabtree Hill. I slipped down a communication trench and my leg broke in the old place. While I was
in the 2nd Eastern General Hospital at Brighton, I heard that
Monty James was leaving King's to be Provost of Eton. In a short
letter to him combining congratulation with regret, I said that I
was tempted to write a farewell sonnet in the manner of A. J.
Mason. Monty, in a postscript to his reply, wrote 'I think I must
have that sonnet' so I sent him the following:

Vale. M.R.J.

His parts were manifold. The open door
The kindly host proclaimed. The room revealed
The bookman—Lo, patristic scripts unsealed,
Fly-sheets (unread), dim antiquarian lore...

Anstey or Philo, which loved he the more?
Patience he had to scan each palimpsest,
Patience he played and humbled every guest.
Alas, they never passed the Provost's score.
The Royal founder, bent on learning's weal,
By Thames and Cam twin edifices set;
Provosts he willed for both. Now Eton rings
With joyous echo and carillons peal
To hail the home-returning one. And yet
For us it is a solitary King's.

From Brighton I was transferred to the 1st Eastern General Hospital at Cambridge (on the site of what is now the University Library) and, on reaching the stage of convalescence, was ordered, much to my annoyance, to report to a convalescent home at Slough. But I had an agreeable surprise. I was met at the station and driven to Stoke Court, Stoke Poges, the vacation home of Thomas Gray. My hosts, Mr and Mrs Allhusen, made me feel completely at home and gave me the run of their library.

When, on 11 November, the news of the Armistice boomed out, a fellow-patient and myself very foolishly decided to go up to London—foolishly, because I was still lame and London on that day was no place for lame dogs. When we tried to get lunch, we found that nearly every restaurant had run out of food. Eventually, about two o'clock, we got something to eat, and when we came out into the street again the crowds were denser than ever and the prospect of reaching Paddington seemed remote. We had the luck, however, to run into my old friend Patrick Laird, then at the Scottish Office, and somehow he found a taxi for us. Out of the vast mass of humanity that thronged the Strand and Trafalgar Square one figure stays in my memory. On the kerbstone opposite Charing Cross was a vendor of what I believe were known as 'ticklers'—elongated brushes made of strips of tissue paper. In a voice of deep gloom the man was shouting: 'Tickle 'em up, tickle 'em up! Let's all go mad!' It was difficult to imagine anything less corybantic than this melancholy, Dickensian figure. When we sat down to dinner at Stoke Court, we found that our host, with characteristic benevolence, had provided each guest with a half-bottle of champagne.

The war was over. Early in 1919 I was discharged from the army and gratefully returned to Cambridge and the University Press.

Chapter 3

POST-WAR CAMBRIDGE

On my return to the Press at the beginning of 1919 I found that there had been some important changes. In particular, there was a change in my own position, in that I was made responsible for bindings and dust-jackets, for advertisements, and for publicity in general. Furthermore, I was to attend meetings of the Syndics.

On the printing side, there had been major developments. For some time before the war there had been considerable criticism of Cambridge printing—not of its accuracy, but of its lack of typographical design. S. C. Cockerell, Stephen Gaselee and Theo Bartholomew were prominent among the critics and the Syndics in 1916 had appointed a committee to consider the question. While the committee's report was still under discussion, the Syndics were faced with a more urgent problem by the sudden death of John Clay, the University Printer. They made a bold, and successful, experiment in appointing one of their own body— J. B. Peace. It happened that, later in the year, Bruce Rogers, the eminent American typographer, came to England to work with Emery Walker and, at Cockerell's suggestion, negotiations were opened, with the result that in the autumn Rogers agreed to act as typographical adviser to the Press.* It was an important landmark in the history of Cambridge printing and it had a certain relevance to my new responsibilities. My knowledge of typography was rudimentary and I realised that I must learn all I could from Rogers while he remained with us. Fundamentally, he was an artist. His favourite definition of 'Art' was 'the disposition or modification of things by human skill to answer a

---

* I have written of this at greater length in *The Evolution of Cambridge Publishing* (1956).

purpose intended', which he regarded as peculiarly applicable to printing.* Apart from his delicate skill in the use of initial letters and printer's ornaments, his main thesis was that Cambridge books, whether mathematical treatises or belles-lettres, should exemplify a Cambridge style. Accordingly, I constantly appealed to him for help in imparting style to a title-page, or a book-jacket or a column of advertisements. I was gratified, of course, that the lay-out of my little book on Johnson (published in February 1919) had been entrusted to him and I think he enjoyed the introduction of some unconventional details into A. E. Shipley's *Voyage of a Vice-Chancellor* and J. C. Lawson's *Litany of the Elves*, a fairy-story which revealed an unexpected side of the author's temperament. More important was the page he designed for the *New Shakespeare*. In the summer of 1919, he returned to America, where later happily I had more than one meeting with him.

I found the Syndicate meetings extremely interesting, especially when the report of Professor A on Mr B's manuscript was read and discussed. But in the years immediately after the war the keenest arguments were on the prices of books. Waller's view was uncompromising. Since printers' and binders' wages had doubled, the public must pay twice as much as before for the finished product. I think he probably applied his rule too rigorously and for a time the Press had an unenviable reputation for high prices. In fact, a learned Press will always have such a reputation and its fiercest critics are those within its home territory. Today they are mollified by the paperback.

The best things said at Syndicate meetings were frequently asides. Waller reported at one meeting that a lady, whose elementary Latin grammar for girls had been accepted, wished to call the book *Virginibus*. The school travellers, being convinced that this would militate against sales, were strongly opposed to such a title and Waller supported them. A discussion followed. In the

---

* John Dreyfus, *Bruce Rogers and American Typography* (1959).

course of it Peter Giles was heard to murmur through his heavy moustache: 'Ye'd better be on the safe side and call it *Puellis*.'

Charles Sayle, meeting me one day on King's Parade, inquired: 'What are you going to do about 1921?' I was puzzled.

'Cambridge printing began in 1521,' he said, 'and someone ought to write a history of the 400 years.'

I reported the conversation to Waller. 'I've no time for that sort of thing,' he said, 'I must leave it to you.'

I went home and thought about it. I had, in fact, written an article on the Press for Ogden's *Cambridge Magazine* in 1912, based largely on Robert Bowes's *Notes on the Cambridge Printers* (1886). In those *Notes* there was frequent reference to Registry MSS. relating to the Press. The Registry was then in the tower of the Pitt Press, and, after dipping into the documents, I decided to make the attempt. I had had no training in 'research' and many of the handwritings were formidable, but, fortunately, I had a quite definite time-limit. The book had to be published not later than 1 October 1921 or not at all. If I had undertaken it just as a leisurely parergon, I might well have spent years upon it. In fact, *A History of the Cambridge University Press 1521–1921* duly appeared at the beginning of the Michaelmas Term. Charles Sayle did not think much of it and said so in the *Cambridge Review*, but other reviewers were kinder and I was pleased when Bruce Rogers wrote from America: 'Your picture of the early succession of printers and their times is as lively as anything I know in the history of printing.'

On 10 November the Vice-Chancellor (E. C. Pearce, Master of Corpus) and the Syndics entertained more than a hundred authors, printers, publishers and academic dignitaries at dinner. Geoffrey Morris (Steward of Corpus) entered into the spirit of the occasion, and amongst the eight courses were *Consommé Richard Bentley* and *Canard Sauvage à la Pitt Press(e)*. The Vice-Chancellor of Oxford (L. R. Farnell), in a lengthy speech frequently interrupted by Ridgeway, proposed the toast of the Press. and Sir Frederick Macmillan replied for the guests.

47

Cambridge, as a whole, presented a lively scene in 1919. There were undergraduates straight from school side by side with colonels and brigadiers; there was also a group of young naval officers distributed among the colleges with a view to absorbing a little of the general culture of which war conditions had deprived them. In the University, as elsewhere, there was a strong undercurrent of feeling that the war had been managed, or mismanaged, by old men and there was a determination that youth should predominate in the reconstruction of university life. Hence the formation of the 'Under Forties', a body which I was induced to join; I paid my guinea and attended one meeting, but I cannot recall any specific activity in which I had a share. There were, indeed, plenty of problems for the young, with the occasional help of their elders, to tackle—compulsory Greek, degrees for women, and, above all, the University's need of financial help. Hence the Royal Commission of 1921 and the new Statutes of 1926.

Having no official responsibilities outside the Press, I was only on the fringe of all this activity. But I found one part of the fringe interesting. As I have already remarked, the Registrary (Dr J. N. Keynes) had his office in the tower of the Pitt Press. One of the Registrary's duties was, and is, the editorship of the *Cambridge University Reporter* and the *Reporter* contains verbatim accounts of discussions in the Senate House. For these discussions a shorthand-reporter was engaged and his script required careful editing. Dr Keynes wanted some help in this and I was nominated as his helper. My job was to attend discussions and to listen with sufficient attention to enable me to check the reporter's versions. Sometimes the debates were dull; but, on the whole, the atmosphere was livelier than it is today—there was more of the rough-and-tumble of debate and less reading of prepared speeches. There was, too, an element of party-politics which has now almost entirely disappeared. The parties were broadly denominated as 'Conservative' and 'Progressive'. The dividing-line was not always a clear one and there were some who were not unfairly taunted with being 'academic Liberals and university Conservatives'. But nominations of candidates for election to the Council of the Senate were normally on a party ticket and, if a special syndicate was appointed to examine a major problem, care was taken to give each party proper representation. Two well-known combatants in this context were Sorley, Professor of Moral Philosophy (Conservative) and Parry, Vice-Master of Trinity (Progressive). Both, I may add in parenthesis, were pillars of strength and sound judgement on the Press Syndicate, where political differences seldom obtruded.

One of the stoutest controversialists of the period was William Ridgeway ('To know Ridgeway', said E. G. Browne once, 'is to realise the Irish problem'). When he fought, he fought with the gloves off, and when, just before the war, the University agreed by a very small majority to accept the first tiny instalment of financial aid from the Treasury, he was violent in his denunciation of so dangerous a step.

The Women's Degrees discussions of 1919–20 brought Ridgeway and all the well-known debaters into the field. On one particular afternoon, J. H. Gray, of Queens', a rubicund clerical don of the old school and an editor of Plautus, made a good hard-hitting speech against the grant of further privileges to women. He was followed by another classic, Harris Rackham, of Christ's, who aptly commented on the 'Plautine geniality of Mr Gray'. The phrase stuck in my mind—and very fortunately, for in the reporter's typescript the phrase had become 'the fatuous senility of Mr Gray'.

There was a dramatic moment, too, when W. E. Heitland of St John's, a champion of the women's cause, was speaking. Stung by some imputations in the speech, Geoffrey Butler (youngest of that famous family of brothers) rose, white with indignation, and in his high-pitched voice cried out: 'I give you the lie, sir.' There was an uneasy stir in the Senate House. Heitland was very deaf. Cupping his ear, he looked about him in a puzzled way until someone strove to enlighten him. Heitland was still perplexed.

'Aspersions?' he murmured incredulously and went on with his speech.

What made the Senate House, and indeed the whole scene of academic controversy, more interesting for me was that I knew many of the participants as authors. With Ridgeway I was fortunate. He was an old ally of Leonard Whibley and had been devoted to my wife's uncle (Frederic Wallis, Bishop of Wellington, N.Z., and formerly Dean of Caius). So I began under good auspices, but Ridgeway could not help fearing the worst about the machinations of his opponents. When he knew that I was sub-editing reports of discussions, he warned me that he wanted every word he said to be faithfully recorded. He mentioned this, he said, in case pressure might be brought to bear upon me from other quarters. Once, perhaps, I had the right to claim the last word. It was when Ridgeway was president and I was treasurer of the Cambridge Classical Society. *The Journal of Philology* had come to an end and a general index to the volumes was badly needed. The Classical Society had some money in the bank and agreed to finance the printing of an index. Ridgeway, always a violent opponent of degrees for women, chose a woman for the job. When the copy for the index came in, it was far from satisfactory and required thorough revision. Ridgeway came to see me in a mood of unusual penitence. 'Oh, I'm sorry about this, Roberts. I'm very much disappointed.' 'Ah,' I replied, 'that's the worst of you, Professor. You will job in one of your *women* friends.'

It was characteristic of Ridgeway that he had proceeded to a doctor's degree not in literature, but in science. His *Origins of the Thoroughbred Horse* had been published in 1905 and he remained faithful to the Press—after his fashion. When a storm blew up on one occasion about the cost of some blocks, he wrote to Waller, asking him to begin his communications in future 'Dear Sir' and not 'Dear Dr Ridgeway'. At other times, as in the controversy about the *Encyclopaedia Britannica*, he would rally to our defence. 'Oh, I'm on your side,' he said to me, 'though I never mind blackguarding you, as you know.'

One of the mysteries of Cambridge in the 1920s was how Ridgeway contrived to cross the road in safety. The traffic, of course, was not what it is today, but, even so, it was formidable for anyone whose sight was as feeble as Ridgeway's. By the door of the Secretary's room at the Press stood a grandfather's clock. On his way out Ridgeway would try to walk through it.

Another half-blind, but indomitable, author was Guy Le Strange, whom I have seen consulting the catalogue in the University Library with his eye-lashes touching the page. He was editing a book of Spanish Ballads for the Press and came one day when Carey was alone in the Secretary's office. Le Strange knew Waller well and me slightly, but Carey not at all. Stumbling into the room, he asked: 'Are you Waller?' 'No.' 'Are you Roberts?' 'No.' And then, despairingly, 'Are you Somebody?'

With W. E. Heitland I had very pleasant relations. His association with the Press went back a long way. In 1874, he had offered his edition of *Cicero*, *Pro Murena* to the Press, having, 'found out that the University Press accepts books'—an interesting reminder of the time when the Syndics first awoke to the potentialities of textbook publishing. Heitland carried his books and papers in a schoolboy satchel slung over his shoulder and, unlike many of our authors, he presented us with MSS. which were a joy to proof-readers and compositors. He wrote a bold, upright hand, leaving always a wide inner margin and what he brought us was literally a fair copy. When we came to the title-page, we ran into one of his idiosyncrasies. He insisted on regarding it as a lapidary inscription and would have no full stops. All his books were by 'W E Heitland MA'. In 1926 I was delighted to hear that he proposed to offer us a book of reminiscences. I had heard from other Johnians of his aptness of phrase at college meetings; how, for instance, during a discussion of the quota of attendances at chapel, he had protested against 'this trafficking in the units of worship'. In fact, his *After Many Years* (1926) was disappointing. It was altogether too discreet. I told Heitland that I wished he had let himself go a little more. I had hoped, for example, for more about Perkins, the famous fox-hunting tutor of Downing. 'Oh,' said Heitland, 'if I'd once started writing about Jack Perkins...' The sentence, like the brief account in the book, was unfinished.

As I have already noted, I had come in the pre-war years to value the Union as a club and for a very short time before I took a commission in 1915, I served as Librarian. The Treasurer of the Society was McTaggart and when he attended a Library Committee, he was more than a financial watch-dog, for he was a voracious novel-reader. At one of the few meetings over which I presided, a particular novel was proposed for purchase and someone remarked that it had been banned in the United States. McTaggart quickly broke in: 'The fact that it was banned in America doesn't suggest a very high standard of indecency.'

When I returned from the war, I found that my short tenure of the librarianship had made me an *ex officio* member of the general committee. Like many others, and especially Theo Bartholomew, I looked forward to the re-opening of the Union dining-room, but when the question was raised in committee, McTaggart, supported by the Steward (E. Bullough) refused to take action. The charge for lunch would have to be raised from 1s. 6d. to 2s. 6d. and that, to undergraduates, would be prohibitive. I disagreed strongly and Theo and I, after discussing the new situation, set about raising a fund which would guarantee the Union against loss. We got good support and when I returned to the attack in committee, the previous decision was reversed. Bullough resigned and I became Steward in the Michaelmas Term of 1920. There was no unpleasantness. Bullough, having done the job for ten years, was glad, I think, of an opportunity to retire. As for the demand for meals at the higher prices, it was overwhelming and on Sundays we had to arrange for two or three sittings. I remained as Steward until the Michaelmas Term of 1922. The Kitchen Committee met at lunch once a term and experimented happily with new dishes and new wines. The most interesting dinner for which, in co-operation with Stanley Brown, the chief clerk, I was responsible was the centenary dinner held before the debate on 15 November 1921. It was a postponed celebration, the Union having been founded in 1815; but enthusiasm ran high and more than 100 sat down to dinner in what was then the drawing-room. Among the guests was H.R.H. the Duke of York (afterwards George VI), Lord Ullswater (formerly Mr Speaker Lowther) and General Seely (afterwards Lord Mottistone) and there were, naturally, many ex-Presidents. But the most remarkable guest was Sydney Gedge, who had been Secretary of the Union in 1852. At the age of 92 he made an admirable speech.

This association with the Union was entirely unexpected and I enjoyed it. Even less had I expected to be drawn into the new school of English in Cambridge. The English Tripos had been established in 1917 and the story of its foundation has been told with much personal detail by Eustace Tillyard.*

The first Tripos list (1919) contained the names of three men and fourteen women, but in the Michaelmas Term of that year many came flocking back to Cambridge delighted to find that they could read for two years for honours in English. The difficulty was that there were very few dons to teach them. There was Q, the Professor of English Literature; H. M. Chadwick, the Professor of Anglo-Saxon; and G. G. Coulton, the learned medievalist. But many more were needed and Chadwick went out into the highways and byways to find them. One of the by-ways was the University Press. One morning Chadwick, whom I knew only very slightly as the author of *The Origin of the English Nation*, came into the Press, harassed and breathless. 'Ye know all about Johnson, don't ye?' he said. I replied that I had written a book about him, but that it was a very little one.

'Well,' he went on, 'could ye take a little class? I can't stop now. I'm boxed for time, d'ye see? But you might see Downs† (ye know him, don't ye?) and have a little talk about it.'

---

* *The Muse Enchained* (1958).

† B. W. Downs, a lecturer both in English and Modern Languages; later Master of Christ's

I thought it might be an agreeable change to take a 'little class' once a fortnight, but when I entered the lecture-room I found an audience of about sixty eager young men and women, and the talk to a little class developed into a course of eight lectures on the Age of Johnson.

For a few years I was also asked to lecture on prose-writers of the seventeenth and nineteenth centuries, but Johnson was my special subject and for twenty-five years I continued to introduce freshmen to him and his contemporaries. At the end of that time I had, in the administrative sense, become unique. Before the statutes of 1926, anyone who was invited to lecture had the responsibility of collecting his own fees. Those who attended the lectures were asked to sign their names on slips of paper passed round. The first lecture could be regarded as a free sample, but for anyone who signed at the second or subsequent lecture, a bill was sent to the tutor concerned. After the establishment of the faculty system in 1926, this method of *per capita* payment was abolished. Composition fees were introduced and those, who, like myself, were not officially university lecturers, were paid an agreed fee by the General Board. Such fringe lecturers became rarer as time went on and I think the Board regarded me as an annoying survival of an older régime. But they had to put up with me until 1945.

In the early 1920s I was an examiner for a few years for the Preliminary Examination in English and I have a clear recollection of some of the examiners' meetings. We were, of course, a mixed body. Chadwick took the chair and, although he insisted that he knew nothing of literature after 1066, he consistently dominated the meeting; Tillyard, F. L. Lucas and Attwater had come over from the classical school; F. L. Attenborough helped Chadwick with the Anglo-Saxon; H. S. Bennett looked after the medieval paper and A. B. Cook made himself responsible for the paper on Tragedy. At the preliminary meeting, Chadwick would read through the questions proposed by the examiners. One of his own was: 'What were the recreations in the Viking Age of (*a*) men, (*b*) women?' For A. B. Cook this was too good a chance to miss. 'Mr Chairman', he interposed in his high-pitched voice, 'would a candidate receive full marks if he answered (*a*) women, (*b*) men?'

Later, I was occasionally invited to be one of the referees for a Ph.D. thesis. The first time I was asked, I felt uncertain about accepting the invitation. I could not pretend to any profundity of scholarship and I was not clear about the standards of judgement. However, being partially reassured by a talk with an experienced examiner, I agreed to act. The subject of the thesis was Journalism and Literature (with special reference to the eighteenth century), and my co-examiner was George Saintsbury. I took pains over my report, and it was a great relief to me, when, later, I was allowed to read Saintsbury's and found that, with a wealth of documentation, he had reached the same favourable conclusion. The reports were duly submitted to the Board of Research Studies and, strictly speaking, they should have asked both examiners to give the candidate a *viva*. But Saintsbury, aged eighty, was living in retirement in Bath and, in view of the concurrence of opinion shown in the reports, further scrutiny of any points in the thesis was entrusted to me. The candidate was F. R. Leavis.

Of the books published at the Press during the later years of the war, two that interested me especially were Cecil Torr's *Small Talk at Wreyland* and Quiller-Couch's *On the Art of Writing*. Torr had sent his MS. to the Press with a view to it being printed for private circulation. But Peace, after looking at the proofs, had very wisely suggested to the Syndics that they might properly put their publishing imprint upon it. Reviewers had been uniformly enthusiastic. One of them (J. C. Squire, I think) wrote that his first thought had been: 'What on earth is the University Press doing with small talk in an obscure village' and his second: 'How enterprising they were to get hold of such an odd and excellent book!' As I pondered this second remark, I felt that such a spirit of enterprise might well be fostered in the future.

Q had been appointed to the Chair of English Literature in 1912. Classical dons had raised their eyebrows at the establishment of the English Tripos. But there was no doubt about the success of Q's professorial lectures. They were written with immense care and marked for emphasis, accent and pause. At the same time they were written with a view to publication and they were welcomed as keenly by readers as by listeners. The chapter on *Jargon* acquired a particular fame and other publishers frequently applied for leave to include it in volumes of selected essays.

There was one series of lectures, that on *Shakespeare's Workmanship*, which Q had felt bound to give to Fisher Unwin in fulfilment of an earlier contract. These lectures had a particular interest for Waller in relation to a plan which he was preparing for a new Cambridge Shakespeare and the textual editor whom he had in mind was John Dover Wilson.

Dover Wilson, after taking his degree in History and winning the Harness Prize for an essay on John Lyly, had in 1909 become a lecturer at Goldsmith's College in the University of London. His *Life in Shakespeare's England* (1911) was one of the first successful textbooks with which I had become familiar and in the later years of the war he had made an intensive study of *Hamlet* and, in collaboration with A. W. Pollard, of the 'Stolne and surreptitious' texts of Shakespeare.

So the way seemed clear for an edition comprising a scholar's text, prefaced by essays written by an accomplished and most readable critic. The proposal was welcomed by the Syndics, some of whom wished to delay publication until the corpus of the plays could be published as a completed work. But Waller had asked Bruce Rogers to design a page with a view to the separate publication of each play and, for once, he used the typographical distinction of B. R.'s lay-out to support his argument. Q and Dover Wilson were brought together and became warm friends. Waller, of course, was delighted and visualised the production of, say, five or six plays per annum. In eight or, at the most, ten years Cambridge would have a text of Shakespeare based on the most recent research and adorned by the most humane of literary professors. *Editoribus aliter visum.* The start was fairly promising. Three comedies appeared in 1921, two in 1922, and two in 1923, but thereafter the pace flagged. Q had trouble with his eyes and the last comedy (*The Winter's Tale*) was not published until 1931. But this part of the story is best described in Dover Wilson's own words:

As I look back to the day eleven years ago when what came to be called 'The New Shakespeare' was first projected, I am amazed at the light-heartedness of those concerned. 'A handy, inexpensive Shakespeare in 40 volumes, each volume to contain a critical introduction, some few textual and bibliographical notes and possibly a very brief glossary'. Such were the original proposals for an edition, six volumes of which were expected to appear annually! The truth is, of course, that none of us knew what we were in for, least of all perhaps the textual editor. And I should like to take the opportunity of this truant excursion to express my gratitude to both publishers and fellow-editor for much long-suffering and great kindness. The former without a murmur saw their thin little volumes padded out to twice the contemplated length with notes and a full glossary, neither of any commercial value, and the pace of production correspondingly slowed down to one or two plays a year. The latter, once he perceived that he was launched on a south sea of discovery with a hare-brained mate on board, threw himself into the enterprise in the spirit of a true Cornishman. Any other captain, seeing the direction of the ship, would have put back to port or at least ordered the mate to keep the stipulated course; this one bade clap on all sail and run before the wind.*

In the earliest stages of the enterprise my own part was slight. The design of the binding was left to me, and Waller had many talks with me on matters of detail. In the later history of the edition I was destined to play a larger part.

In the summer of 1922 Waller's health failed. Shortly after the last Syndicate meeting of the term he retired, much against his will, to bed and during the period of what turned out to be

* *Modern Language Review*, xxv (1930), 397.

his last illness I carried on as his deputy. Of the books in hand or under consideration at that time, two remain most clearly in my memory. The first was a small book on *The Beggar's Opera* by Frank Kidson recently accepted by the Syndics. It seemed to call for a piece of period printing and I enjoyed collaborating with F. G. Nobbs, overseer in the composing room, in making full use of the initials and ornaments to which Bruce Rogers had introduced us. I also devised an unacademic binding (canvas back with label, ornamented paper sides) and prescribed a bright yellow paper for the jacket. The admirable man responsible for ordering paper brought me a sample which I regarded as anaemic. 'Oh, I see, Mr Roberts', he said, 'you want something beyond canary.' I did.

The second arose out of a letter to Waller from A. C. Benson, who was then just recovering from a breakdown. In the letter he explained that he wanted 'some literary work of a mild kind'. Did the Press want a little book of selections, prose or verse? In reply I suggested *Selections from Ruskin* as a possibility. Benson responded very favourably and a little later asked me to dine with him in Magdalene. I thoroughly enjoyed the evening. Benson's talk was entirely free from the introspective sentimentality of some of his essays. In particular, we exchanged many anecdotes of A. J. Mason. The Ruskin book was published in the following year.

On 19 July 1922 Waller died. The obituarist of *The Times*, after a proper tribute to the *Cambridge History of English Literature*, of which Waller was the principal architect, rightly stressed the value of his constant awareness that the Press was not an institution specifically endowed for the publication of works of scholarship, but a business which had itself to endow such works by a careful garnering of profits on textbooks.

Certainly I learnt a great deal from Waller, especially about the economics of publishing. In matters of typographical taste, we frequently disagreed, but he was always willing to listen and, having delegated the business of binding to me, he remained loyally aloof even when he deplored my choice. He thought I was too fond of printer's ornaments and intensely disliked the brown cloth I chose for the new Shakespeare.

During the later part of July I was, naturally, in a state of some uncertainty. Was I too obviously an 'Under Forty' to be entrusted with the Syndics' business? At the vacation meeting in August the Syndics took the risk and made me their Secretary.

Chapter 4

SECRETARY TO THE SYNDICS

The man who meant most to me in my early years as Secretary was Hugh Kerr Anderson, Master of Caius. He had first made a reputation as a physiologist and had been elected a Fellow of the Royal Society in 1907. But both his college and the University had noted his exceptional ability in what is called administration, and when he succeeded M. R. James as chairman of the Press Syndicate he was the dominating influence in its deliberations. Yet dominance was the last quality one would have attributed to him. He was lovably, even absurdly, modest. When the mastership of Caius fell vacant on the death of E. S. Roberts in 1912, Anderson confided to a colleague that he was a little hurt because no one had asked for his views about a suitable successor. The obvious reason for his being left out of the discussion had not occurred to him. At the Press, as at the Council of the Senate and the Financial Board, he grasped the essential points of a problem with unerring judgement. He pretended to know little about literature, but he had a fine taste and a sure instinct for quality. When he approached a financial question he would compile sheet after sheet of figures, always clearly set out and always written in Indian ink.

Since my return in 1919 I had improved my knowledge of printing and publishing; but when I became Secretary, I knew that I had much more to learn and it was to Anderson that I constantly turned. Although the Press was only one of his many responsibilities, his study door was always open to me and when we had finished our business, he frequently pressed me to stay for lunch and a gossip—for he was as deeply interested in human beings as he was in budgetary estimates. One of his major pre-occupations was his membership not only of the Royal Commission on Oxford and Cambridge but of the Statutory Commission for Cambridge and I believe that it was he, more than anyone else, who was responsible for the introduction of the faculty system under which all lecturers were to be university lecturers.

Though not so intimately connected with the University Library as with the Press, he was in fact one of its most notable benefactors. When negotiations were opened in 1927 with the Rockefeller Foundation for help in building the new library, the Council of the Senate wisely made him the university's plenipotentiary and his work is fittingly commemorated in the entitlement of the Anderson Room.

Like other mortals, he had his heel of Achilles—the making of a public speech. He refused to be nominated for the vice-chancellorship, but he could not always escape from the duty which he most deeply hated. One morning I found him in his study in a state of profound depression.

'Read this,' he said, handing me two sheets of paper, 'it's awful, I know it is, but read it and tell me candidly what you think.'

It was the draft of what he proposed to say at the annual Perse Feast. After reading it, I suggested one or two insignificant alterations, but it was a perfectly adequate piece of composition and I said so.

'Oh no, it isn't. You're only saying that to please me. I think I shall resign.'

J. F. Cameron, his successor both as Master of Caius and as chairman of the Press, told me afterwards that such threats of resignation were common form.

Firm and confident in matters of organisation and finance, Anderson quickly retired into his shell of diffidence if he felt that he was not qualified to deal with an item on the Press agenda. The publication of the Revised Prayer Book of 1928, notwithstanding its rejection by Parliament, raised some awkward constitutional questions and Anderson felt uncomfortable in the chair. The Vice-Chancellor in 1928 was the Rev. T. C. Fitzpatrick, President of Queens', and a few days before the Syndicate meeting Anderson said to me: 'I'm going to make the V-C take the chair on Friday for the Prayer Book discussion. I'm only a damned Presbyterian.'

I loved working with Anderson; even more I loved the man.

When sessions of the Statutory Commission prevented Anderson from attending meetings at the Press, we had a good vice-chairman in W. R. Sorley. A moral philosopher and a man of staunch conservative principles, he could always be relied on for a sound judgement of men and books. Like Anderson, he was willing to spend much time and trouble on financial detail; unlike Anderson, he rather enjoyed making a little speech when the occasion demanded it and he could state a case with great clarity.

Another Syndic who gave me valuable help, especially in the technique of accounting, was G. H. A. Wilson, Secretary of the Financial Board. Under the new Statutes of 1926, he was the first holder of the title of Treasurer of the University and it was at my suggestion, some years later, that the Treasurer became an *ex officio* member of the Syndicate. Wilson went on to be Master of Clare, member of Parliament for the University and Vice-Chancellor. He had a very quick brain and an equally quick sense of humour. Gradually we became intimate and had some entertaining holidays together in Norfolk and North Wales, playing golf by day and bridge by night.

I had already been long enough at the Press to appreciate the fundamental importance of school and university textbooks and my first proposal at the time of my own appointment was that Gordon Carey should assume responsibility for that side of the business with the title of Educational Secretary. He had a wide knowledge of schools and schoolmasters and this, I knew, would be of value not only in selling books but in securing authors. For the post of Assistant Secretary the two candidates finally considered were R. J. L. Kingsford, of Clare, and Sir Richard Rees, Bart., of Trinity. Liking them both, the Syndics decided that there was room for a young man in London as well as in Cambridge. Richard Rees did not stay long. We all liked him, but it soon became clear that he would not settle down to the routine of a publishing house. Kingsford, on the other hand, showed himself from the first to be the man made for the job and we worked together in complete harmony for twenty-five years. Apart from the basic necessity of good textbooks, there were other matters of policy in my mind. I was, for instance, anxious to show that not all the products of a university press were learned treatises. For an academic imprint has a double edge: it is, or ought to be, a guarantee of sound scholarship; but it also is frequently regarded as a guarantee of unreadability. All that I wanted to prove was that, given the opportunity, the Press could sell an unacademic work of good quality as successfully as any other publisher.

Broadly speaking, manuscripts offered to the Press were in three classes: first, there were those which were rejected out of hand either because they were rubbish or because they were wholly unsuited to the Press catalogue; I never ceased to marvel at the persistent optimism of those authors who submitted work so remote from the standards of a university publishing house. Secondly, there were the manuscripts of serious intention on every kind of subject; for these the first thing to do was to choose the most competent referee, or, if the choice were not obvious, to ask one of the Syndics for advice. Lastly, there was the manuscript of general interest, or of what the author thought would be of general interest. It was this class which had a special interest for me and when, very soon after I became Secretary, the manuscript of George Sturt's *The Wheelwright's Shop* arrived, I took it home to read myself. Naturally, the work contained many technicalities, but, as I read it, I appreciated its intensely human interest as well as its value as a document of social history. I presented my report to the Syndics, adding that they might well wish to obtain another opinion; but Anderson brushed the suggestion aside and the book was accepted.

When it was published in the spring of 1923, I was greatly pleased by its reception. Unfortunately I never met the author. He was a sick man at the time, but just well enough to enjoy the welcome which the book received. On 6 May he wrote to me:

I am very feeble (after another slight stroke) but I cannot quite forego the pleasure of saying thank you, which I have long promised myself. Long ago, before it was finished, I thought I should like the Cambridge Press to publish it, but I hardly hoped, and never expected, to see it got up so beautifully. You have really made me a man very much to be congratulated and it is only common decency to acknowledge my great obligation to you.

After Sturt's death we also published *A Small Boy in the Sixties*, for which I got his devoted friend, Arnold Bennett, to write an introduction. *The Wheelwright's Shop* went into many editions and received the rare distinction of a blessing by *Scrutiny*, which judged Sturt to be 'incomparably more intelligent and more important than the conventional classics...as potently evocative of what we have lost as Lawrence'.

One reader in a thousand of Sturt's book may possibly have been stirred to curiosity by the imprint on the last page: 'Printed by the Syndics of the Press at the University Press.' Why 'the Syndics' instead of the name of the University Printer? The explanation is tragically simple: in January 1923 J. B. Peace, appointed Printer in the middle of the war, went home after his day's work, sat back in his chair and died. A powerful oarsman in his early days, he had had no cause to consult a doctor for many years and the suddenness of his death was truly shattering. He had had no specific training as a printer, but he was a good man of business and a good engineer; above all, he knew how to handle men and perhaps the finest tribute to him was the spontaneity with which the whole staff of the printing house marched in column of fours from Great St Mary's Church to the graveside after the funeral service.

For the Syndics, and for me, the situation was serious. Peace had loyal and efficient heads of departments, but he had no deputy and for four months I was, in effect, Acting Printer. In that capacity I attended a conference on printing design at the Royal Society of Arts—not an important affair, but for me memorable because I ventured upon an argument with the eminent G. W. Jones and because I met Stanley Morison for the first time.

But the important thing was to find a University Printer. Anderson, as always, was the embodiment of sympathy and strength. We went to London together and first had a talk with Richard Austen-Leigh, who was admirably clear and frank: 'What you want, of course, is a university man who is also a first-rate printer. Any such men are probably directors of private printing houses and the salary you can offer would not tempt them away. Your only hope is to find a works manager and promote him.'

'But do you know of such a man?' Anderson asked.

'Well, there is a good man named Lewis who was with us [i.e. the Ballantyne Press] for a time and then ran a press in Manchester. I rather think he's not in a good job at the moment.'

We went on, at my suggestion, to see G. H. Grubb, head of Putnam's London house, whom I had got to know very well. He had not much to offer, but he, too, said 'There used to be a man named Lewis...'

In the end, the Syndics considered several candidates, but before the official interviews at Cambridge, Anderson and I had a talk with Lewis at Fetter Lane. When he had left us, Anderson seemed worried. Very tentatively he said to me: 'I rather liked that chap.' 'Oh, so did I, Master', I replied. Anderson's face cleared at once and in March Lewis came to a full Syndicate meeting and was appointed University Printer.

It was an important day in the history of Cambridge printing. Lewis had learned his trade under his father's eye at Butler and Tanner's and had risen to be works manager of the Ballantyne Press and, later, manager of the Cloister Press at Manchester. The old hands in the printing house at Cambridge welcomed him politely, but reserved judgement; it was not long before they recognised that they were in the charge of a master-craftsman. If at any time they seemed dubious about the operation of some technical improvement, Lewis would demonstrate precisely what he wanted. If there was any demur, he made it abundantly clear (for, when roused, he had a powerful vocabulary at his command) that his instructions were final. Accustomed as he was to the fluctuations and anxieties of the printing trade, he was astonished at the normally even flow of work at the Press and at the long and continuous employment which the men enjoyed. 'Gawd in heaven,' he would say, 'you chaps seem to come here and bring your tombstones with you.' Of university life he had no experience, but he had an instinctive and profound respect for scholars and scholarship.

One morning, soon after his arrival, John Oman, the learned Presbyterian, came to see me. He brought with him the manuscript of a short work on the text of Revelation and explained that he wanted the printing of the text to correspond exactly with the manuscript on which it was based. 'This is a typographical problem,' I said, 'come and meet our new printer.' So we went across to Lewis's room and Oman began his explanation of the Greek text afresh. Lewis interrupted him: 'I'm a printer, sir. I know my Greek alphabet, but that's all.' 'Ah, weel,' said Oman, 'there are a guid many people in this univairsity who don't know any more.'

After Lewis had settled into his work, he talked to me about Stanley Morison, with whom he had worked at the Cloister Press. 'You'd like him,' he said, 'he's the academic type.' So Morison lunched with me in the grill room of the old Holborn Restaurant and the upshot was that in October 1924 he was appointed typographical adviser to the Press.

Lewis and Morison made a wonderful pair. Morison, after heading towards the extreme Left in his youth, had joined the Church of Rome and liturgiology was one of the many subjects in which he rapidly acquired the authority of a scholar. Lewis was a stalwart old-fashioned Liberal with little interest in ecclesiastical affairs as such. So they found plenty to argue about and, as they warmed to their work, they could be heard shouting each other down from the other side of the Press courtyard. Lewis had a keen appreciation of Morison's inspired typography ('I'm not a typographer,' he would say, 'I'm just a printer') and Morison had a deep respect for Lewis's integrity both as craftsman and as man of business.

Officially, Morison was employed by the printing business, but on his visits to Cambridge he would often come first to my room for a talk. After ten minutes I would hear Lewis's voice on the house-telephone:

'You got a chap called Morison with you?'

'Yes.'

'Well, ask him who pays his fare.'

Then, with a burst of Homeric laughter, Morison would slap his thigh and hurry off to Lewis's room, to be greeted with 'Well, old tin-ribs, how many cancels are you going to want for this job?'

The early 1920s were, in fact, marked by a typographical renaissance which had a notable influence upon book-production; or perhaps it would be more accurate to say that the war interrupted a movement which had already begun. Gerard Meynell at the Westminster Press was a pioneer and was responsible both for a new type, the 'Imprint', and for a typographical journal to which he gave the same name. The journal had a brief life of nine numbers in 1913. By that time hand-setting was giving way to monotype keyboards and casters with the result that the printer's scope and the publisher's choice were immensely widened. It is true that during the 'nineties new standards had been applied to the printing of poetry and belles-lettres, but it was not until after the war that publishers as a whole began to recognise that the basic principles of book-design could, and should, be exemplified as clearly in a half-crown textbook as in a three-guinea *édition de luxe*.

With Lewis as printer and Morison as typographer, we were well equipped to take a share in the movement and examples of Cambridge printing were prominent in exhibitions of contemporary book-production organised by the Bibliographical Society and other bodies.

One by-product of the movement was a dining club—the Double Crown. The first president was Holbrook Jackson and in 1924 I was invited to join the original committee in company with Frank Sidgwick (founder of Sidgwick and Jackson); Hubert Foss (manager of the music department of the Oxford Press); Oliver Simon (of the Curwen Press); G. Wren Howard (director of Jonathan Cape); and Gerard Meynell. The *raison d'être* of the club was quite simply defined as the exchange of ideas on good printing and the rules provided that it should meet for dinner not more than six and not less than four times a year. The name given to the club was ambivalent. 'Double crown' is familiar to printers as a size of paper; but the club also proposed to 'crown' two books a year: (1) a book published in the ordinary way at not more than fifteen shillings, (2) a *biblion abiblion*. This proposed coronation was the one notable failure in the club's activities. In 1925 a 'crown' was awarded to a slim volume of poems, with wood-engravings by Eric Gill, printed in a limited edition at the Golden Cockerel Press. Copies were duly distributed to members, but were not welcomed. In particular, I remember Lewis's scornful comments and his even more scornful markings in the book itself. In 1927 there was another 'crowning', which again provoked a storm of caustic criticism. 'The club', wrote Frank Sidgwick, 'may be thankful that no verbatim record exists of what was said on either occasion', and coronations were thereafter abandoned.

But the main purpose of the club was amply fulfilled. For each dinner one member was made responsible for the typography of the menu. Oliver Simon was the designer for the first dinner on 31 October 1924 and presented us with a very delicate piece of printing and a still-life decoration by another member, Thomas

Lowinksy. For the second dinner we had a brochure entitled 'Familiar Faces' with the menu printed in a series of caricatures of four different typographical styles. Gerard Meynell, the designer, evidently had enjoyed his little exercise in burlesque. The subject of discussion was 'Type Faces of To-day' and the club guest was Emery Walker. Paul Nash produced something entirely different for the next dinner—a single sheet with a bold woodcut at the head, printed by Philip Sainsbury. Will Rothenstein was the guest of the club.

Some of the most interesting papers were those read by guests —Charles Whibley for instance, who spoke about the printing of the Bible and was roused to indignation by Humbert Wolfe; Osbert Sitwell on Baroque printing; Walter de la Mare on the printing of poetry. This last was afterwards printed for the club at Cambridge and is a perfect example of what an after-dinner discourse should be—intimate, urbane, discursive, yet not wholly irrelevant. 'Some men', he said, talking of his own collection of poetry, 'are born with a library, some acquire a library, others become reviewers.'

When Lewis was induced to read a paper, the title was announced as 'The Technique of Machining', but Lewis preferred to call it 'Making Ready' and gave us an essentially practical talk. 'Good, even colour' was the highest praise he ever gave to what he called a 'decent job'. Morison, with whom I collaborated in a menu descriptive of the work of Ichabod Dawks, was naturally prominent in propounding new ideas on 'prelims' and other topics. Coming away from one dinner, I remarked to him that we had had a paper with a pleasant literary flavour. 'I'm not interested in literature', he replied, 'I want information.'

I derived great pleasure, and perhaps some information, from the dinners I attended, but by 1934 I found it difficult to be a frequent diner and resigned my membership. Soundly based upon Johnson's definition ('an assembly of good fellows, meeting under certain conditions') the Double Crown Club still flourishes, as I found when, in 1964, I was invited to a dinner to celebrate its fortieth anniversary. Two other original members (Tom Balston and Geoffrey Keynes) were there; Morison and Francis Meynell made tape-recordings for the occasion.

In general, Morison was a superb guest and one night in Pembroke I arranged that he should sit next to Bethune-Baker after dinner. Theologically, they were poles apart, but Morison had a profound respect for Bethune-Baker as the editor of the *Journal of Theological Studies*. They got on very well and Bethune-Baker said to me afterwards: 'I liked your friend. Bring him to dinner with us the next time he comes.' So, some time later, my wife, Morison and I dined with the Bethune-Bakers at their house in Cranmer Road. The only other guest was Alexander Nairne, Regius Professor of Divinity, and at dinner the talk was on general topics. After dinner it drifted into theology and at one point Morison burst out: 'That's the sort of church that I belong to—a great, driving, persecuting church...'

'Quite so', said Bethune-Baker in his iciest tones; 'years ago I had hopes that it might become a *Christian* church.'

Nairne was clearly distressed. 'Oh dear,' he pleaded, 'can't we all say our prayers together?'

Nairne, as we all recognised, was the embodiment of Christian charity. One afternoon at the Press, Lewis and I watched him as he crossed the courtyard. 'There goes a real saint', I said.

'Yes, mister [Lewis had an engaging habit of substituting "Mister" for "Sir"]. He's for heaven all right—unless the Lord don't know his job.'

In 1924 Nairne took part in the preparation of an important schoolbook. The Cambridgeshire Education Committee, inspired by its remarkable Secretary, Henry Morris, had issued a new Syllabus of Religious Instruction which was welcomed and adopted by many other authorities. The Syllabus was published at the Press and led to the production of two anthologies: the *Children's Bible* and the *Little Children's Bible*. The editorial triumvirate was carefully chosen: Nairne as Professor of Divinity; Quiller-Couch as Professor of English; and T. R. Glover representing the Free Churches. The choice of passages naturally involved some differences of opinion and Q told Glover that he regarded himself as 'the pure white leaf in the Bible dividing the Old and New Testaments'. Gordon Carey handled all the details of publication and my old friend Marjory Whittington did some pleasing and unconventional drawings for the illustrated edition. The books were produced in various styles of binding, some of them peculiar to the Bible trade. Q was tickled by the varieties offered and sent me the following on a post-card from Fowey:

> The Children's Bible
> In this climate is li'ble
>   In 'Cloth Limp'
> To be damp as a shrimp;
>   'Cloth Boards'
> No protection affords
>   Against water spilt.
> Even less, Cloth Gilt.
>   'Pluviusin'
> Lets J. Pluvius in.
>   Moroccoette
>   6s net...will yet
>   let wet get
> Thro' to the text.
> Wherefore, O perplexed
>   And Christian friend
>   The Syndics recommend
>   POLISHED LEATHER
>   DEFIES EVERY WEATHER

The two schoolbooks were followed by a more substantial anthology, the *Cambridge Shorter Bible*, about which Q wrote to me in 1925:

I understand that in these halcyon days the Regius Professor of Divinity and the Public Orator are both sitting on the final egg of Father Carey's Chicken. The balance is insecure and the egg is like to be a Curate's Egg unless Carey and I (I say it modestly) do a bit of adjusting.

However, the adjustments were made and the book was published in 1928.

In my early years as Secretary I had from time to time to deal with proposals which involved research into the unfamiliar past. In 1923, for instance, I received a curt note from Wallis Budge, Keeper of Egyptian Antiquities at the British Museum, stating that his work on Egyptian mummies, published in 1893, had long been out of print and would I let him know without delay whether the Press would be interested in a new edition? I looked up earlier correspondence; what little I could find was of a frigid character and I felt that it would be politic to have a talk with what appeared to be a militant author. So I made an appointment to call upon him at the British Museum. The journey to his room seemed endless and when I finally reached it, I saw a tubby little figure crouching over a kettle and a spirit-stove. Having briefly greeted me, he said:

'The last man I dealt with at the Cambridge Press was a damned scoundrel. How old are you?'

'I'm 36.'

'I'm 66. Like a cup of tea?'

Over the tea-cups he became more genial. The new edition of *The Mummy* was duly accepted by the Syndics and Budge quickly forgot his old grievance. He came up to Cambridge and had lunch with me and I discovered that Cecil Torr was an old friend of his. Budge was evidently very fond of him, but complained that he was extremely fussy and old-maidish. Some time later, when my wife and I had lunch with Torr in his beautifully appointed house in Devonshire, I mentioned Budge's name. 'Yes,' said Torr, 'he's a very old friend of mine, but when he comes to stay with me, he will smoke very strong Burmah cheroots all day.'

Another author who caused me to refer back to ancient files was J. S. Reid, Professor of Ancient History. Elsewhere* I have recorded how in 1923 he apologised for the lateness of the com-

* *The Evolution of Cambridge Publishing* (1956).

pletion of his edition of Cicero, *de Finibus*; and how I eventually found that the delivery of the manuscript had been expected in the Long Vacation of 1879.

At the other end of the scale, it was pleasant to receive proposals from friends and contemporaries. Geoffrey Keynes, for instance, submitted an edition of Milton's *On the Morning of Christ's Nativity*, with six unpublished illustrations by Blake, which was published in time for Christmas 1923. As well as the ordinary edition we printed 150 copies on hand-made paper, which were quickly subscribed. Geoffrey's other proposal was for an edition of Donne's *Devotions*. The editor, he said, was a schoolboy, but he would vouch for the quality of the editing. Thus was published the first work of John Sparrow. Geoffrey himself is an insatiable collector and bibliographer and his *Bibliography of Sir Thomas Browne* (1924) was the first of several that we published for him.

In 1924 H.I.H. Taffari Makonnen (now Emperor of Ethiopia) received an honorary degree from the University. Stephen Gaselee, then Librarian of the Foreign Office, wrote to me to say that the Ras Taffari would like to see something of the University Press, but that he would probably not have more than twenty minutes to spare for it. He went on to advise me to show him some old-fashioned hand-composition and not to worry him with complicated machinery. The Ras was courteous, dignified and silent, but I contrived to have a little talk in French. We took him and the six chieftains who accompanied him to watch a compositor setting up the Lord's Prayer in Amharic, but they did not seem deeply impressed. As we came through the courtyard, the door of the large machine-room was open and immediately the party became alert and interested. One of the chieftains (whom I afterwards discovered to be the Foreign Minister) surprised me by speaking in halting English: 'What is book?' he asked, pointing to the machine. I told him that it was a volume of the *Cambridge Modern History*. 'Can I have copy?', he asked. 'Of course', I replied. But after consultation with Gaselee, I sent him two volumes of my *Picture Book of British History* and in due course received a charming letter of thanks.

In 1926 I was invited to join the Family, the oldest dining club in Cambridge. The precise date of its foundation is unknown, but in origin it was almost certainly a Jacobite club. Quite certainly it was well established in the time of Richard Farmer in the 1780s. There are twelve members and each is host once a year. Some of the members (Hugh Anderson, G. H. A. Wilson, E. C. Pearce) I already knew well, others only slightly. 'From the day I joined it', wrote M. R. James in his book of reminiscences (*Eton and King's*), 'its meetings were things to look forward to'— a feeling which I shared. The senior member was J. J. Thomson, whose *Conduction of Electricity through Gases* had been published at the Press before my time. At a Family dinner he never talked about physics, but he could tell a good story—sometimes against himself. Once, he told me, the College had decided to offer the Clark lectureship in English Literature to someone called Chambers. 'I went back to my study,' he said, 'looked up *Who's Who* and found a Chambers who was a Professor of English in the University of London. That seemed all right and I invited him—but it was the wrong Chambers!'

Meanwhile the problem of the American market was very much in my mind. In 1920 a ten-year agency contract with G. P. Putnam's Sons had expired and the Syndics had reverted to the Macmillan Company of New York. In Waller's time I had met George Haven Putnam (a gallant and slightly garrulous veteran of the civil war) and also George P. Brett, president of the Macmillan Company. The argument was always the same. Our agents urged that they would sell more of our books if only they could buy them at a lower price; to which the reply was that we were not interested in selling books below cost. But, our agents argued, it will cost you practically nothing but the paper to run off a few hundred copies for us; yes, was the reply, but why should the heavy initial cost be borne only by the English buyer?

Another problem was the author's very natural demand for a higher return on American sales, and feeling that it was time for me to study the problem at first hand in New York, I booked a passage in the *Olympic* in the spring of 1925. Later I heard that R. W. Chapman and Humphrey Milford of the Oxford Press would also be on board and I was pleased at the prospect of congenial company. With Chapman I was already on common Johnsonian ground and in the previous year we had both been elected to membership of the Arcades, the Oxford and Cambridge dining club founded in 1900 by J. L. Myres, Leonard Whibley and others. Of Milford I had seen less, but by the end of the voyage we were old friends. Chapman was already at work on Johnson's *Letters*; Milford and I played deck-tennis. Milford generally had a World's Classic in his pocket and although he did not re-read a book, as Chapman did, 'in the hope of finding a corruption in the text', I noticed that every now and then he would bring out a pencil and correct a misprint.

We parted at New York, where I was warmly welcomed, in the first instance, by Bruce Rogers, who had become printing adviser to the Harvard University Press and was also working with W. E. Rudge at Mount Vernon. Although he had complained at Cambridge about 'the unpromising kind of books' with which the Press was normally concerned, it was clear to me that he looked back on his time at Cambridge with a certain measure of affection. But my main objective, of course, was the Macmillan Company. I wanted to see for myself how our books were handled and to devise, if possible, some improvement in their circulation. George P. Brett treated me very courteously and regarded me, I think, as a young man in a hurry, but I assured him, quite honestly, that I had come to learn. I arranged special terms for certain books and appreciated, more keenly than I could ever have done at home, the difficulties of distributing our highly specialised academic publications over a vast country. Good bookshops were rare and the importance of the mail-order department was something new to me.

I left New York for Boston with plenty to think about. Bruce Rogers came with me and introduced me to Harold Murdock, chairman of the Harvard University Press. At Harvard, W. W. Buckland (Professor of Roman Law at Cambridge and a Syndic of the Press) was in residence as visiting professor and with him I paid courtesy calls upon President Lowell and Professor Roscoe Pound. He also took me to a dinner organised by the Rhodes Trustees at which Chapman and Milford were present. Inevitably, I was asked to say a few words and I recalled the form in which I had been welcomed by one American publisher: 'Glad to get a grip of Mr Roberts; the Oxford outfit was here yesterday.' It seemed to me a sad symbol of the priority of Oxford publishing in the minds of Americans at that time.

From Boston I went on to New Haven, where for the first time I met the distinguished Yale printer, Carl Rollins; then, via Buffalo, to Toronto, where we were also represented by the Macmillan Company, and then to Chicago. There the position was in part reversed. The Chicago University Press acted at that time as agents for our journals, but their own publications were handled by us in Great Britain and it was my turn to explain why we did not sell more of them. The officials of the Press were most friendly and gave me a round of golf on a beautiful course. At Cincinnati I spent a night with one of my earliest author-friends, B. A. G. Fuller, and broke my journey at Washington on my way back to New York. Combined with my publishing pilgrimage were many entertaining encounters with Johnsonians, which are recorded in another chapter.

I rejoined Chapman and Milford in the *Homeric* and found that they had collected another fellow-traveller—Sir Hugh Allen, Professor of Music at Oxford. I know little about music, but that did not militate against our companionship, though he sometimes found it hard to bear the orchestra's favourite tunes—'Tea for Two' and the 'Indian Love Lyrics'. Chapman and Milford went off in a car from Southampton and Allen and I took the boat-train in the afternoon. Half-way through the journey he said suddenly: 'By Jove, I've got to go to the Royal Academy dinner to-night.' Whereupon he disappeared into the lavatory and came back fully dressed for the evening.

One of several introductions to American scholars which I had taken with me was from E. G. Browne, with whom I had had a most friendly talk before I left. At that time he was convalescent after a severe illness and in June 1925 he was shattered by the sudden death of his wife. He never recovered from the blow and died six months later. His first book, *A Year amongst the Persians* had been published in 1893 by A. and C. Black, Adam Black having been a contemporary of Browne's at Pembroke. Like Doughty's *Arabia Deserta* before it, the book had been a commercial failure. Browne was then young and unknown, but long before his death he had been recognised as the greatest exponent of Persian life and letters and I welcomed the suggestion of a new edition. Sir Denison Ross agreed to write an introductory memoir and we did our best to make the book typographically worthy of its author. The new edition was widely praised for its format as well as its content; little did I think that I should one day spend a fortnight amongst the Persians myself in celebration of Browne's achievements.

A publisher writing about his books is tempted to record his successes and to forget his many failures—failures, that is, from the commercial point of view. In 1927, for instance, I hoped that J. C. Squire's *Cambridge Book of Lesser Poets* might be as success-ful as it was interesting. 'No lover or student of British poetry', wrote one reviewer, 'can do without it.' But most of them did. Another small book which deeply interested me was Bethune-Baker's *The Way of Modernism* (1927). I had heard, and been impressed by, one or two of his sermons and, knowing that he had frequently written papers for clerical and other societies, I suggested that he might make a book of them. He was surprised and, I think, rather pleased; but the book had little more than a *succès d'estime*. Similarly my own edition of Browne's *Christian Morals*, including Johnson's *Life*, was praised as a pretty little book, but I ought to have known that it deserved the epithet I had applied to many of the manuscripts offered to us—it was a born remainder.

In 1928 the Clark lectures at Trinity College were given by André Maurois. His subject was 'Aspects of Biography' and I was pleased when he agreed that the lectures should be published at the Press. Later, he wrote and explained that although he had spoken in English, he was not satisfied that it was good enough English for publication in book form. He had therefore revised the lectures in French and would we please have it translated? My first thought was to find a good French scholar for the job. Then I began to read the French text and found it quite easy and straightforward; I was keenly interested in the subject and proposed myself as the translator. This time there was no question of a remainder. Arnold Bennett gave the book a long review in the *Evening Standard* and found room for a good word for the translation.

By this time it had become painfully clear to me and my colleagues that a building designed to accommodate the Secretary to the Syndics and his clerk had become quite inadequate to our needs. So I pressed for an additional storey and this was duly completed in 1927. One particular advantage was that it enabled me for the first time to engage a private secretary.

The year 1929 was one of several changes in the Press staff. Gordon Carey was devoted to the Press and especially to the reading of proofs ('prooves' as the old hands called them), but I knew that the one job that would tempt him away was the headmastership of his old school, Eastbourne College, and when the post was offered to him, he naturally accepted it. About the same time Kingsford, who had most efficiently taken over a large measure of responsibility for production and publicity, moved to our London house.

Carey's place was filled by Charles Carrington. An Oxford man, he came to us from Haileybury, where he was sixth-form history master. He was a brilliant writer and had just completed

A Subaltern's War, the record of a young soldier who, in contrast to the *All Quiet on the Western Front* school of authors, had enjoyed the war. His school *History of England*, written in collaboration with J. Hampden Jackson, was highly successful; more substantial was *The British Overseas*, but he is perhaps best known as the biographer of Kipling, of whom, as of the concept of empire, he was a fervent champion. After twenty-five years at the Press during which he visited many parts of the Commonwealth on the Syndics' behalf, he was appointed Professor of British Commonwealth Relations at Chatham House, where he enjoyed everything except the title of Professor.

In 1930 George Barnes joined the staff as an assistant secretary. He was a man of discerning taste and wide interests. Publishing was new to him, but he gradually developed a keen bibliographical sense. He loved books as books, whether ancient or modern, and it was a sad day when in 1935 John Reith took him away from us. But I could not blame him for accepting a post which offered a wider scope, and later the secretarial staff was strengthened by the appointment of F. H. Kendon and of R. W. David. At the B.B.C. Barnes's rise was rapid. He was largely responsible for setting up the Third Programme and was afterwards Director of Television. Personally, I rejoiced when he returned to the academic world as Principal of Keele and with countless others mourned his untimely death. George was a man of rare quality and lovable withal.

On the printing side, F. R. F. Scott, of Magdalene, had been appointed as assistant University Printer in 1923. At the time I warned him that he would be concerned with business rather than with literature. This he fully appreciated and was happy and successful in his work until A. B. Ramsay, Arthur Benson's successor at Magdalene, pressed him to return to the college as Tutor. Later, his place was taken by Brooke Crutchley, who, after working many years with Lewis, succeeded him in 1946. Since then he has become a master-printer of repute on both sides of the Atlantic and it was after my time that his long-cherished plan of a new printing house built on modern lines was fulfilled. Today it serves the traveller from Liverpool Street as an impressive introduction to Cambridge.

In the spring of 1930 I paid my second visit to the United States. The agency contract with the Macmillan Company was about to expire and I was determined that, if it should be renewed, there should be some change in its terms. Before I left, I had a talk with Sir Frederick Macmillan over lunch and outlined my ideas to him. He was wholly sympathetic and when I got to New York I explained to Mr Brett that I wanted a more definite recognition of Cambridge books as such. My first visit had shown me very clearly how much better Oxford books were known in the United States than our own. The advantage of the Oxford branch in Fifth Avenue was obvious and from the first Mr Brett suspected that I was aiming at a similar establishment for Cambridge. But at that time I had no such intention, since I could not envisage that our turnover could carry the overheads of a branch of our own. On the other hand, I was tired of receiving letters from a variety of departmental heads in the Macmillan house; what I wanted was one man who would be responsible for the sale of Cambridge books and for nothing else. To this end I suggested the formation of a Cambridge department within the Macmillan organisation in charge of a Cambridge man, to whose salary we would be prepared to contribute. My proposal was not well received.

'Such a man as you suggest, Mr Roberts,' said Mr Brett, 'would spend his time running round our various departments.'

'Mr Brett,' I replied, 'that is precisely what I want him to do.'

'Very well. We don't like your scheme. But you prepare a memorandum and we will have another conference.'

So I went back to my hotel and got down to detail. In due course I presented my plan in more precise terms. Mr Brett, still frankly disliking it, but clearly unwilling to lose the agency, accepted it with a good grace.

'Now, what about the man who is to take charge of this new

department?' I asked. 'Would you prefer an Englishman or perhaps an American with first-hand knowledge of England and English universities?'

'Oh, but this is your scheme. You must find the man.' The ball was now definitely in my court; but it was a member of the Macmillan staff (Curtice Hitchcock) who helped me to play it. Hitchcock had some sympathy with my ideas and told me about a Corpus man (F. R. Mansbridge) who was at that time teaching at Barnard College and wished to settle in the United States. 'Why not take a look at him?' said Hitchcock. I gratefully agreed and the look was entirely favourable. When I returned to Cambridge, I had no hesitation in recommending Mansbridge's appointment and in 1931 the Cambridge branch was duly established in the Macmillan house. From the beginning I had warned Mansbridge that he would have a difficult job: he would be serving two masters, one of whom did not really want him; Cambridge would complain that he was too cautious in ordering stock; Macmillans would abuse him for being too venturesome. My forecast of these and other difficulties was amply fulfilled, but Mansbridge stuck manfully to his work; his final reward was to come later.

Chapter 5

PEMBROKE IN THE
NINETEEN-TWENTIES

At the Pembroke High Table of the 1920s there were several changes, though not so bewilderingly rapid as those of today. Though saddened by the loss of his elder son in the war, Hadley, now at the Lodge, was as genial as ever. Whibley, for long regarded by all of us as an essentially bachelor don, astonished us by announcing his engagement to be married. He moved to Surrey, but frequently came up for college meetings and feasts. Far from losing touch with him, I often stayed with him at Frensham and was intimate with him until his death in 1941. Kenneth Mozley left to be head of the Leeds Clergy School; Alex Seaton had been killed in France in 1915. Even so, it was characteristic of a small society in the 1920s that Edward Wynn, who was elected Fellow and Dean in 1921, remained the junior Fellow for seven years. It was a long time since Pembroke had been obliged to seek a Dean from outside and Edward's task was not easy. The vigilant eye of Bethune-Baker was upon him in his conduct of chapel services and in those days junior Fellows were not expected to initiate proposals for change. It was many years before Edward persuaded his colleagues to abolish compulsory chapels.

One of the first post-war elections was that of Aubrey Attwater, who had taken a first in Classics in 1914, and had also won the Charles Oldham Shakespeare prize. He had intended to read for the bar but, instead, he found himself a subaltern in the Royal Welch Fusiliers, serving in the same battalion as Siegfried Sassoon and Robert Graves. Early in 1915 he received the wound which crippled and eventually killed him. When he was elected to a fellowship in 1919, there was no obvious opening for him in

82

Classics and he threw himself with enthusiasm into work for the English Tripos. It was at his suggestion that Pembroke took the lead in offering scholarships in English and for many years I took a small share in the examination. Permanently lame, Aubrey could hobble as far as the Senate House to do his duty as Praelector, but not much farther. His rooms in Pembroke (the rooms where Thomas Gray and William Pitt and E. G. Browne had lived) were open till all hours of the night—and morning. Too lame to explore libraries, he amassed a fine collection on his own shelves. Elizabethan drama was his special, though not his exclusive, interest and he formed a small play-reading society, primarily for the benefit of his pupils. But it was soon enlarged to include what would now be called the two cultures. Twice a year the meetings were preceded by a dinner, to which I was usually invited, and the choice of play was suited to the after-dinner mood.

Sometimes we followed the beaten track and read *The Critic* or parts of *A Midsummer Night's Dream*; at other times we unearthed *The Vampire*, a romantic drama by J. R. Planché or *The What D'ye Call It*, a tragi-comi-pastoral farce by John Gay; and, of course, we seized upon the *Savonarola* of the unfortunate Ladbroke Brown. One of our gayest evenings was when we read Fielding's *Tragedy of ... Tom Thumb the Great*. Initially there was a difficulty, since there was no separate text available. The problem was solved very simply. In great haste I arranged for an edition of twenty-five copies to be printed at the Press—'Very privately printed for the *Tenth Dinner* of the Spenser Society of Pembroke-hall in Cambridge.' Amongst those who read parts at various times were R. A. Butler, Pierson (Bob) Dixon, Roy Pascal, George Pickering, Douglas Lowe, Patrick Browne and H. R. Stevens. None of these, it may be noted, were reading English. In particular Stevens, afterwards senior Science master at Cheltenham, told me many years later how much the Spenser Society had meant to him.

The mention of R. A. Butler's name brings to my mind a meeting of another society—the University French Society. I was not a member, but Rab was secretary and persuaded me to take part in a French debate. Oliver Prior, Professor of French, was in the chair and I spoke in support of the motion 'Que la politique est néfaste'. The motion was carried.

But to return to Aubrey Attwater. Immobile as he was, he was no recluse. He served on the General Board, the Press Syndicate and other bodies; he was Treasurer of the Union and edited the *Cambridge Review*. Every year he was to be seen at Lord's and Twickenham and Henley and in September he would spend a week or more seeing the plays at Stratford-upon-Avon. His Shakespearian learning was wide, but he published little. He contributed a chapter to the *Companion to Shakespeare Studies* and was pressed, especially by Q, to undertake a new edition of the Temple Shakespeare. But he refused. What he really wanted to do was to write the history of Pembroke on the grand scale. He worked hard upon the college archives and was at length persuaded to give us, without prejudice to the larger work, a short history of the college. It was practically finished when he died in 1935 and it fell to me to see it through the press.

It was in the 1920s that I got to know Comber really well. Not being a Marlburian or a skilful games-player, I had known him only slightly as an undergraduate, but I now realised that his interests were far from being confined to the playing-fields. In particular, he was a superb host. One of my favourites among Max Beerbohm's essays is *Hosts and Guests* and I always think of Comber, who was restless and fidgety as a guest, as the supreme example of the born host. Undergraduates flocked to his rooms as to those of a benevolent uncle and to them he became the 'Old Man' of their permanent affection. His small dinner-parties for senior members of the college were also convivial occasions and a shy guest was quickly made to feel at home. Of no one was this more true than of G. P. Moriarty.

Moriarty was not a Fellow, but he was one of the most interesting characters at the High Table. A Balliol man, he had been adopted by Pembroke when the University appointed him as teacher of Indian history and director of Higher Civil Service studies. For this work he was very poorly paid and through the good offices of Hadley and Whibley he was given some college teaching. It happened that I had known his name, and those of his brothers, on the honours boards of Brighton College and as a freshman I attended his lectures on essay-writing. He was acutely conscious of his deafness and almost painfully shy. A plump figure of medium height, he wore an 'imperial' and liked to describe himself as 'an Irishman—born in Dieppe'. At Oxford he had won the Stanhope Prize, but had missed his first in History and I suspect that this was a keen and lasting disappointment. He wrote a life of Swift (1893) and ten years later his first novel, *More Kin than Kind*, was published over the name of Gerald Fitzstephen and dedicated to Comber. It was very much a novel of Oxford in the 'nineties and a reviewer in the *Cambridge Review* wrote: 'If the author knows Cambridge equally well, a novel from his pen would be read with trembling avidity.' That novel was never written and we had to be content with papers read to the Martlets on such subjects as 'The Nonconformist Conscience' or 'Victorianism: its cause and cure'.

In 1910, however, *Griffith Colgrove's Wife*, by Gerald Fitzstephen, was published. It was a clever projection of the story of the Carlyles about thirty years forward. I bought a copy and told the author I had done so. 'Splendid,' he said, 'that will be ninepence for me.' But he was fully prepared for the book's commercial failure. It had, he said, too much of the unity of a Greek tragedy to please the public.

Diffident as he was, Moriarty loved congenial company. On the strength of the old school tie (a phrase at which he would have shuddered) I had introduced myself to him soon after I came up and I did essays for him in my fourth year. In the early years of my first marriage he would find his way to my villa and enjoy the simplest kind of domestic party. He had rooms at No. 1 Mill Lane, immediately opposite the front gate of Pembroke, and was rigidly methodical in his habits. At the beginning of each term he informed the Buttery of the two nights a week on which he would dine in Hall and nothing would induce him to change those nights—probably because he was terrified of upsetting his landlady. From time to time he could be seen posting a letter, addressed to someone in college, in the pillar-box by the college gate. Once, years before, a note handed in at the porter's lodge had gone astray and he was unwilling to risk a second mishap.

He was too badly paid to be able to afford a proper holiday, but in vacations he would spend a week in London at the Thackeray Hotel where, as he said, in the late evening all the bloods drank cocoa. Occasionally he would give a little dinner-party at Frascati's. 'How did it go?' I asked him once. 'Oh, very well,' he replied, 'we had a good dinner and just before the brandy was served, I asked the conductor of the orchestra to play Gounod's *Ave Maria*, which he did with exquisite modulation.'

Conversation was for Moriarty a serious art and he was faithful to the 'nineties in his search for the *mot juste*. When Comber one night after dinner put some leading questions about the landlady's niece at 1 Mill Lane, Moriarty hesitated for a fraction of a second. Then—'She is slim, virginal, and slightly provocative.' On another evening the talk was of contemporary authors and the works of Jack London were mentioned. 'Oh, awful,' said Moriarty, 'I once picked up a book of his and it seemed to be nothing but a prohibitionist tract.'

'But', said someone, 'you must remember that the poor chap died of drink.'

'A great artist wouldn't die of drink. He'd enjoy it.'

In 1924 Moriarty himself died after a brief illness. Comber was his executor and I inherited all his books and manuscripts, including an unpublished novel based on the story of Medea. After the funeral, it was comforting to be told by Louis Moriarty, a housemaster of Harrow, that we had made his brother supremely happy at Pembroke.

In my undergraduate years George Birtwistle kept immediately below me. He was always friendly, but seemed curiously diffident. All I knew of him then was that he had been Senior Wrangler, but when I joined the High Table, I soon realised that he had many interests besides mathematics. He was a good golfer, a keen fisherman and a regular follower of cricket. He complained bitterly when a college meeting was fixed for one of the days of the Yorkshire match and nothing was allowed to interfere with his fishing plans for the vacation. In manner he was extremely nervous and, when I first sat next to him at dinner, he alarmed me by suddenly laying aside his knife and fork and putting his hand to his head. But no one seemed to take any notice and I gathered that it was a familiar mannerism induced by slight flatulence. He was also liable to occasional attacks of claustrophobia. Once, during the time that he was Praelector of the college, he was overcome by the crowd and the heat of the Senate House, so he quietly walked out of the east door, sat down on the steps and smoked his pipe—an offence for which he was duly admonished by the Registry (Dr J. N. Keynes). As a mathematical lecturer he had in his later years a high reputation and his *Principles of Thermodynamics* (1925) and *New Quantum Mechanics* (1928), both published at the Press, were very successful.

Both at the Press and in college I saw a good deal of Ellis Minns. I turned to him for advice about any manuscript relating to Slavonic literature, but he would never accept the customary fee. Instead, he would ask me to send a copy of *Scythians and Greeks* to some impoverished scholar in Hungary or Finland. He could appreciate good typography, but a printed book never gave him the thrill that he got from a manuscript. Nor did he neglect modern calligraphy. He kept a range of pens with which to practise various forms of writing and chose 'Writing' as his subject when he gave the Sandars lectures in 1925. Two years later, when he was elected Professor of Archaeology, he maintained that the University, after rejecting him for more than one office which would have been congenial to him, had chosen him for a post for which he was quite unfitted. In college we were familiar with this kind of remark. If you asked him about some antiquarian matter which was not in his special field, he would reply that he was quite ignorant of the subject and then proceed to tell you all about it. At meetings of the Cambridge Antiquarian Society he would frequently interject audible criticisms that were disconcerting to strangers, but in college we were used to them. As Whibley once said in a speech: 'Mr Minns will correct me if I'm wrong—and probably if I'm right.'

Two fine scholars, whom I knew well, were elected to fellowships towards the end of the decade: Pierson (Bob) Dixon, who, after a brilliant diplomatic career, rose to be our Ambassador in Paris and died very soon after his retirement; and Bryan King, now one of the senior law lecturers in the University and fervent champion of many good causes outside it.

Hadley died suddenly on Christmas Day 1927, and his successor, Arthur Hutchinson, was elected with unusual speed and unanimity. Originally a Christ's man, he had come to Pembroke in 1892, the first Fellow to represent the natural sciences, and in 1926 had been elected Professor of Mineralogy. At the time when he became Master, he was not widely known amongst old Pembroke men, other than those whose studies he had directed, but very soon he won affection as well as respect. On the surface, his manner was rather grave, but he had a fund of dry humour. I enjoyed a story he told about Ralph Straus, who had been up at Pembroke just before my time. As an undergraduate, Straus, whom I knew fairly well in later years, frequently aimed at shocking the bourgeois, and Hutchinson, as his tutor, had from time to time to reprimand him. After the discussion of one of his escapades, Hutchinson concluded: 'It's no good, Straus. We're not going to send you down; we're not going to make a Shelley of you.'

In the summer of 1929 Hutchinson told me that the College proposed to elect me to a non-stipendiary fellowship. As a fellow-commoner for the previous eighteen years I had received nothing but kindness, but to be admitted to full membership of the society meant a great deal to me.

At that time the most important item on the agenda of a college meeting was the future of the Master's Lodge. There was general agreement that we needed more rooms in college, but there was a clear division of opinion about the best means of providing them. One party favoured the erection of a new building, the other, the conversion of the Lodge into undergraduate rooms and the building of a new and more economical Lodge for the Master in the south-eastern corner of the garden. No one, I think, held a brief for the architectural quality of Waterhouse's Lodge, but its main rooms looked south upon the garden and some of the fellows felt that it provided the right sort of accommodation for a Master. Others, with whom I personally agreed, urged that a future Master might find it a burden and that the opportunity should be taken of building a manageable house better suited to modern conditions. Hutchinson, not unnaturally, was opposed to a move, but when a decision was finally taken in favour of the conversion of the old Lodge, he accepted it, not perhaps with alacrity, but with characteristic good humour. The new Lodge was completed in 1932.

Chapter 6

JOHNSONIANA

I have already described the circumstances in which my *Story of Doctor Johnson* was written and published. I was genuinely surprised, and of course delighted, by the amount of attention it received and was encouraged to pursue the study of Johnson and his age. Naturally, I began to buy such books as I could afford. In the Charing Cross Road I got a copy of the first edition of the *Dictionary* for 30s. The binding was in a very poor state, but the pages were quite clean; at David's stall I picked up a copy of the first impression of Mrs Piozzi's *Anecdotes* (boards, uncut) for 1s. and I also bought a first edition (or so I thought) of Johnson's *Journey to the Western Islands*. As I have recorded elsewhere,* this latter purchase led to my first contact with R. W. Chapman. It also led booksellers to distinguish the two issues of the book in 1775—one with an eleven-line, the other with a six-line errata.

I joined the Johnson Society of Lichfield and attended the annual supper for the first time in 1921. The president in that year was J. F. Green and Dean Inge sat opposite to me at supper. There I met many Johnson enthusiasts whom I was to know well in later years—in particular, Lord and Lady Charnwood who, with Alderman W. A. Wood, contributed most to the success of the annual meeting.

For the *Cambridge Review* during the period of Aubrey Attwater's editorship I wrote an account of a few imaginary visits of Dr Johnson to Cambridge. These sketches, with some additions, were published in 1922. They made but a small book, which had a similarly small sale, but I have found that it serves as an acceptable item on a guest-room shelf.

More substantial were my editions of Boswell's *Tour to*

* Article on R. W. Chapman (*Essays and Studies*, 1961).

Corsica (1923) and of Mrs Piozzi's *Anecdotes* (1925) which led to correspondence with enthusiasts on both sides of the Atlantic, and on my first visit to the United States I took the opportunity of introducing myself to some of the well-known collectors. At Boston I found that I had much in common with Harold Murdock. He was an enthusiast for good printing and had tried his hand, as I had, at Boswellian imitation. He gave me a copy of his *Earl Percy dines abroad* (1924), but told me that his own collection of eighteenth-century books was hardly worth looking at; in fact, I contemplated it with admiration and envy. At the little luncheon-club to which I was introduced in Boston, we had most interesting talk. Murdock deplored the local politics of Boston and was wholeheartedly Anglophile.

A more famous collector was R. B. Adam, who had written to me very kindly about my first book. I travelled to Buffalo by the night-train from Boston and presented myself at Adam's house. At first I was a little nonplussed and wondered whether I was really welcome. 'What have you come to see?' Adam asked. I hadn't come to see anything in particular, but I said quickly: 'I believe you have a large number of Johnson's letters.' So the letters were produced and I pored over them. By lunch-time Adam was entirely genial. In the afternoon he took me into the town to see his store, which I took to be the Harrods of Buffalo. When we got back to the house, he told me that his wife and daughters would be going to a dance in the evening. Would I mind staying in the library with him? The dance-party would, of course, be late and we need not wait up for them. When the dancers returned about 2 a.m., we were still in the library. As the evening had worn on and the glasses of rye-whiskey and ginger ale had been replenished and Adam had taken book after book from the shelves, I had begun to realise something of the richness of his collection, which was by no means confined to Johnsoniana. The next day was Easter Sunday. 'I expect you'll have to go to church', Adam said to me, 'I don't go. I'm too deaf.' I assured him that I should like to go to church and Mrs Adam invited me to go with her in her electric brougham. 'I'm too stupid to drive an automobile', she confided in me. 'It's Presbyterian,' she went on, 'that's what you have in England, isn't it?' I explained that I was in fact a member of the Church of England, but that I should be quite happy to go with her. 'Oh now, that's funny,' she said, 'I thought Presbyterian was what you had.' In the end I was rewarded by listening to a magnificent Easter sermon.

In the afternoon we went to Niagara Falls and on the Canadian side were regaled with beer of which the alcoholic content was said to be one per cent. On our return to the American side, the car was searched to make sure that we were not smuggling any of this powerful liquor into the land of prohibition. After dinner Adam said to me very solemnly: 'We were very late last night; to-night we must go to bed early.' At 1.30 a.m. we were still in the library. Adam grew more and more active in showing me books and in delivering his opinions on eighteenth-century writers. Gray, he thought, was inferior to Collins as a poet and he quoted with gusto the line:

And Hope enchanted smiled and waved her golden hair.

Before we went to bed he insisted on giving me a few souvenirs. One was a tiny little almanack of 1795, beautifully bound and containing engravings of the Prince of Wales and Mrs Fitzherbert, and also of Dr Johnson and Mrs Piozzi.

As all Johnsonians know, Adam made his own catalogue in four volumes. Bibliographically, it is glaringly defective. The items are not numbered; there is no index; and there are misprints which no decent printer's reader would have passed. But Adam liked to handle his matchless collection in his own way. To my great regret, I did not meet him again. He called on me once at Cambridge, but he had given me no notice and I happened to be away at the time. He was badly hit by the slump of 1929–30 and was obliged to mortgage his collection. Years later, every Johnsonian rejoiced when a large part of it became the property of Donald and Mary Hyde.

I do not remember exactly when I first met A. Edward Newton, but I think it must have been in London in 1923 or 1924. But certainly I called on him in his office in Philadelphia in 1925. He gave me lunch and then we drove out to his home at Berwyn. His wife was away from home, so we had an entirely bookish evening. Thanks to his success in the manufacture and sale of a highly complex electrical apparatus, Newton had been able to retire from business at a comparatively early age and had plunged into book-collecting on the grand scale. He never professed to be a scholar, but he had a genuine, sometimes an almost idolatrous, love of literature. Of course, like any other collector, he sought for first editions and tall copies and, above all, he loved an 'association copy'. When he described his book-hunting adventures in a series of essays entitled *The Amenities of Book-collecting* in 1918, he was astonished by its success. He had written the book for fun, but he infected his readers with his own enthusiasms. He was a devoted Johnsonian, but his range was wide— Blake, Lamb, Dickens, Trollope, Hardy, to name just a few— and he collected an author because he loved and admired his writings.

So I enjoyed a memorable evening and was delighted when, in the following August, Eddy Newton's rubicund face suddenly appeared round the door of my room at the Press. Having rebuked him soundly for not giving me warning of his visit, I asked him where he was staying and what his plans were. 'I'm staying at the Bull,' he replied, 'and my wife's with me. You haven't met her, have you? She's a faithful old thing.' Newton accepted a cup of tea, but curtly refused an invitation to look round the printing house. Machinery no longer interested him. I arranged that he should dine with me in Pembroke and that after dinner we should collect Mrs Newton and take her up to my house.

Before dinner I showed Newton a bit of Pembroke and took him into the Buttery for a glass of sherry. Chapman made an immediate appeal as 'an old Colledge Butler' and served as a fitting introduction to the evening's enjoyment. It was the year in which the Hall was in the builders' hands and we were dining in the Old Library. Comber was the senior fellow present and fortunately I had an opportunity of introducing Newton to him in Old Court. They took to each other at once. 'I don't know how you feel, Mr Newton,' said Comber, 'but it's a chilly evening and I think we might have a glass of champagne.' Newton's eyes glistened. 'My dear sir,' he replied, 'I'll follow you anywhere.' Half-way through dinner Newton whispered to me: 'D'you have a dinner like this every night?' I explained that I dined in college only once or twice a week, but that he might take the evening's menu as a fair sample. 'Oh, I'm going to be a don', he said.

After dinner we adjourned to Comber's rooms for port. Newton grew happier and happier. 'How d'you like your coffee, Mr Newton?' asked Comber. 'My dear sir, that's the one form of alcohol I never touch', was the reply. But Comber was not to be put off. 'Wait a minute,' he said, 'I've got something here that I think you'll like' and he brought out from a corner-cupboard a bottle of Van der Hum. 'Try a glass of that.' Newton sipped it with evident pleasure. 'How long are you staying here?' asked Comber. 'Only to-night. To-morrow we're going on to Norwich.' 'Well, if you come through Cambridge on your way back, just drop in and take pot luck.' Newton held up his glass. 'Pot luck,' he said, 'my God!'

A few years later Newton and his wife stayed a night with us in Barton Road. We had a small lunch-party for them at which Newton, as usual, talked with fluent gaiety. 'Come, Mr Newton,' said my wife, 'you're not eating anything.' 'Madam,' he replied, 'I can buy food; I can't buy conversation.'

Besides Adam and Newton, I met two professors who were good Johnsonians, C. G. Osgood of Princeton and C. B. Tinker of Yale. Osgood had a wide range of learning. His *Concordance to the Poems of Spenser* had been published in 1915 and when he later visited England, it gave me great pleasure to give him lunch in Pembroke and to show him Spenser's name in the Buttery book.

Tinker had recently come forward as Boswell's champion and I had been deeply interested in his *Young Boswell* (1922) and his edition of Boswell's *Letters* (1924). Though I did not know it at the time, he had reason to believe that the mass of papers left by Boswell had not, as everyone thought, been destroyed, but were preserved at Malahide Castle, County Dublin, the home of Lord Talbot de Malahide, whose mother had been a Boswell. In the summer of 1925 Tinker visited Malahide and was shown the contents of Boswell's famous ebony cabinet, but did not succeed in making any arrangements for their publication.

The rumour about the papers did not reach me until a year later. I heard it first from M. R. James, who gave me an introduction to J. H. Bernard, Provost of Trinity College, Dublin; the Provost kindly put me into touch with the Rector of Malahide who conducted me to the castle. There, on an afternoon late in June 1926, I saw laid out on a refectory table a dozen or more Boswelliana. They were only samples, of course, but I noted Goldsmith's reply to Boswell's letter of congratulation on the production of *She Stoops to Conquer*, Boswell's account of his interview with George III and other fascinating pieces. I told Lord Talbot that I should be delighted to co-operate, if he should consider publication of the papers. Lord Talbot was extremely courteous but, as I expected, quite non-committal. On 5 July he wrote to me: 'I will bear in mind your kind offer of help regarding publication of the Boswell MSS. I have certain rather indefinite plans already but am making no more just yet.' In fact another inquirer, Ralph Isham, had arrived at Malahide a week earlier. He was interested not only in investigation, but in purchase and, as all the world knows, acquired the whole collection.

Some time in 1925 or 1926 I was elected a member of the Johnson Club. Before that I had been taken by Arundell Esdaile as a guest to a meeting at which Sir Frederick Treves had been invited to read a paper on Johnson from the physician's point of view. Other eminent medical men had also been invited and the discussion became more and more drearily technical. The most picturesque figure in the room was Augustine Birrell. As one physician after another made his contribution to the post-mortem examination, I noticed Birrell's restlessness. At length he got up. 'With the greatest respect', he said, 'to the learned members of the medical profession, I believe that Johnson was a thoroughly healthy man. How many of you, in middle age, are prepared to stop a dog-fight or to jump into a dangerous pool and swim through it?' In a few minutes the atmosphere of the discussion was transformed. Birrell was, I think, the best impromptu after-dinner speaker I have ever heard. At a later meeting someone had read a paper on the unfortunate Dr Dodd. Birrell recalled that in the *Cambridge University Calendar* Dr Dodd was described in a footnote simply as 'Author of *Thoughts in Prison*'. 'The delicacy of it', he murmured. Much later, after a summer meeting of the club in Oxford, he described a dinner given by J. M. Barrie. 'Barrie loves politicians,' he said, 'but as Baldwin hates the Conservatives and Ramsay MacDonald hates Labour, he couldn't have either of them. So we had Edward Grey instead. And what do you think he talked about? Nature! Fly-fishing!! Dry fly-fishing!!!' The crescendo of scorn rose finely to its climax.

But, of course, Birrell was not the only good talker in the club. Sir Frank (afterwards Lord Justice) MacKinnon's talk had the same clarity and incisiveness as his writing; R. W. Chapman was laconically witty, especially in the correction of any textual inaccuracy; A. W. Evans (a clerk in holy orders who had become head of Elkin Matthews's bookshop and eventually returned to the work of a parish priest) was a mine of bibliographical information; J. C. Squire, who did not attend very regularly, was always lively when he came; and there were others like Roger Ingpen and Geoffrey Russell, who did not make many speeches but were admirably clubable.

The club had been founded in 1884 and one of the founders,

T. Fisher Unwin, was a regular attendant at the time of my election. Originally, meetings were held in various Fleet Street taverns, but, thanks to the foresight and generosity of Cecil (afterwards Lord) Harmsworth in restoring Johnson's house in Gough Square, the club was able, from 1913, to take supper in the 'upper room' in which the *Dictionary* was compiled.

One of the earliest papers I read to the club was on 'Johnson's Books' and being anxious to verify which books were in Windham's library at Felbrigg, I got into touch, for the first time, with Wyndham Ketton-Cremer, then a Balliol undergraduate. It was the beginning of a lasting friendship.

I went with fair regularity to the annual Lichfield supper and got to know Lord and Lady Charnwood very well. Charnwood, who bore a strong physical resemblance to his brother, Frank Benson, always seemed to me by nature a don. He had in fact been a lecturer in Philosophy at Balliol in his early days, but later entered Parliament as a Liberal and was raised to the peerage in 1911. At Stowe House (the lower house on Stowe Hill, just below that in which Johnson enjoyed the company of Molly Aston) he and his wife were most kindly hosts. Lady Charnwood seemed to me a sad illustration of the vanity of human wishes. Rich, beautiful, intelligent, widely read and a vigorous conversationalist, she was doomed by a carriage accident to years of pain and immobility. But she never gave in and the house-parties which she arranged year after year for the Johnson week-end were gay and memorable. In 1929 I succeeded Chapman as president of the Society and entitled my address 'The Focus of the Lichfield Lamps'. Lady Charnwood was pleased that she had, for once, induced the Dean of Lichfield (H. E. Savage) to come to the dinner-party on the Friday night. The Dean was a recluse, but on that evening he was very good company. A year or two before he had produced a good edition of Johnson's *Prayers and Meditations*.

In the spring of 1930, when I visited the United States for the second time, I made a point of inviting F. A. Pottle, who had succeeded Geoffrey Scott as editor of the Boswell papers, to dine with me at my hotel. As we talked, we discovered that we were both to be the guests of Newton for the following week-end. When to my surprise Pottle remarked that he had never met Newton, I told him that there was some fun in store for him. Newton had sent me a post-card telling me that I should take the train to Philadelphia North; that I would meet a number of fellow-guests on the train; and that we would be met at the station by a chocolate-coloured car driven by a chocolate-coloured coachman.

When we reached Oak Knoll, Newton was standing at his front door clad in one of his check suits and exuding Pickwickian hospitality:

How are you, my dear Roberts? How are you, my dear...oh, and here's Mr Pottle. My dear old friend Tinker said to me that Mr Pottle was the greatest scholar of the age. I said 'My God, what an age'—come in, Mr Pottle!

It was a characteristic introduction to a hilarious week-end. On the Sunday morning there was what Newton called a bibliographical stag-party and from about 11 o'clock onwards librarians, booksellers and bibliophiles poured into the library.

'Eddy's got some nice books,' said one of them to me, 'yes, sir. And they're in good condition. And I'm a condition man, sir.'

'Quite so', I replied, thinking of my shelves at home and of some of the shivering folios, in Charles Lamb's phrase, which they contained.

We had a fork lunch in a sort of conservatory and, as I feared, Newton could not resist making a little speech in my honour. To my relief he talked most about Comber, whom he described as an 'exquisite man'. It struck me as a curious epithet for a man who weighed about 18 stone, but I knew what he meant.

Later in the year, to his great satisfaction, Newton succeeded me as president at Lichfield and enjoyed referring to me as an extinct volcano. His successor in 1931 was Anthony Hope

[Hawkins] and after our return from the Johnson Supper he was induced to read one or two of the *Dolly Dialogues* to us. The book had always been one of my favourite minor classics and it was a delight to hear a few chapters read by the author in his deep and resonant voice.

1931 was also the year in which it was my turn to be 'Prior' of the Johnson Club. Our summer meeting was always held somewhere away from London and I arranged a dinner in Pembroke. By that time Leonard Whibley, who after his retirement had devoted himself to the eighteenth century and particularly to Thomas Gray, had become a member of the club; Ketton-Cremer was another new member. At a hint from Chapman, I invited two American enthusiasts who were known to be in England—Ralph Isham and W. S. ('Lefty') Lewis. Isham's contribution to the evening's enjoyment was a little unfortunate. He arrived when we were half-way through dinner, and after an excellent paper read by Andrew Gow on 'the unknown Johnson' I announced that, as usual, we hoped our guests would join in the discussion. Isham, very naturally, took the opportunity to tell us something about his acquisition of the Malahide papers; unfortunately he chose to dwell upon a number of bawdy passages from them and these did not go down so well as he had hoped. On the following day, when I showed him round some of the colleges, he was in a less excited state. I did not meet him again.

For me the most memorable feature of the week-end was my introduction to Lefty Lewis. From that time onwards he developed a warm, even a passionate, affection for Cambridge and his friendship with both Whibley and myself grew into intimacy. Whibley, when his turn came to preside over the Johnson Club, characteristically insisted on abolishing what he called the mumbo-jumbo of 'Venerable Prior' and 'Learned Scribe' and substituted the normal 'President' and 'Secretary'— which reminds me that Theobald Matthew, a witty and most engaging speaker, once held the office of secretary. With his pince-nez half-way down his nose, he had a roguish, Dickensian manner which was completely captivating. One evening he announced very formally: 'I have to apologise to the club; I have forgotten the minute book.' Then, with equal solemnity: 'All I can say is—damn the bloody book!'

On the scholarly side, the club was greatly strengthened by the election of L. F. Powell, who has now for many years been one of its most faithful and learned supporters. Of him and of some others I shall have more to say in a later chapter.

Chapter 7

SCIENCE A BEST SELLER

Though my own tastes were literary and historical, I realised from my earliest days at the Press the supreme importance of the mathematical and physical section of the Cambridge catalogue. Those massive dark blue volumes with such titles as *Matrices and Determinoids* or *The Theory of Functions of two Complex Variables* were recognised as characteristic products of Cambridge and had a steady sale all over the world.

In 1913 the last of the three volumes of *Principia Mathematica*, by Bertrand Russell and A. N. Whitehead was published. New types had to be cut for the new ideography which the authors had developed and the whole work has been described as the greatest single contribution to logic since Aristotle. Meanwhile, in 1910, Whitehead had left Cambridge for a Chair of Mathematics at Imperial College, London. He visited the Press from time to time, especially when he had a new book ready for publication. Such visits saved him the trouble of letter-writing, an activity which he disliked. In 1924 he resigned his post in London to become Professor of Philosophy at Harvard. Before he left, he came to see me. 'I shall probably write some more books for you,' he said, 'but don't send me any agreement-forms—just the usual, you know.' I was perfectly happy with this endorsement of 'the usual', though the Authors' Society would scarcely have approved.

Whitehead's earlier books had done well from our point of view, but their appeal had been to mathematicians and philosophers. The first product of his time at Harvard was *Science and the Modern World* (1926), based on the Lowell lectures of the preceding year. The book was initially published by the Macmillan Company of New York and I must confess that in the first instance we were not alive to its importance. We ordered 500 copies in sheets and soon realised that it was a ludicrous miscalculation. The work was hailed as the most important contribution to its subject since Descartes and we hastened to set up our own edition, which was many times reprinted.

I visited Whitehead more than once at Harvard. It was in 1930, I think, that having given me dinner at the Graduate Club, he apologetically explained that it was an evening when he was 'at home' to his students. So we went to his room and gradually young men and women, eager to imbibe his wisdom, gathered round him in a semi-circle. It was quite a Socratic scene.

As I have already hinted, a letter from Whitehead was a rare event. Once, however, he seemed to feel a twinge of conscience. In November 1936 he wrote from Harvard:

In reply to your letter of July 1st respecting a 3/6d edition of my 'Religion in the Making' by the Cambridge Univy Press, I am quite agreeable, if you still think it worth while after my delay in replying. I note that the royalty will then be 10 p.c. on sales of the cheap edition. I apologise for my inexcusable omission to reply. I can only plead the habits of a life-time, not to be remedied at the age of 75. Also incidentally, when I write a letter, it spoils my thought for the day— perhaps no harm is done by that.

It is only fair to add that when I cabled our congratulations on his O.M. in 1945, he replied promptly—and in his own hand.

During the last years of the First World War mathematicians and astronomers were deeply concerned with the problem of the equilibrium of the stars, and two of the protagonists were A. S. Eddington and J. H. Jeans. Both had already published important books at the Press, but they were not books for the general reader. When, however, Eddington's *The Nature of the Physical World* was published in 1928, the general reader devoured it. The first edition was quickly exhausted and it was many times reprinted. Eddington came to see me from time to time and was always courteous and uncomplaining. But a Quaker silence seemed to impregnate the atmosphere and I never achieved any kind of intimacy with him.

With Jeans it was a very different story. He, too, had published a large work *Astronomy and Cosmogony*. It was a highly technical work and I was a little surprised when Ralph Fowler came into my room one day and asked me if I had read it. I reminded him, in reply, that I was not obliged to read everything I published. 'Ah, yes,' said Fowler, 'but you should read the last chapter.' It was a timely rebuke; I ought to have spotted that chapter. A passage from it, as Kingsford reminded me, had been included by Q in his *Oxford Book of English Prose* and I sought to make up for lost time and opportunity. At that time I frequently drove to Worthing, where my parents lived. Jeans's house at Dorking was very near the main road and one day I proposed myself for lunch. He was very friendly and in his study after lunch I sounded him about the possibility of a popular book. He looked at me rather quizzically. 'Oh, several publishers have approached me about that', he said. 'Well,' I replied, 'what about us?' 'Oh,' he said, 'you're the finest mathematical printers in the world, but you couldn't sell a popular book.' 'Have you ever written one?' I countered. But I could see that Jeans was nibbling. I think the success of Eddington's *Nature of the Physical World* was an additional spur.

Jeans never haggled over royalties and *The Universe around Us* was published in September 1929. By the end of the year more than 11,000 copies had been sold. At the Press, of course, we were delighted and so, in his own way, was Jeans, but his shyness made it difficult for him to express pleasure or enthusiasm. He would rap out a caustic comment on anyone or anything in a way that chilled his hearers and dried up conversation; when he was genuinely pleased, he was awkward and embarrassed. With an effort he said to me: 'I always thought the book would do well, but you've sold more copies than I thought you could.'

One result of the success of *The Universe around Us* was that

Jeans was invited to deliver the Rede Lecture in 1930. I wrote at once to say that, of course, we should like to publish the lecture and would he please send the manuscript in good time, so that we might publish immediately after delivery? Jeans played up well and suggested that the book might be considerably longer than the lecture. Better and better, I thought, and some weeks before the date of the lecture we had 10,000 copies of *The Mysterious Universe* printed and bound. The lecture was to be given in the Senate House at 5 p.m. on 4 November. Two days before, I was rung up by Harold Child of *The Times*. 'S. C.,' he said, 'the whole office is buzzing about Jeans. Can you let me have an advance copy of the lecture?' I told him that I could, but warned him that review copies of the book, as distinct from the lecture, had been distributed to all newspapers. So *The Times* had its early sight of the lecture and on the following morning there was a 'turn-over' on the middle page together with a leading article. Jeans came into my room in the middle of the morning. He had the embarrassed air of a sixth-form boy who had just won a scholarship and wanted to thank his form-master for his help. 'I've got a very good show this morning,' he said, adding jerkily, 'thanks to you, I expect.'

For the next few weeks our main problem at the Press was to keep *The Mysterious Universe* in stock. Lewis cleared the decks with gusto and we sold 1,000 copies a day for a month. By now, Jeans was in great demand as lecturer and broadcaster. *The Stars in their Courses* (1931) was an expansion of a series of broadcast talks and *Through Space and Time* (1934) was based on Royal Institution Christmas lectures. In the higher reaches of philosophical thought Jeans had plenty of critics, but no one could deny his clarity as an expositor or his fine command of the English language. *The Stars in their Courses* involved us, temporarily, in a commercial controversy. We had sold the first serial rights to the *Sunday Express* and the first article resembled the talk as printed in *The Listener* fairly closely. The manager of the *Sunday Express* felt that he had a grievance, which the legal adviser of the B.B.C. would not admit. I think it was Moray McLaren who eventually found a formula of compromise, for which Jeans and I, who had spent most of the day between Fleet Street and Broadcasting House, were profoundly thankful.

In 1932 my wife died after an intermittent illness of several years; two years later Jeans had to bear a similar blow. Soon after his wife's death, he asked me to spend a night with him at Dorking and for the first time the barriers of shyness were broken. His daughter was ill in bed and he was desperately lonely. 'Sometimes', he said, 'I wish I'd been a games-master at Eton.' Later, he stayed a week-end with me and in the following year he made a further tentative approach. 'You never go abroad, do you, Roberts?'

'I haven't been lately, but before my wife's illness we often went to France for ten days or so. Why?'

'Well, I wondered whether you'd care to come for a holiday with me this year.'

After discussion of trips to Istanbul and other places which were beyond my resources, we settled on Pontresina. It was my first visit to Switzerland and I was too old to learn to climb in the technical sense; but I was pleased to find that one could do quite a lot by stout walking. Jeans's knee was not very reliable and once or twice I went off on my own. Helen and Harley Granville-Barker were staying at St Moritz and asked us over for the day. After an exquisite lunch in the woods, described as a picnic, we drove over the Maloja Pass and explored the picturesque corners of Soglio. In spite of the poor quality of the beer at the inn, it was quite a hilarious party and Barker proposed that we should send a picture-postcard to someone whom all of us knew. We fixed upon D. A. Winstanley, of Trinity, and sent him some verses beginning:

> As duodecimo to folio
> Bears very slight affinity,
> So is the beer of Soglio
> To Audit Ale at Trinity...

It was a memorable day, but not so memorable as those of our second trip over the Italian border. Jeans seemed keen to drive over the Stelvio Pass and spend a few days at Solda, adding that he had been asked by his friend Lady Heath to look up a young musician who would be there. At the time I did not appreciate the significance of this supplementary motive.

We reached Solda in the late afternoon. After being allotted a room, I came down to the entrance-hall of the hotel. Most of the guests were Italian, but suddenly an elegant figure approached— a tall girl in a white climbing-suit. She looked inquiringly at me and we introduced ourselves; she was Susi Hock, the young Viennese musician whom Jeans had met at Lady Heath's. She had just done a little climb (about 10,000 feet). Jeans then appeared and we went to change for dinner. After dinner we strolled out on to the terrace of the hotel. It was a brilliantly clear evening and Susi asked Jeans many questions about the stars, which he was only too ready to answer. Then they embarked upon musical topics. 'Jeans,' I said, 'we've had a long day. I think I shall go to bed early.' 'Right oh, Roberts,' he replied briskly, 'see you at breakfast.' The situation was becoming quite clear to me.

The next morning we climbed up to a near-by hut. Jeans did not move quickly and it was easy, and convenient, for me to act as pathfinder. Later in the day Jeans asked me, with some of his old embarrassment, whether I would mind if Susi came back with us to Pontresina. I replied, quite honestly, that I should be delighted. I had never imagined that a holiday with Jeans would acquire a romantic element. As we prepared for our return journey, I announced firmly that I wished to sit in front with the driver. Our arrival at the hotel provoked some interest. Two days before, we had left—a pair of detached and unromantic widowers. Now we returned with our elegant prize and the dowagers of the Kronenhof were agog with curiosity. But our gaiety was not damped. In the evenings a dance-band played, but the average age of the guests was high and not many took the floor. Jeans's bad knee debarred him, so Susi and I enjoyed one or two Viennese waltzes, Jeans looking on with bland magnanimity. One morning we went up the Schafberg by the funicular and had lunch in a hut on the way down. There were some odd characters in the hut and we rioted over the silliest jokes. Never before had I seen Jeans shaken with helpless laughter.

After a few days I returned to England. Some ten days later Jeans wrote to me from Vienna:

Just a line in haste to tell you—before you see it in *The Times*—that I hope soon to marry Susi Hock. I expect this is no surprise to you and fear you must think I owe you an apology for Pontresina and Solda. I am really sorry if you felt it broke up into a 2 + 1 party, but I had not quite foreseen how things would turn out. Anyhow I hope we may all three meet again soon.

The apology was unnecessary and the hope was soon fulfilled. A year later I stood godfather to Jeans's elder son Michael, afterwards an undergraduate at Pembroke. Some time before his death Jeans had asked me to be one of his executors, but not until his will was read did I learn that I was a co-guardian, with Susi, of his three children. It was characteristic of him that he had not brought himself to the point of asking me during his life-time.

There was no trace of shyness in Ernest (afterwards Lord) Rutherford. His work on Radioactivity had been published before my time, but a new edition, revised in collaboration with C. D. Ellis, came out in 1930. Rutherford was not really interested in writing books, but he enjoyed pulling my leg about other people's.

'Hello, Roberts,' he said once, as he burst into my room at the Press, 'makin' your fortune out of Jeans, eh?'

'His books are doing very nicely,' I replied. 'Why don't you write a popular book?'

'Oh, it's not our business, Roberts. All this mystery...'

'But it *is* a mystery', I ventured.

'I know it is, but it's not what laboratories are for.'

There was something extremely refreshing about an encounter with Rutherford. 'How's Hutchinson getting on as Master?' he asked me once. 'Very well,' I replied, 'he's excellent in the chair of a college meeting.' 'Good. I'm very fond of Hutchinson. I remember asking him soon after his election how he liked his new job and he replied that he spent a good deal of time greasing the wheels. "Ah well," I said, "like the rest of us—a bloody mechanic, eh?"' Anywhere, at any time, he could be breezily indiscreet. Travelling to London, he would discuss (*sotto voce*, as he imagined) forthcoming elections to the Royal Society; at the Trinity High Table someone (Ernest Harrison, I think) murmured plaintively about 'the loud speakers from the Cavendish'.

After his untimely death, his son-in-law, Ralph Fowler, discussed with me the question of a biography and asked me to approach A. S. Eve, who had worked with Rutherford at McGill. Eve, whom I knew a little as a member of my own college, was a devoted admirer of Rutherford, but he was a compiler rather than a biographical artist. His manuscript needed a good deal of pruning and revision, which was, in fact, gratefully and gracefully acknowledged. I was able to add one or two anecdotes to Eve's narrative and am, perhaps, entitled to repeat one of them here:

Invited once to dine at Pembroke he [Rutherford] arrived early and found the Master's drawing-room empty except for an ecclesiastical personage. The two men introduced themselves and were soon in friendly conversation. Later, in the college hall, Rutherford was called on for a speech and described the meeting: '"I'm Lord Rutherford" I said, and the other man said "I'm the Archbishop of York"—and I don't suppose either of us believed the other.'

Lady Rutherford was pleased with the book, except with the frontispiece, which was a reproduction of Oswald Birley's portrait.

'What's wrong with it?' I asked.

'Well, it shows him with his mouth closed. But he was always either smoking or talking.'

Science a Best Seller

A famous book published in the middle of the First War was D'Arcy Thompson's *Growth and Form* (1917). Soon after I became Secretary, it was urged upon me that it was scandalous that the book should be allowed to remain out of print. I wrote to the author at St Andrews. He replied that he would shortly be in London and asked me to meet him at the Athenæum. We sat together on one of the benches in the entrance hall and I pressed for leave to put a reprint in hand. 'Certainly not,' he replied, 'There is a great deal that needs re-writing. I'm not going to let the book circulate as it is.' 'But', I urged, 'we shouldn't advertise the book as a second edition. We should make it quite clear that it was a plain reprint for the time being.' But I made no impression. The book remained out of print and its price soared in the second-hand catalogues. Years afterwards the author came to see me at the Press. He was in an amiable mood, having greatly enjoyed a Commemoration dinner at Trinity the night before. 'Ah,' he murmured, 'God meant me to be a don.' Then, without any prompting from me, he confessed that he had been foolish and improvident in his veto of a reprint. However, he had at length completed his re-writing and asked what terms the Press would offer for the new edition. I suggested what I thought would be a suitable royalty. To my astonishment he leapt up from his chair, held out his hand (not in acceptance but with a gesture of farewell) and, with a severe 'Good morning', moved towards the door. A few words of explanation, uttered as gently as I could, soon restored his equanimity and we parted in an atmosphere of comparatively sweet reasonableness. Later, another storm blew up over the cost of proof-correction of the new edition. It was vastly in excess of the generous allowance provided in the agreement and I took care to sound an early note of warning. 'I know,' he replied, 'but I've got to make this book as good as I can and I rely on you to do your best for me.' I did what I could and obtained authority to halve the amount for which he was liable, but my appeasement was not appreciated. D'Arcy Thompson was a great man and I always welcomed a chance of meeting him; but there was an element of quicksilver in him which, from a publisher's point of view, made negotiation difficult.

'Best sellers' are exciting; they are talked about at dinner-parties and justify extended advertisement It is only within a publishing house that the true 'best seller' is recognised. A good example is G. H. Hardy's *Course of Pure Mathematics*. It was first published in 1908. When I left the Press forty years later, its sale was steadily increasing and in the current catalogue I note that it still survives and flourishes. I never knew Hardy well, but our negotiations were always friendly and I had a profound respect not only for his eminence as a pure mathematician, but for the quality of his writing and for his passionate love of cricket. With his tickets for the four or five days of a test match pinned to the lapel of his jacket, he would look as serious as when expounding the theory of numbers. In 1940 I was delighted to publish a small book by him, which I could read and enjoy and, I think, understand—*A Mathematician's Apology*. The essence of the aim and the achievement of the pure mathematician is distilled, for the layman's benefit, with remarkable lucidity.

Elsewhere I have referred to the 'stimulating atmosphere of selling books as quickly as they could be printed'; but such stimulus should never be allowed to obscure the importance of textbook longevity.

Chapter 8

HISTORIES AND HISTORIANS

I suppose that, apart from the Bible, the first book that made the Press well known to the general public was the *Cambridge Modern History*. When I joined the staff of the Press in 1911, the work was virtually completed—only the index to the volume of maps remained to be done. It was in 1896 that the Syndics approached Lord Acton with a view to the publication of a universal history. Acton prepared a detailed plan, but died before the first volume was published and the general editorship was entrusted to A. W. Ward, G. W. Prothero, and Stanley Leathes.

As Wright had initiated the proposal for the *Modern History*, so Waller, in association with A. W. Ward, was responsible for the *History of English Literature*, completed in 1916. With this I had little concern, except that in 1927 I fortunately persuaded H. S. Bennett to undertake the labour of a general index.

Meanwhile, the *Medieval History* had had a chequered career. The work was planned by J. B. Bury and under the editorship of H. M. Gwatkin and J. P. Whitney two volumes were published before the First World War. Gwatkin died in 1916 and it was hoped to obtain the help of G. T. Lapsley, but ill-health compelled him to resign and Whitney, who had succeeded Gwatkin as Dixie Professor, was left to carry on. There were many difficulties: in a wave of patriotic feeling, contracts with specialist scholars who happened to be enemy aliens were cancelled; Whitney was a poor organiser and came away from interviews with Waller in a state of some disarray. The situation was saved by the addition of J. R. Tanner, C. W. Previté-Orton and, later, Z. N. Brooke to the editorial body; Previté, as someone said, was the soul of Whitney.

The *Ancient History* was planned in Waller's time and the first volume was issued in 1923, the original editors being J. B. Bury, S. A. Cook and F. E. Adcock. Of all the Cambridge histories, it probably had the smoothest passage from the publishing point of view and this was mainly due to Adcock's remarkable tact and efficiency in driving his teams of contributors. The last volume was published in the spring of 1939 and I gave a short broadcast talk to commemorate the completion of the series which had grown out of the suggestion put to Lord Acton in 1896.

A smaller work in progress at the time of Waller's death was the *Cambridge History of British Foreign Policy*, edited by A. W. Ward and G. P. Gooch. Ward was 85 when the first volume was published in 1922, but he took the work comfortably in his stride. Ever since he had presided over my first interview with the Syndics in 1910, he had been extremely kind to me. Like some other distinguished men of letters, he showed to much greater advantage in his talk than in his writing. 'His lack of colour and his lengthy sentences limited his appeal', wrote G. P. Gooch of him; but his talk was easy and far from colourless. When his five volumes of collected papers were published, I marvelled at his range. His professorship at Manchester had involved responsibility for English language and literature as well as for history and, when he became Vice-Chancellor, he continued to be dramatic critic of the *Manchester Guardian*. His glossy white beard and his majestic gait made him an imposing figure in the Cambridge scene. Quite simply, he preserved the manners of an earlier generation. Frequently, in the afternoon, he would order his brougham with a view to paying calls, properly equipped with morning coat and silk hat. On his way he would sometimes drop in to the Press. He came in once when I was busily engaged with Sir Thomas Jackson in sorting drawings and photographs for one of his architectural books. Ward halted at the door, but I begged him to come in.

'I expect you know Sir Thomas Jackson?' I said.

'I know his work, of course, but I don't think I've ever had the pleasure...'

Jackson, two years older than Ward, replied in exactly the same terms and it was a charming sight to see the two old gentlemen, both very deaf, bowing to each other in mutual gratification.

On another afternoon Ward came in to talk about the *History of Foreign Policy*. 'How is it going, Master?' I asked.

'Fairly well, but I've had a bit of trouble with Algernon Cecil's chapter.'

'What's wrong with it?'

'It's a bit lively.'

I could readily visualise the blue pencil at work.

One of the Cambridge histories with which I was more closely associated from the beginning was the *History of the British Empire*. It was announced in 1925 and the editors were J. Holland Rose, A. P. Newton (of the University of London), and E. A. Benians. Benians was the effective editor, but Rose was senior and the fact of his seniority weighed heavily upon him. Benians later described him as 'somewhat important in manner and speech'. It was a charming and charitable understatement. Rose, after many years of extension lecturing, had firmly established his reputation as a historian by his books on Napoleon and on William Pitt. He was the first holder of the Chair of Naval and Imperial History and he took his editorship, as he took his professorship, with high seriousness.

One morning he came to my room and, at some length, reported progress, or lack of progress. His explanations were not wholly clear to me, and in my innocence I suggested that it would perhaps be more satisfactory if he reported to the Syndics personally at their next meeting. I said it would be convenient if he came in at the tea-interval. I think the suggestion appealed to him, and he was careful to inquire whether gowns were worn. As we reassembled round the table after tea, Anderson whispered to me: 'What do we do now?' 'Ask the professor for his report', I replied. So Rose cleared his throat and began:

'Well, gentlemen, we have had many conferences, anxious conferences, especially concerning our New Zealand adviser,

Professor Scott—Professor Ernest...I *think* his Christian name is Ernest...yes, Professor Ernest Scott. We had for some time noticed a falling-off, a decline, in the vigour of his correspondence, due to his failing health, until in fact he...er...died. We do not propose to communicate with the widow until her grief is assuaged, or mitigated...'

Such was the beginning of a speech which was of considerable length and I was afterwards warned that my experiment of a first-hand report to the Syndics need not be repeated. Rose's manner of speech and writing was not reserved for official occasions; it was equally evident in personal communications. As Professor Newton was in London, we had agreed at the outset that when he was summoned for a conference, one or other of us would give him lunch. On one such occasion, Rose wrote to me asking me to entertain Newton and explaining why he could not do so himself: 'Mrs Rose and I are so incapacitated by our new teeth-plates, that we are avoiding company for the present.'

Later, on a September morning when I was walking down the Barton Road, I was surprised to see a figure in cap and gown approaching. As I drew nearer, I recognised that it was Holland Rose and remembered that the Master of his college (A. E. Shipley) had recently died.

'Ah, good morning', said Rose. 'I've just been viewing the remains of our late Master—prior to cremation.'

Phrases of this kind came from him with complete spontaneity, but the most serious announcement he made to me was that he was beset by so many difficulties that he had decided to resign his editorship. I was a little disturbed by this and told Benians at once. Benians received my news with his attractive, slow smile. 'Don't worry,' he said, 'there's a drawer in my desk full of Rose's resignations. Leave him to me.' Which I gratefully did.

Apart from his help in reorganising the *Medieval History*, J. R. Tanner did much valuable work for the Press. He was the first editor of the *Student's Handbook* and in 1917 compiled the

Historical Register of the University to 1910. I found him as genial a Syndic as I had found him a lecturer and his books on Tudor and Stuart documents had a good sale. His special interest was in Samuel Pepys, whose letters and other documents he had edited, and when he left Cambridge to live at Aldeburgh, he looked forward to writing the definitive *Life* for publication by George Bell and Sons. But at the time of his death in 1931, he had done little more than amass material and some time afterwards Guy Bickers, head of George Bell, wrote to say that his firm felt unable to grapple with the contents of the packing-case which had been sent to them. Would the Press be willing to take over the material and to find an editor? On general grounds the Syndics welcomed the opportunity of publishing a *Life* of Pepys, but they had some difficulty in finding the right author. In Cambridge, it appeared, there was no obvious candidate and I think it was Keith Feiling who recommended us to consider Arthur Bryant, author of *Charles II*, recently published by Longmans.

Arthur Bryant was, and is, a man of remarkable energy, with a vivid sense of history which in his early days he had displayed as a pageant-master. When he came to discuss the Pepys proposal with me, we had lunch in college and I was interested to learn that he had first been destined for Pembroke, but that after serving in the army in France he had decided, in view of family traditions, to go to Oxford. He undertook the work on Pepys *con amore*. Tanner had not begun to write the book, so that Bryant had a free hand from the beginning. The first volume, dealing with the period of the Diary, was highly successful and was followed by *The Years of Peril* and *The Saviour of the Navy*. Save for one little incident, everything went smoothly. Bryant's agreement was made direct with the Press. After the publication of the first volume he had put his affairs into the hands of an agent, who, without reference to us, sold the serial rights of the second volume to one of the Sunday papers. When I remonstrated with him and reminded him of the rights of the Press under the terms of the agreement, he naïvely replied that he had assumed that a

University Press would not insist upon its legal rights. It did not take me long to dispel his illusion.

The third Pepys volume was published in 1938 and all three continued to have a good sale, but the rigours of wartime paper-rationing made it difficult for us to reprint them in adequate numbers. The greater part of our ration was required for text-books, but Collins, who published other books by Bryant, had more paper available and, with great regret, I felt that it was but fair to the author to negotiate a transference.

After the war I served for a time on the Ashridge educational council, of which Bryant was chairman. I enjoyed the work and lectured once or twice at Ashridge at the invitation of the director (Sir Bernard Paget). Later, when a storm arose over a major question of policy, the members of the council supported Bryant and resigned with him.

J. H. Clapham became a Syndic of the Press in 1916 and so remained until his retirement in 1938, frequently serving as vice-chairman. He was the first Professor of Economic History and his three-volume *Economic History of Modern Britain* became a standard work. He took a keen and practical interest in the economics of publishing and his literary judgement, as well as his financial shrewdness, were of great benefit to the Press and to me. In parenthesis I recall the remarkable career of his son, Michael, who, after taking a classical degree, had a keen desire to be a printer. He worked for some months in the printing house and Lewis, being impressed by his qualities, recommended him to the Kynoch Press, owned by Imperial Chemical Industries at Birmingham. There his rise was rapid, so rapid that with some regret he left printing behind him and in a relatively short time became a director of I.C.I.

Another notable, and highly individual, historian was G. G. Coulton, the 'remote and ineffectual don' of Belloc's poem. In fact, Coulton was neither remote nor ineffectual. His best friends deplored the amount of time and energy he devoted to contro-versy, but he was a crusader for truth as he saw it and if he discovered error or evasion in Gasquet or anyone else, he felt himself in duty bound to proclaim it. He had been a candidate for the Chair of Ecclesiastical History when Whitney (a 'safer' candidate) had been appointed. Undaunted, he remained on good terms with his successful rival and threw his energies into the editorship of the *Cambridge Studies in Medieval Life and Thought*. Among the contributors to the series, all personally devoted to him, were Eileen Power, H. S. Bennett and Margaret Deanesly and his own four volumes of *Five Centuries of Religion* serve as a monument of his vast and tireless learning. My relations with him were very happy and at the Press we always marvelled at the form in which his manuscripts came to us. They were written on the back of examination scripts and held together with enormous safety-pins. Absorbed in his medieval research, he made no effort to keep abreast of later, and lighter, literature. He told Stanley Bennett one day that in Deighton Bell's shop he had picked up a pamphlet by S. C. Roberts which, he said, 'seemed to be about a private detective'.*

Only once did I have trouble with him of a controversial kind. In 1931 we announced a cheap reprint of the fifteen volumes of the *Cambridge History of English Literature*. Our advertisements made it abundantly clear that it was not a new edition, but a plain reprint. The whole object was to make the volumes available to students at 5*s*. each.

Coulton heard of this and came to see me:

'I hear you're bringing out a new edition of the *C.H.E.L.*', he said.

'No,' I replied firmly, 'just a plain reprint of the text.'

'But aren't you going to correct it?'

'Certainly', I said unwarily, 'we shall take the opportunity, as we always do, of correcting a date or a purely factual error, but nothing more.'

Coulton brightened at this and, even more unwarily, I agreed to send him a set of sheets of R. H. Benson's chapter in volume III on 'The Dissolution of the Religious Houses'. About a week later

* See pp. 227 ff.

the sheets were returned with heavy corrections, some of the statements being neatly amended by the insertion of the word 'not'. When I told Coulton that we couldn't possibly print a revised version of one particular chapter, he was greatly upset. In vain I repeated that we had announced not a new edition, but a cheap reprint. 'Very well,' he said, 'but I must warn you that I am shortly to deliver a lecture on historiography at the British Academy and you mustn't mind if I expose you.' I assured him that I would face it.

The exposure, when it came, was politely veiled. A 'press of great distinction' was criticised for 'reprinting a bulky work of reference...without the least warning to the public that particles of poison may be found in the good wholesome food'. Coulton had a keen nose for particles.

During part of the Second World War he held a temporary professorship in Toronto and there he wrote his autobiography, *Fourscore Years*, which we undertook to publish on condition that the proofs were read and passed for press in Cambridge. With the help of Stanley Bennett, Frank Kendon and the author's daughter, Mary, this was done and the book was published in 1943. Coulton died in 1947 and in the following year his daughter's *Father, a portrait of G. G. Coulton at home* shocked some readers by its frankness. But its candour, at once caustic and benignant, was in the authentic Coulton tradition of truth at all costs.

Eileen Power was one of the most distinguished of Coulton's followers. Her substantial work, *Medieval Nunneries*, was published in 1922 and I did not then have occasion to meet her. A few years later I noted the announcement by another publishing house of her small popular book, *Medieval People*. With Clapham's help I arranged to meet the authoress and asked her why she had deserted the Press.

'Oh, but do you really want that kind of book?' she incredulously inquired, 'of course I always bring my tombstones to you, but I had no idea that you would care about a little book.'

'And how', I asked, 'do you think we can provide the money for your tombstones if we don't have the chance of making it on something more popular?' After a little more badinage, Eileen became constructive: 'I'll tell you what', she said, 'my sister Rhoda is very good at writing for the young and I'd guarantee that the history was sound. But have you any ideas about the sort of book Rhoda might write for you?'

'Well', I said, 'what about history seen through the eyes of children in various centuries?'

It was a purely tentative suggestion, of which the outcome was *Boys and Girls of History*, *Great People of the Past* and other books —certainly they compensated for the tombstones. More important was Eileen's collaboration with Clapham in the planning of the *Cambridge Economic History of Europe*. Her work was cut short by her sudden and untimely death, but I treasure the recollection of a gay lunch we had together in a New York speakeasy in 1930.

Of all Coulton's disciples perhaps the most faithful was Stanley Bennett, but I think of him quite independently of the books we published for him and his gifted wife. From 1919 onwards our friendship grew into intimacy, for we had much in common. Frequently, and particularly in Aubrey Attwater's rooms, we talked over the affairs of the English faculty, of the Union Society (of which he was librarian) and of the University in general. Very fittingly he succeeded Aubrey as a Syndic of the Press in 1936 and gave me constant help; but his most valuable contribution was made when, after my time, he served as chairman throughout the period in which the new printing house was planned and built.

G. M. Trevelyan returned to Cambridge as Regius Professor of History in 1927. As an author he was loyally attached to the house of Longman, as his father (G. O. Trevelyan) and his great-uncle (Macaulay) had been before him. But he was most friendly towards the Press and always ready with advice about historical publications. When in 1940 I wrote to congratulate him on his appointment as Master of Trinity, he replied: 'I greatly appreciated your note. I hope it will turn out all right. I have had grave doubts about it, but the war and Winston have resolved them. I am so very glad that the Press continues to pour out good books...'

Having settled into the Lodge at Trinity, he wrote a short history of the College, primarily designed for the benefit of freshmen. His first intention was that it should be printed for sale within the college, but I persuaded him to let us publish it in the ordinary way, being confident (and my confidence was justified) that it would have a much wider sale.

Longmans suffered very badly in the blitz and I remember Trevelyan telling me that of the many books of his in their catalogue only two were in print. The stock of the others had been destroyed. 'I suppose', he added, 'that it is a judgement on me for not publishing at the Press.' Publishing apart, both he and Mrs Trevelyan were always most kind to me and, as it happened, it was after my retirement in 1958 that I saw most of him. I had moved to the Loke House, West Road (a house originally built for A. N. Whitehead) and found myself next door to him. By that time his eyesight was failing. He could not see well enough to read and frequently consoled himself by reciting long passages from Milton or Wordsworth or Meredith. The best service that his friends could offer was to read aloud to him and I was pleased to find that he could always enjoy half-an-hour or more of Boswell. But the reading that he most regularly enjoyed was that of his faithful nurse-housekeeper. Once, when he was lunching with us, my wife said:

'Sister Thomas reads a lot to you, doesn't she?'

'Yes,' he replied in his most decisive manner, 'and much better than the dons.'

He was a warm-hearted neighbour, but no one could have described him as an easy conversationalist. Once, when I had exhausted my topics and there was still some time before tea would be ready, I asked whether he would like me to read some-

thing to him. 'No,' he replied, 'I think I'd rather sit and chat.'
Whereupon a long silence ensued. E. M. Forster, who was among
his regular visitors, told me that he rather enjoyed the silences.

On the other hand, an attack upon one of his literary heroes
would rouse him to fluent indignation. He revered Milton and
fulminated against any disparagement of him. At closer range he
revered Macaulay. When I suggested that the full text of
Macaulay's diary, preserved in the library at Trinity, ought to
be published, I was surprised by the vehemence of his outburst:
'Over my dead body,' he said, 'I'm not going to have those
Bloomsbury people laughing at my great-uncle.' Meredith was
one of his favourites. Dover Wilson has often told me how on
Sunday mornings in his undergraduate days Trevelyan would
lead a party of walkers over the Gogs, vigorously reciting Meredith's poetry as he went. In my time he would quote Max
Beerbohm's *Euphemia Clashthought* with similar enthusiasm.

In his later years the anti-clericalism of his youth was appreciably diluted. One of his regular visitors was M. D. Knowles, for
whom he had the highest regard, and when I asked him how he
liked having an episcopal son-in-law [the Bishop of Ripon], he
replied: 'Well, if you've got a parson in the family, it's very nice
that he should be a bishop.' To the end, he preserved his forthrightness. During his last illness a cousin came to visit him. 'Now
you sit down', he said, 'and talk about yourself and that will
send me to sleep.' But I like to remember that the last words he
spoke to me were words of sympathetic inquiry about my
daughter, who had been gravely ill.

Academical history has for long been one of my special interests
and one of the most impressive series of volumes which the Press
issued in my time, and after, is *Alumni Cantabrigienses*. The first
volume of Part I, which covers the period from the earliest times
to 1750, was published in 1922. I had known the compiler, J. A.
Venn, ever since my return to Cambridge in 1911, when he was
secretary of the 'Cock and Hen' tennis club, and in 1915, as I have
already noted, he was a fellow-member of the M.A. Platoon.

After the war he became a lecturer in agricultural economics and a Fellow (and later President) of Queens', but he had inherited from his father a love of university archives and when the four volumes of Part I of *Alumni* were completed in 1927, he was delighted that the Syndics agreed to continue the record down to the year 1900. As he says in his preface, the procession of *alumni* forms a microcosm of the country itself and personally I find the six volumes of Part II a fascinating storehouse.

Another academical historian was D. A. Winstanley of Trinity. I begged him at one time to write the modern history of the University. J. B. Mullinger's three massive volumes brought the story down to 1670, but there is no full-dress history of Cambridge from that date onwards. Winstanley, however, said he must do his own work in his own way, which was 'to survey certain activities and inactivities, mainly educational' and this episodic treatment resulted in three volumes *Unreformed Cambridge* (1935), *Early Victorian Cambridge* (1940) and *Later Victorian Cambridge* (1947). There is plenty of information in these books about educational reform and religious tests and statutory commissions, but what gives them their special character is such chapters as those entitled 'Trouble at the Fitzwilliam', 'Robinson's Vote' and 'The Judges and Trinity College'. Winstanley was a man of wit as well as of learning. At Merchant Taylors he had been a schoolfellow of R. V. Laurence, who, even in his thirties, had the look of an old man. 'We were boys together,' said Winstanley once, 'at least I was.'

Laurence was a notable figure in Trinity and in the history faculty. He had contributed to the *Cambridge Modern History*, but I never had the opportunity of publishing a book for him. He was essentially a bachelor don and served as Tutor of Trinity for many years. 'These married fellows', he said to me once, 'don't understand what it means to live as a tutor in college, always exposed, week-days and Sundays alike, to pupils or their parents. D'you know, when I was Tutor, I often used to take the train to London, simply to have a little snooze at the club.'

Professorial interchange between Oxford and Cambridge occurs quite frequently and in 1927 Ernest Barker was elected as the first holder of the Chair of Political Science. In his *Age and Youth*, he has described in detail his feelings as an Oxonian in Cambridge. He is full of praise for the open access and the borrowing rights provided by the University Library, but I am afraid he never felt quite so warmly towards our Press as he did towards that of his old university. Nevertheless, our relations were very cordial. We published several books for him in his later years and he frequently advised about manuscripts offered to us. His reports were clear and informative and had the great, and rare, merit of punctual delivery. During the war he was an energetic general editor of a series of small books on 'Current Problems', of which by far the most successful was Sir Richard Livingstone's *The Future in Education*. Barker was always brimful of ideas. He was in advance of his time in his plea for the extension of graduate studies and rather sadly saw himself in retrospect as 'buzzing about with notions before the right avenues had been explored and the preparations properly made'. But he appreciated the leisure which retirement gave him for reading and writing and I enjoyed many a talk with him in Cranmer Road—a road categorically and characteristically commemorated in his memoirs.

Chapter 9

POETS AND CRITICS

Contemporary poets do not figure prominently in the Cambridge catalogue, but there are dons who write poetry as well as criticism and one of these is F. L. (Peter) Lucas, for whom we published several books of poems between 1930 and 1935. 'The difficulty with poetry', he once wrote with engaging frankness, 'is to read it. There are so many easier things to read—books about poetry among them', and certainly we found it easier to sell his *Eight Victorian Poets* (1930) and his *Decline and Fall of the Romantic Ideal* (1936) than his own poetry.

I once urged him to write a new series of 'Lives of the Poets', beginning where Johnson ended, but he refused to be deflected from the many other projects he had in mind. He has for some years been retired and I never cease to marvel at his continued energy and productivity.

I think I first met A. E. Housman about 1924, when an enterprising secretary of the Martlets caught him in a good mood and invited him to be the 'distinguished stranger' of the year. The subject of the paper was Robert Burns, but towards the end of it Housman delivered some caustic comments on Scotsmen in general. As the president of the society (David MacMyn) was a fervent Scottish patriot, the discussion which followed the paper was more than usually lively.

A year or two later Housman came to see me about the publication of a volume of essays by Arthur Platt. Platt had been Professor of Greek at University College, London, and Housman had been his devoted friend. Consequently, he was prepared to break his normal rule and to write a preface to the book, in which he paid full tribute to Platt's gaiety and versatility as well as to his scholarship. But he felt bound to add:

124

In conclusion it is proper to mention his vices. He was addicted to tobacco and indifferent to wine, and he would squander long summer days on watching the game of cricket.

So I was not surprised to find Platt occasionally using a cricket metaphor or referring to famous batsmen in his essays. What did surprise me was that Housman thought it necessary to annotate them. Fry, Gunn and Shrewsbury were carefully explained to be 'cricketers of the day'. When I queried the necessity of these footnotes, Housman was quite firm. On 27 April 1927 he wrote:

At p. 66 Roger Fry's 'average' will be a great puzzle. You are old enough to know who Gunn and Shrewsbury were, but the number of those who do is always lessening and they are on their way to join the celebrated Mrs Rudd who was a subject of conversation at General Paoli's on April 28, 1778 and is not in the Dictionary of National Biography.

But my true object in adding the notes was to win a smile from Platt's beautiful spirit and mitigate the tedium of Paradise.

Housman's edition of Juvenal had been published in 1905 by Grant Richards. By 1929 it had been out of print for some years and the Syndics invited Housman to publish a new edition at the Press. The terms offered were gladly accepted and Housman added: 'They [the Syndics] will not be able to offer the work to the public at 4/6d net as I did, but the price had better be moderate, as even the pleasure of buying copies for less than they cost to print did not induce mankind to take more than 18 per annum.'

The Juvenal was followed by a one-volume edition of the *Astronomica* of Manilius and here we ran into a little trouble, first about the printing of the *apparatus criticus* and then about the wording of an advertisement. On 20 November 1932 Housman wrote:

Hospitality will protect you from violence, so do not be afraid to come on Friday; but what you make me say in your advertisement in the *Classical Review* is the exact opposite of what I said, and intrinsically idiotic...

125

But the most exciting of our Housman publications was *The Name and Nature of Poetry*. I think it was Will Spens, Master of Corpus and Vice-Chancellor at the time, who persuaded him to accept the invitation to deliver the Leslie Stephen Lecture in 1933. Housman agreed that we should publish it and his MS. arrived in good time. It happened that I had leisure to read it straight through and in my acknowledgement I was bold enough to add that, if the author had no special intentions with regard to the MS., I should be proud to have it. I did not expect a reply and none came.

The delivery of the lecture was a great occasion. Housman had consented to give the lecture with reluctance; but, having consented, he recognised that he had been invited not as the editor of Manilius but as the author of *A Shropshire Lad*. He did not shrink from describing the emotions which poetry induced in him: 'As for the seventh verse of the forty-ninth Psalm in the Book of Common Prayer, "But no man may deliver his brother, nor make agreement unto God for him", that is to me poetry so moving that I can hardly keep my voice steady in reading it...' At the end of the lecture he went further: he told his audience how his own poems came into being. As he began the famous passage ('Having drunk a pint of beer at luncheon...') there was a slight stir, followed by the complete hush which betokens a wholly attentive audience. Finally came the dismissal: 'Farewell for ever...I shall go back with relief and thankfulness to my proper job.'

Most listeners came away from the Senate House with expectations more than fulfilled, but the *avant-garde* of the English faculty were heard to murmur that it would take many months to undo the harm the lecture had done to youthful students of the meaning of poetic meaning.

Meanwhile the lecture was already printed, but we delayed publication for a short time in the interests of American copyright. When the date (31 May) was fixed, I suggested to Housman that he might like to dine with me in celebration of the event.

He agreed with alacrity and I arranged a small party in my rooms in Pembroke—Harold Child, Aubrey Attwater, my son John (then an undergraduate) and his friend Denys Haynes, of Trinity. I gave Housman a Burgundy he liked (probably Chambertin 1923) and he made one remark which gave Child particular pleasure: 'The only form of Christianity I profess is anti-Protestantism.' Quite late in the evening he suddenly turned to me: 'I believe you asked for the manuscript of the lecture. Some parts of it are very bad, but I'll send it to you.' It came with the following letter:

I congratulate you on your salesmanship. I enclose the MS, which however lacks 2 pages. Probably I destroyed them as containing things too bad to be read.

In fact, four pages were lacking. Even so, it is, I think, the only prose MS. of Housman's which survives. His essay on Burns and similar papers written for literary societies, which the Press had sought in vain to publish, were destroyed in accordance with the terms of his will.

It was fortunate for me that just at the time when I was dealing with Housman as an author I was elected to the Family. An intelligent interest in food and wine was regarded as one of the necessary qualifications of membership and no one insisted on this more firmly than Housman, who, when he was host, designed his menus with great care. Under the mellowing influence of a good dinner conversation became quite easy. I remember his telling me that he had rather ruefully agreed to be a pall-bearer at Thomas Hardy's funeral. One of his companions was Galsworthy, of whose books he had a low opinion. 'He', said Housman, 'represents humanitarianism; I represent pessimism.' I took the opportunity, rather rashly, of putting in a good word for Galsworthy's short stories, particularly for *A Stoic*, the story of the rascally old financier who dies after a sumptuous meal ordered in defiance of his doctor's warnings. Housman admitted that it was a good dinner.

He could also enjoy entertainment on a more modest scale. Tentatively, I invited him to a small party when I was living in the Barton Road. I was then a widower and my elder daughter, Molly, who had not long left school, was terrified when I told her that he had accepted the invitation: 'Daddy', she said, 'I'll probably have to sit next to him. What on earth shall I have to talk about?' But she need not have worried. Housman put her at her ease at once and was entirely amiable. At a similar party in the following year I was astonished and gratified when at the end of dinner he turned to me and said: 'Kindly convey my compliments to your cook—the best Scotch Woodcock I have ever tasted.'

My last meeting with him remains vividly in my memory. On 24 April 1936 I was host to the Family in Pembroke. On the 22nd Housman wrote: 'I still hope to be there, though I am not so sanguine as I should like to be.' But he came. He looked terribly ill and, shortly after we had sat down to dinner, he confessed to me that he felt sick. I took him into the bedroom and asked him whether I should get a taxi to take him back to Trinity. No, he said, he would rather come back to the table. Having nibbled a little toast and drunk a glass of Burgundy, he left early. The next day he went to a nursing home and on the 30th he died.

At his funeral service the hymn ('O thou that from thy mansion'), which he had written for the occasion, was sung and the lesson was appropriately taken from the last two chapters of Ecclesiastes, unfortunately misprinted on the hymn-sheet as 'Ecclesiasticus'. Housman might well have taken it as a final justification of his mistrust of editors and printers.

Many books, too many perhaps, have been written about Housman; but there is no better portrait of him than the biographical sketch preceding Andrew Gow's *List* of his writings which was published at the Press at the end of 1936.

In an earlier chapter I have written briefly of the beginnings of the *New Shakespeare* and of the happy co-operation of Q and

Dover Wilson in the production of the comedies. When Q, who was having trouble with his eyesight, resigned, the first inclination of the Syndics was to appoint a new co-editor in his place and, at Dover Wilson's suggestion, I sounded Lytton Strachey. At lunch in the old Cavendish Club he seemed inclined to go further; but in the end, and to my satisfaction, it was agreed that Dover should be sole editor. In 1924 he had been appointed Professor of Education at King's College, London, and I stayed more than once with him at his house in Purley, playing golf on the Banstead Downs and prodding him into greater speed of Shakespearian production. Early in 1931 Faber and Faber invited him to write a short *Life* of Shakespeare. With instinctive loyalty, Dover asked me whether this would be in order. Unhesitatingly I replied that it would not. If the editor of the *New Shakespeare* contemplated such a book, it should be published at Cambridge. So we discussed its scope and size and agreed that it should be a small one, to be sold at 3*s*. 6*d*.

On 23 April 1932 the new Shakespeare Theatre at Stratford-upon-Avon was to be opened with a great flourish by the Prince of Wales and that day was clearly the right day for publication. Accordingly, I told Dover that we must have 'copy' by Christmas 1931. The year came to an end and I wrote urgently demanding the MS. No answer came. I then sent a reply-paid telegram, pressing for a date of delivery. This had its effect and *The Essential Shakespeare*, duly published on 23 April 1932, has been one of the most successful of Dover's books.

In 1935 he moved to Edinburgh, having been appointed Professor of Rhetoric and English Literature in succession to Sir Herbert Grierson. He was full of hope that his release from the study of education would enable him to devote more time to Shakespeare. It was a vain hope. The comedies being finished, he had turned to *Hamlet*. Alas for Waller's vision of concise annotation and an annual output of five plays. Dover discovered so much, that two volumes on the text and one volume on the plot (*What Happens in Hamlet*) were necessary to supplement the edition of the play itself. When he turned to *Richard II*, he assured me that things would be different, since the text had already been settled by A. W. Pollard. But further examination showed that there were many textual problems still to be tackled and in the end *Richard II* contained 70 pages of introduction and 130 pages of notes. The study of *Henry IV* led Dover to choose Falstaff as the subject of his Clark lectures in 1943 and *The Fortunes of Falstaff* had a good sale. But by now it was clear that a busy professor could never, with the best will in the world, hope to complete the edition and I had a talk with my chairman (J. F. Cameron) about the possibility of some drastic action. Cameron was sceptical, but he gave me a free hand to negotiate and on an afternoon in the summer of 1944 Dover and I settled down to a talk in the Athenæum. We began sadly. Each of us had recently lost an only son in the war and, having given each other what comfort we could, we turned to business. Dover was 63 and was due to retire at 70; but, if it were made financially possible, he would be willing, and indeed happy, to resign and to devote his whole time to Shakespeare. This made things easy for me and I was pleased to note, years afterwards, that Dover, in the preface to his *Shakespeare's Happy Comedies* (Faber, 1962), described the terms of our arrangement as generous. He had come to love Scotland and the Scots, and freedom from professorial duties gave him a new lease of editorial optimism. He added a spacious study to his house at Balerno and liked to regard himself as a whole-time employee of the Press.

I made many visits to Balerno. Mrs Dover Wilson was the daughter of Canon Baldwin, sometime Vicar of Harston, who, after his retirement, lived for many years in Scroope Terrace, Cambridge. His small, stooping figure and his picturesque white hair gave one the impression of an early Tractarian and his clerical cape concealed a great store of vigour. He was a keen chess-player and a keen Shakespearian. From time to time he would invite his friends to a Shakespeare reading, adding at the bottom of the card: 'No refreshments other than intellectual.' In his drawing-room on the first floor were rows of chairs for his guests; the room was unlit and when the curtains had been drawn, the Canon retired to a recess by the fireplace and proceeded to recite from memory. But 'recite' is a feeble word. Out of the dark corner came the trial scene from *The Merchant of Venice* or Mark Antony's speech over Caesar's coffin, with the murmurs of the crowd rising to the crescendo of 'Read the will'. It was all very Irvingesque and a remarkable *tour de force*. On the Canon's ninetieth birthday I was invited by the Dover Wilsons to dinner at the Garden House Hotel. He was in good form and I cannot pretend to recall his anecdotes, except that one related to wine (which he treated with proper seriousness) and that the story rose to a climax of tragedy—'it was CORKED'.

But to return to Balerno—Mrs Dover Wilson was a woman of many parts. She was a chess-player (like her father) and also an enthusiastic bird-watcher. As a housewife she was punctilious and had a deep suspicion of the carelessness and unreliability of males as such. 'Which of you two men left the light on outside?' was one of the first remarks I heard her make. Fundamentally, I think, she approved of me; and especially because I worked in a good cause. Her business sense was keener than Dover's and she applauded my efforts to accelerate his editing. With some of my tastes (for beer and tobacco, for instance) she was less sympathetic. 'John,' she said one evening, 'are you going to have cocoa to-night or more of that *everlasting* beer?' Not that we drank a great deal, but we frequently had a round of golf at Baberton and Dover always laid in a good supply of his favourite brew. But, of course, the main object of my visits was to extract more, and if possible slimmer, volumes of the *New Shakespeare*. In particular, I protested once against the bulk of one of the glossaries. Printing costs apart, I honestly felt that a considerable number of entries were otiose. Under protest, strong protest, Dover agreed—but he has since told me in triumph that they have all been restored in a later edition. Dorothy Dover Wilson died in 1961. The sadness was not in her death, but in the period of partial paralysis and blindness which preceded it. Her spirit and her forthrightness persisted to the end.

Dover's eightieth birthday was fittingly celebrated by a dinner at Prestonfield, a noble house in which Sir Alexander Dick had entertained Dr Johnson in 1773. The Vice-Chancellor of Edinburgh (Sir Edward Appleton) took the chair and there were friends and colleagues from Oxford and Cambridge as well as from Edinburgh. It fell to me to propose Dover's health and eighteen months later, to my astonishment, I found myself doing it again on the occasion of his return to Edinburgh after his second, and very happy, marriage to his cousin Elizabeth.

From all this it will appear that my retirement from publishing was very far from weakening our friendship. I have little doubt that it was Dover who was primarily responsible for my appointment as a trustee of Shakespeare's Birthplace. We often met at Stratford-upon-Avon, where he knew many of the leading actors; but, to my surprise, he had never met Dame Edith Evans. At the time of one of our visits she was playing in *All's Well that Ends Well*, and after the play we went to her dressing-room. I said a brief word of introduction, but it was made superfluous by Dover's felicitous self-presentation. 'I've never met you,' he said to Dame Edith, 'but I've loved you for years.'

From Stratford we went on more than once to Marlborough, where the school literary society always welcomed a talk on a Shakespearian subject—and on other subjects, as I afterwards discovered.

The most striking feature of Dover's exposition was its freshness. I only once heard him give a formal lecture and that, oddly enough, was in Paris in 1946. Kingsford and I were concerned with an exhibition of books published by the University Presses during the war. Dover came with us as representative author and, very naturally, was asked to give a lecture. A distinguished French savant was in the chair, but the audience was not primarily academic and I have no doubt that Dover gave us one of his stock pieces designed for popular delivery. But he spoke like a young man who had just discovered Shakespeare for himself and was eager to communicate his enthusiasm to others. Neither old age nor modern criticism could depress his buoyant spirit.

When I heard that the plays were completed and that 'copy' for the *Sonnets* had been delivered, I recalled with some satisfaction our talk at the Athenæum in 1944.

In a note in his edition of *Henry V*, published in 1945, Dover paid an affectionate tribute to Harold Child, who up to that date had written the stage-history of each play. I, too, mourned the loss of an old friend, for I first met Child in 1912. In that year the *Oedipus Rex* was the Greek play chosen for performance at Cambridge, and Child, whom Waller knew well, came up for it as dramatic critic of *The Times*. Waller, who was not very well at the time, suggested that I might like to accompany him to the theatre, which I did. But it was not until after the First World War that we became intimate. Child's own story of his career fascinated me. Coming down from Oxford, he had been articled to a firm of country solicitors. In the country he was happy enough, but when he was sent to the office of the firm's London agents, he ran away and joined a theatrical touring company, playing the 'Light Juvenile Gentleman' with Harry Paulton in *Niobe*. Eventually, I persuaded him to write the story of his stage adventures and *A Poor Player* was published in 1939. It was not a propitious time for publishing, but I valued the 'Epistle Dedicatory' which he addressed to me. As one of his obituarists remarked, Harold was by nature a man of letters and the main course of his later career was determined by his association with Bruce Richmond in the founding of *The Times Literary Supplement* in 1902. Of that journal he became a mainstay, as indeed of *The Times* itself, and his 'light leaders' possessed an individual charm. There was scholarship underneath his lightness of touch, and before my time he had contributed many chapters to the *Cambridge History of English Literature*.

He was the easiest of companions. Like me, he enjoyed driving a car and would come up to Cambridge in his A.C. to spend a night with me; and, if there were time, we would explore some of the countryside. Driving through the fenlands was simple enough, but Harold had a proper feeling for the personality of a car. At the end of a description of an exciting mountain-drive in Switzerland, he wrote: 'Worse luck, you cannot pat a motor-car and give it a bran-mash or a lump of sugar.' From time to time I had lunch with him at the Garrick. He had a fine taste in Burgundy and it was a delight to talk with him. At one time he shared a cottage at Thakeham, near Storrington, with Hugh de Selincourt (author of that enchanting story, *A Cricket Match*), and when I was on holiday at Worthing I occasionally went over the downs to have a cup of tea with him. In the later part of his life asthma, which had always troubled him, became more insistent. In 1942 he was seriously ill, but his gentle, humorous spirit persisted. From hospital he wrote to me:

I only see people whom I must see or whom there is no chance of my seeing when I am at home again. And as laughing is as much discouraged as talking, you are one of the very last people I should think of asking them to let in.

You and I and a bottle of Burgundy—it is an entrancing, a rosy prospect! But when, Lucius, when? I am Perfect Patient Number One. Doctors and Sisters and such come and gloat over my chart, which seems to have, like some modern poetry, an inner beauty appreciable only by the initiates...

My last memory is of him sitting up in bed, very wheezy, but quite cheerfully writing a review of a book of Shakespearian criticism. He died in 1945. In *The Times* office was a series of large press-cutting albums containing his contributions for forty years back—an impressive memorial of a scholar-journalist. Into these volumes I dipped and made an anthology, entitled *Essays and Reflections*, which was published in 1948. Very few people bought it, but I was content to have Bruce Richmond's approval of it.

Publishers and booksellers frequently disagree about discounts and other matters, but the judgement of a bookseller who is also a bookman can be of great value. I think it was through Charles Young, of Lamley's, that the manuscript of *The Wheelwright's Shop* was sent to Cambridge and it was John Wilson, of Bumpus, who first put me into touch with another Shakespearian authority, Harley Granville-Barker. Barker had been made Professor of Drama in the Royal Society of Literature. This and similar titles have now been abandoned, but Barker was tickled by the notion of being a professor and determined to mark his tenure of office by something out of the ordinary. So he secured from Fellows of the Society a series of essays relating to the life and literature of the 1870s. All my early play-going had been provincial and, alas, I had seen none of the famous Vedrenne–Barker productions at the Court Theatre. But I had inherited from Moriarty a copy of the first edition of *Mrs Warren's Profession* (1902) and was familiar with the photograph of Barker as Frank. When he came to lunch with me at the old Cavendish Club in 1928, he did not look markedly different. Some of the youthful twinkle had gone, but his rich brown hair was no thinner and there was no trace of greyness in it. Towards a publisher he instinctively adopted an 'Authors' Society' attitude, but we came to terms without difficulty and his list of contributors, which included de la Mare, Saintsbury, Drinkwater and Pinero, was attractive enough from the publishing point of view. By the time that the book was published, I was on very good terms with Barker. Twice I visited him at Netherton Hall, a lovely manor house, some miles inland from Sidmouth. Helen, his wife, was a gracious hostess and seemed to me like a character in a Henry James novel. She was clearly anxious to preserve the tradition of the country house and insisted on Harley putting his theatrical work behind him. Personally, I longed to get him to talk about his early days, but I always drew blank. However, my heart warmed to Helen over one little incident. On my first visit I had my son John with me. He was only about fifteen, but he looked much older. When the wine came round at dinner, he was careful to ask my permission before his glass was filled. I readily agreed and thought no more about it, but the next morning Helen told me that the 'May I, daddy?' coming from a self-possessed and debonair young man was the most surprising and the most charming thing she had ever heard. On the Sunday we drove over to see Henry Head, whom I had got to know well while his monumental work *Aphasia* (1926) was going through the press. But he was already a sick man, himself afflicted by the disease to the study of which he had devoted two large volumes.

After *The Eighteen-Seventies* had been successfully launched, Barker broached the idea of a *Companion to Shakespeare Studies* to be edited by himself and G. B. Harrison, a Brightonian whom I had known well in his undergraduate days just after the First World War. A number of prospective contributors and myself were invited to lunch at the Garrick and, characteristically, Barker insisted that publication should be on a royalty basis with each contributor receiving his appropriate fraction. To this I demurred, in view of the accounting work involved, but as Barker (or rather his agent) undertook to make the individual distribution, I withdrew my objection. The *Companion* was published in 1934 and was very successful. I have a particular affection for it as it contains the only published essay by Aubrey Attwater. In the same year we also published *The Study of Drama*, a lecture given by Barker to a summer school at Cambridge. As a supplement to the lecture, he added some lively notes on the Censorship and the New Psychology and Sunday Cinemas and other engaging topics. His Clark lectures, given at Trinity College in 1930, were unfortunately pledged to Sidgwick and Jackson. Barker enjoyed his time at Trinity and told me a pleasant little story of 'J. J.' Leaving the college after his last lecture and expressing his thanks to the Master, he added: 'I believe, Master, that I shall shortly have the honour of receiving an honorary degree at Edinburgh in company with you.' 'Oh yes,' J. J. replied, 'as a matter of fact, I thought I'd had one there 20 years ago—but I suppose they know.'

In 1937 Barker became director of the British Institute in Paris and, when France fell, went to America. In New York he worked for the Ministry of Information and lectured at a number of universities. He wrote many long letters to me, full of lively comment on the state of the world and also full of home-sickness. 'One feels', he wrote, 'that one has no right to be living over here in at least physical comfort.' He came back to England in 1945 and I had lunch with him in London. He and his wife wanted to break with Sidgwick and Jackson and he just wondered whether the Press might take over their books *en bloc*. He was not surprised when I expressed some doubts, and the possibility was not further explored, for Barker died in the following year. But I had been gratified by his inquiry. He was an author who felt it to be a moral obligation to haggle with a publisher, but he could appreciate some of the facts of publishing life. 'It is a pleasure as well as a duty', he once wrote to me, 'to bargain with you a bit...But I know well enough what would happen to the Press if you did not keep the balance true.'

When I meet and talk with poets, I am always conscious of my own limitations. I enjoy listening to them and reading their autobiographies, but I feel that their minds are exploring a wider range of imagination than I am able to absorb. But it is also my experience that many poets write uncommonly good prose and I think the first time I met Walter de la Mare was at dinner with the Sewards when he came to lecture at Cambridge in 1923. Certainly, as I have already recorded, he spoke beautiful prose at the Double Crown Club in 1927 and a year or two later I saw more of him as the editor of *The Eighteen-Eighties*, the volume which followed Granville-Barker's *Eighteen-Seventies*. He assembled a good team of contributors and had the usual experience of delays ('Eliot', he wrote, 'has a little way, with which I cordially sympathise, of leaving his correspondence to mature'). He himself contributed an essay on Lewis Carroll as well as an editorial introduction. In the Lent Term of 1930 he and Housman dined with me at a Pembroke feast, after which he wrote: 'I enjoyed the Feast immensely. So clear and pearly in memory is its atmosphere that I can still count the oysters on my plate. And I was so very glad to get those last few words with A. E. H.' I also saw something of him in his home at Taplow. My two daughters were successively at Wycombe Abbey School and in the middle of each term I used to drive over on leave-out day. Every parent is familiar with the problem of finding something fresh to do on such days and it was a joy to take them to Hill House for tea.

When de la Mare was elected an honorary Fellow of Keble, I sent him the following:

> We've loved the gentle de la Mare
> In story, song and dream;
> We've wondered if his fancies were
> Exactly what they seem.
>
> The beams of academic light
> Now gratefully have shone:
> Breathless we ask: 'And will he write
> The "Memoirs of a Don"?'

To which he replied:

> Dear S.C.R., alas, too far
> The waters of the Don
> Flow the green fields of learning through
> Ever to shed their gentle dew
> *This* frosty paw upon.
>
> A Fellow—with that great big F!——
> Smile not: the diadem
> No more befits untutored wits
> Than Koh-i-Noors 'Miss M'.
>
> But how the Others now will shine:
> Since KEBLE, just for once,
> Has, with a gesture so benign,
> Proffered its Attic salt and wine
> And welcomed in a dunce!

In later years I did not see much of de la Mare, but I was pleased to be invited to contribute to the book offered to him on his seventy-fifth birthday. 'With what clearness and happiness', he wrote in July 1953, 'I recall my visits to you at Cambridge in the now-so-far away.' I visited him once or twice in his last home at Twickenham and found his sense of wonder and his sense of fun undimmed. To the end it was the simple, yet miraculous happenings of life which he contemplated with an eager reverence—the song of a bird, a child asleep, 'the unfolding of the petals of an evening primrose'.

In 1929 I received a MS. entitled *The Small Years*. The author was Frank Kendon, who had, I think, attended my lectures just after the First World War. But he was virtually unknown to me and, at that time, very little known to the general public. Having read the MS., which was a record of the author's childhood, I had no hesitation in recommending its publication. In general, I was never enthusiastic about commendatory forewords and Frank's good wine needed no bush. Nevertheless, the book seemed to me so clearly one which would appeal to Walter de la Mare, that I asked him whether he would like to introduce it. He agreed willingly and the book's reception showed that neither of us had made a mistake. The quality of Frank's story of his early days at Goudhurst and of the school over which his father presided was quickly recognised and one of the most prominent reviews was that by Lord Stamp, who had himself been a pupil at the school. The book was published in 1930. Some years later, we had a vacancy on the secretarial staff and in the circumstances we needed a man with experience of publishing rather than a young man straight from his degree. Kingsford, who had moved to our London house and for whose judgement I had a high regard, strongly recommended Kendon, who was then on the staff of *John o' London's Weekly*. The prospect of exchanging Fleet Street for work in an academic publishing house was to him an attractive one; not that he had any deep interest in university affairs as such, but he welcomed the chance of designing and editing substantial books instead of preparing 'copy' for a weekly journal against the clock. He knew, of course, that he would have to handle all sorts of books and that many of them would have little appeal beyond a small circle of specialist scholars. But when he was entrusted with a manuscript in which imagination played some part, he was immensely happy in the help he gave to the author—and it was so gently done that the author was hardly conscious that his book had been re-written for him.

Frank was a poet and a quietist. To and from his house at Harston he bicycled at an incredibly slow pace, observing the trees and the meadows and the birds as he went. His Christmas card usually embodied a poem and he took as much care about the typography as about the writing. Here are some lines from one that gave me especial pleasure:

> Shepherds, shepherds, wake as I do. See!
> A star is down and wanders over the plain,
> Must we go to it? Is it a sign for us?
> Come and search with us. Come and see.

In one capacity Frank bade fair to rival Christopher Smart, the Pembroke poet who won the Seatonian Prize five times between 1750 and 1755.

Thomas Seaton, Fellow of Clare, who died in 1741, left money for a prize to be annually awarded to the Master of Arts who, in the judgement of the Vice-Chancellor, the Master of Clare and the Professor of Greek, should compose the best English poem on the attributes of the Supreme Being or other sacred subject. 'Other sacred subject' is now interpreted with some liberality and Frank was the Seatonian prizeman in 1942, 1945, 1946 and 1949. Though the Master of Clare and the Professor of Greek have now been replaced by examiners appointed *ad hoc*, the Vice-Chancellor remains and Frank was amused to hear that I should be one of the three to sit in judgement on his entry for 1949. The poems are, of course, judged anonymously and my co-examiners had no doubt in making the award to a piece which was to me easily recognisable. 'I was resolved', Frank wrote to me after the award was made, 'when I knew you were one of the adjudicators (Posh for "judges") to do my best in my late taskmaster's eye.'

Frank's judgement sometimes surprised and did not always convince me; but when it was a matter of imaginative literature, he was more likely to be right than I. When, for instance, Christopher Fry sent us the MS. of *The Firstborn*, Frank was more enthusiastic than I had ever known him. So the MS. was accepted and Frank commissioned an admirable jacket for the book. Similarly, when Ronald Searle came out of captivity in Japan, it was Frank who urged the publication of his drawings, gruesome as many of them were, of Japanese prison-life; *Forty Drawings* (Ronald Searle's first book) was published in 1946. Poet though he was, Frank had enough experience to realise that the money to publish a new book must come from the profit made on an old one and that the interest of the public must be stimulated by intelligent presentation. Gradually we entrusted jackets and their all-important blurbs to him. He had a flair not only for choosing the right sort of drawing or photograph, but for composing a blurb which really meant something. I had written many blurbs myself in earlier days and often, I fear, they were little more than paraphrases of the author's preface; but Frank's had a highly individual quality. His novel, *Martin Makesure* (1950), did not make an appeal to me. Frank knew that it was not my book, but I liked what he wrote on the fly-leaf of my copy: 'For S. C., who never judged harshly.'

In January 1947 I attended a conference in London at which, under the chairmanship of the Bishop of Truro (the late J. W. Hunkin), proposals for a new translation of the Bible were discussed. The history of the *New English Bible* is no part of my story, since I left the Press soon after the preliminary work had begun, but I was pleased that Frank was chosen to be one of the panel of literary advisers to whom the translators' work was submitted. After the publication of the New Testament in 1961, Frank was entrusted with the Psalms and in his last years they were his main concern. At the time of his death he had completed his versions of thirty-six of them. These were separately published in 1963 and form as fitting a memorial as Frank would have wished.

Chapter 10

PLAY-ACTING

Though domestic miming had always been a hobby of mine, I had never been a member of a dramatic society and I think my first appearance upon a public stage was at the Theatre Royal, Worthing. During my convalescence in the spring of 1918, my mother introduced me to Nancy Price. Nancy's energy was tireless and amongst other activities she was organising a mixed bill for a charity performance under the patronage of H.H. Princess Marie Louise. She herself gave a spirited recital of Henry V's speech before Agincourt; another item was a curtain-raiser, *Postal Orders*, which had not been played out of London before. I played in this with Joan Chard (afterwards Lady Harwood) and thoroughly enjoyed it.

In the years after the First World War I regularly took my family to Worthing for a summer holiday. When we arrived in 1923, I found my mother and other active spirits busily engaged in organising a pageant at Arundel Castle. The Worthing members of the committee were responsible for the Civil War episode and I was cast for the part of Sir William Waller. We had a few rehearsals and, with an imperfect knowledge of my lines, I rode at the head of the Roundhead troops and received the surrender of the castle. The weather was good and the cricket-ground provided a splendid amphitheatre. A mixed lot of horses had been placed at our disposal by local owners and as soon as the Elizabethan episode was over, there was a rush to grab a good mount. Knowing that a powerful bombardment was a feature of our episode, I took care to secure a quiet horse. At one of our performances my aide-de-camp was less fortunate. His horse bolted with him at the first explosion and he was not seen again that day. After the last performance there was a ceremonial parade of the whole cast led by the young Duke of Norfolk in Elizabethan dress. Years afterwards, when I met the Duke at a Brighton College speech day, I could not resist telling him that I had once captured his castle.

In Cambridge, too, I was brought to the fringe of pageantry. Camille Prior, indefatigable producer of every kind of dramatic and musical show, wanted someone in the guise of Dr Burney to speak a prologue and epilogue to a pageant of music. So, with a wig and a Mus.Doc. gown borrowed from C. B. Rootham, I said my piece. Purists criticised the appearance of Burney in a Cambridge gown, but as I won the general approval of E. J. Dent, I did not worry.

The performance was given in Nevile's Court in Trinity College and I suppose it was the first time that I played with Donald Beves. He was cast for the part of Henry VIII and it was interesting to watch him studying the portrait in the Hall for his make-up. The result was entirely convincing. Thereafter, and especially in Long Vacations when Cambridge was full of conferences and summer schools, I played many times with Camille Prior and Donald not only in pageants, but in the light comedies beloved of amateurs—*The Dover Road, Mr Pim Passes By, A Hundred Years Old, The Mask and the Face.*

I think the part I most enjoyed was that of 'Mr Pim', especially as I had the opportunity of discussing details of the play with Irene Vanbrugh, to whom I had been introduced by her nephew, George Barnes. She was extraordinarily kind and encouraging. Two really 'fat' parts were those of the Mayor in *The Mask and the Face* and of Alonso in *A Hundred Years Old*. 'Tut! Tut!' wrote Granville-Barker when I told him I was cast for the latter part, 'What must the Syndics think? A serious man like you, whose mind should be on nothing but Palaeo-botany and Astrophysics and the early Sumerian civilisation...'

Apart from his skill and versatility as an actor, Donald Beves was an exceptionally good producer. Amateurs are notoriously liable to arrive late at rehearsals with a sketchy acquaintance with their parts, but Donald was extremely tolerant. He never stormed and his good humour ensured the enjoyment of everyone.

A more ambitious production was that of Purcell's *The Fairy Queen* in 1931. Primarily, of course, it was a production by musicians for musicians, but Donald Beves undertook to produce the clowns and I was asked to play Peter Quince. 'What sort of dialect do I attempt?' I asked Donald, 'Mummersetshire?' 'Yes, if you like', he replied. So I tried out the speeches to myself. They sounded very stagey and I reflected that Peter Quince and his party would be yokels from the Midlands. I read some lines aloud in what I hoped was a Midland accent and the result seemed more promising, especially in such lines as:

> Whereat, with blade, with bloody blameful blade
> He bravely broached his boiling bloody breast.

Whether or no it was a good imitation, it made the audience merry. Bottom was played by Humphrey Jennings, a Pembroke undergraduate who became a well-known figure in the film world and died as a result of an accident while filming in Greece.

One of the pleasantest sequels to my play-acting in Cambridge was an invitation to stay, in company with Camille Prior and Donald Beves, at Cranmer Hall, near Fakenham, the home of L. E. (now Sir Laurence) and Lady Evelyn Jones. It was a delightful house and a delightful holiday. We combined rehearsals with an occasional round of golf at Brancaster and at the end of the week played *Mr Pim* and, on another visit, *Belinda* to an appreciative audience.

Two familiar figures of the Cambridge amateur stage were those of C. J. B. Gaskoin and the Rev. Kingsbury Jameson. Gaskoin was immensely industrious and immensely good-natured. He worked hard as a history teacher and did a great deal of civil service examining, but was always eager to take part in any dramatic production. He had a curiously penetrating voice and his walk and gestures were highly individual. Consequently, whatever his part, he was just Gaskoin, except perhaps, in *A*

Hundred Years Old, in which with little movement he took the centre of the stage—a dignified great-grandfather.

Kingsbury Jameson, an Anglican clergyman, belonged to a class now virtually extinct in Cambridge—that of the private coach. Clad on week-days in a Norfolk jacket and Victorian knickerbockers, he had a room (and, I believe, a small laboratory) above the Hawks Club and liked to regard himself as honorary chaplain of the A.D.C. He had no desire to act himself, but welcomed any job, however humble, in the mechanics of production—properties, noises off, the curtain, anything provided that it gave him a part in the show. He was very deaf and at the end of a performance Donald Beves and I had more than once to remind him in hoarse whispers: 'House lights!' Jameson, cupping his ear and eventually grasping the situation, would rush with apologies to the switchboard.

From 1916 to 1930 Jameson was Vicar-chaplain of St Edward's Church. St Edward's is a 'peculiar' and so independent of episcopal jurisdiction. Jameson accepted the vicar-chaplaincy on the understanding that his own preaching would be reduced to a minimum. Being free to invite laymen to the pulpit, he used his freedom to the full. ('Jameson expects', it was said, 'that every man will do *his* duty.') Quiller-Couch, T. R. Glover, E. G. Browne and many other local figures (including myself) were brought in, until Winstanley was provoked to remark that anyone who had not preached at St Edward's was a social pariah. Jameson also succeeded in attracting distinguished strangers; I particularly remember sitting under Sir Oliver Lodge and Lord Hugh Cecil.

Jameson left St Edward's in 1930, but his enthusiasm for the theatre was undimmed. On his eightieth birthday in 1936 Sheppard, Provost of King's, gave a luncheon-party in his honour and Jameson declared that he felt much better than he had felt at seventy—so much better, in fact, that three years later he determined to arrange a production of *Candida*. He cast me for the part of Morell and the *Cambridge Review* was good enough to say that I avoided the worst faults of parody. My curate was Charles Albery, the brilliant young Orientalist of Christ's who later joined the Air Force and was killed.

During the war we revived *The Dover Road* for the benefit of R.A.F. camps in the neighbourhood and shortly after the end of the war I was asked to play Gayev in *The Cherry Orchard*. Chekhov is really too difficult for amateurs, but this particular production somehow attracted the attention of London critics. Eric Keown wrote enthusiastically in *Punch*, and the *Observer* also gave us a good mark.

Amateur productions tend to provide more fun for the players than for the audience. The number of performances is generally small and I often felt that at the end of the week I was really beginning to act, instead of just waiting conscientiously for my cues. But I console myself with what Harold Child said at the end of his 'Epistle Dedicatory': 'I failed as a professional actor; you have merely succeeded as an amateur.'

Chapter 11

A MISCELLANY OF AUTHORS

I have already written of the part played by T. R. Glover in the production of the *Children's Bible*. His participation gave me much satisfaction, for it led to the healing of a breach. His first book, *Life and Letters in the Fourth Century*, had been published at the Press in 1901. When, two years later, he offered his work on Virgil, the Syndics, or some of them, treated it not so much as a manuscript offered to a publisher as a thesis to be appraised by the strictest academic standards. The book was rejected by 8 votes to 5. Glover took it to Edward Arnold, who successfully published many editions.

Outside the Press I had several points of contact with Glover—the Classical Society, the *Cambridge Review* committee, David's stall in the Market Place. He always maintained that the severer type of classical don disapproved of him because his books were too readable—an objection which I could hardly be expected to share.

When, in the spring of 1930, I was preparing to make my second visit to the United States, I heard that Glover was sailing in the *Aquitania* about the time that suited me. Publishing apart, I always enjoyed an argument with Glover and I gladly arranged to travel with him.

As we travelled second class, we found an interesting group of fellow-passengers, among whom were Miss Sperry, daughter of Dean Sperry of Harvard; R. E. Balfour of King's (afterwards killed in Holland whilst serving with the 60th Rifles); Walter Starkie, of Trinity College, Dublin; and Beverley Robinson, of Toronto. I had already met Starkie, and Robinson knew Glover a little, so the four of us shared a table in the dining-saloon. Glover had been trained in a Puritan tradition which excluded alcohol, tobacco, card-playing, the theatre and other worldly delights. But he was not indifferent to the pleasures of the table, especially if they were salted with argument, and with Walter Starkie he had plenty to argue about. In fact, Glover's enthusiasm for his favourite authors (Herodotus, Horace, Cervantes, Charles Lamb) sat rather oddly on a Puritan; in his book entitled *Poets and Puritans* he even contrived to include James Boswell. So we enjoyed hilarious meals, except for one day when I succumbed to a brief attack of sea-sickness. Glover came into my cabin and sat on the end of the bed. 'You know,' he said, 'there are times when books fail to satisfy me—and then I really wish my parents had taught me to play cards or something.' It was a revealing confession. Loyal Baptist though he was, there was something in him to which Starkie's stories of gipsy life in Spain or Hungary made an instinctive appeal. Amongst the passengers, moreover, there were plenty of characters to arouse his interest—an eminent violinist from Roumania, a magnificent negress with a contralto voice of great depth and power, an 'eccentric' dancer from the Palladium, and the champion tight-rope walker of the world. Their names have escaped me, but there was also a couple whose names were known to everyone—Naughton and Gold, of the Crazy Gang. At the ship's concert Glover took the chair. Naughton and Gold, wearing ordinary evening dress ('We work in dinner jackets' they told me) did a delightful little act as two British workmen and I rejoiced to observe Glover's enjoyment of a really good music-hall turn. On my menu-card he wrote:

> O Roberts, 'mid the Ocean's fury
> Packed with Panjandriots and Jewry
> Some fleet the time with Walter Starkie,
> Some look towards the beauteous darkie,
> And some more quietly make merry
> With Balfour and the bright Miss Sperry,
> But I for one would chiefly bless
> The Secretary of the Press.

and that in spite of my prompt rejection of many books (including a volume of his Latin orations) which he offered for publication as we paced the deck of the *Aquitania* after breakfast.

In fact, we published several books for him before his death in 1943. Most of them related to the ancient world and to Christianity's place in it, but I also conspired with him to issue a tiny book of tributes to David, the market-stall bookseller, to whom we were both devoted.

Glover was by nature controversial, and the cordiality of our relations did not exempt me from criticism. On his return from one of his Canadian trips he came storming into my room at the Press in high indignation. As a result of the intransigent attitude of our Canadian agents in a Toronto trade dispute, he said, none of his books were being sold and what was I going to do about it? My reply was: 'Nothing, until I have heard the other side of the dispute.' Gradually he grew calmer and slightly apologetic. 'I didn't come in here to quarrel with you', he said. 'You wouldn't have succeeded if you had', I replied—and the storm was over.

The last book we published in his lifetime was *Cambridge Retrospect* and I was glad that he lived to read a *Times* third leader on it. In spite of his many differences with his colleagues in the classical faculty, and of his frequent desire for re-invigoration on the other side of the Atlantic, he had a deep love of Cambridge—which, perhaps, was one of the foundations of our friendship.

In the years immediately following the First World War, one of the most valuable editors of English texts in the Press catalogue was George Sampson. Sampson had begun life as an elementary school-teacher; he had risen to be a headmaster and, later, a school inspector under the London County Council. A voracious reader from boyhood, he had an acute critical sense and expressed his criticism in clear and pungent prose. Both Waller and Q held him in high regard and it was through their influence that the University made him an honorary M.A. in 1920. His *English for the English* (1921), in which he maintained that it was the purpose of education not to prepare children *for* their occupation, but to prepare them *against* their occupation, was written as a tract for the times, but has attained a longevity not usually enjoyed by tracts.

About the same time Waller invited him to condense the fourteen volumes of the *Cambridge History of English Literature* into a one-volume handbook. If the task had been entrusted to the wrong man, it is easy to imagine the dreary compilation that might have resulted. But after many years of delay caused by his poor health, Sampson achieved a *tour-de-force*. He conscientiously followed the sequence of the original work, but infused a miraculous freshness of his own into the condensation and thoroughly enjoyed the opportunity of adding a chapter on the post-Victorians. It is a book one may use as a literary Bradshaw; but whenever I turn to it for a simple piece of factual information, I find myself reading two or three pages before I return it to the shelf. 'Who is the George Sampson', wrote Tinker to me from Yale, 'who has written the best history of English literature that exists?'

It was one of Sampson's books (*Selections from Hazlitt*) that gave me my one experience of copyright litigation. After a few years in which it had a modest sale, the book was specifically prescribed for the London University Matriculation examination, which, of course, gave a substantial fillip to sales. Another firm thereupon produced an edition of such flagrant similarity that we had no difficulty in securing an order for its destruction without going to court. The same firm then proceeded to publish an edition with some additional essays and a fresh series of notes and the new book was offered for sale as the edition prescribed for the examination. I felt that, while breach of copyright in selection might be difficult to establish, our case for 'passing off' was still strong.

The case was heard in April 1928 before Mr Justice (afterwards Lord) Maugham. Mr H. K. Archer, K.C., and Mr E. J. MacGillivray appeared for us and Mr H. B. (afterwards Mr Justice) Vaisey, K.C., and Mr Trevor Watson for the defendants. In cross-examination Mr Vaisey strove to emphasise my commercial approach:

Q. You have published some epoch-making books from your Cambridge University Press?

A. I hope so, yes...

Q. Is it not right to say that it [Sampson's *Hazlitt*] is quite a small matter to the Cambridge Press compared with the magnitude of their other concerns?

A. No, the other concerns which you have in mind do not always sell 20,000 copies.

Q. I see. It is just a matter of pounds, shillings and pence?

A. No, not entirely... but the University Press has to live in order to produce its works of magnitude.

In his summing-up, Mr Justice Maugham was evidently not at ease. He had only recently been made a judge and was not convinced that prescription for an examination was a quality which would entitle us to a judgement for 'passing off'. He therefore gave no judgement, but added that he could not approve in all respects of the defendants' conduct, and ordered each side to pay its costs. It was a disappointing result, but I think it was recognised in the publishing world that we had struck a worth-while blow for what, in my evidence, I described as 'the amenities of competitive publishing'.

The last book we published for Sampson (*Seven Essays*, 1947) is a good illustration of his wide range. In it he takes Mozart, Henry Irving and the hymn-writers of the eighteenth century comfortably in his stride.

After his retirement he went to live at Hove, where I visited him several times. His house was full of books—not a collector's library, but a splendid array of the books that really matter to an English scholar, and somehow one had the feeling that he had read them all. Once he took a slim volume from the shelf. 'Here's something that will make your mouth water', he said. He was right, for it was the first edition of the first published adventure of Sherlock Holmes—*A Study in Scarlet*, originally issued in *Beeton's Christmas Annual, 1887*. It was not, alas, in its original paper covers; but, even so, I handled it tenderly and enviously. 'You can leave me that in your will', I said.

Some time after his death in 1950, his wife sent me the book. 'I have found a note in George's handwriting', she wrote, 'desiring that this book should be sent to you. He apparently had some reason for believing that it would interest you.' He had, indeed.

I think it was in the Christmas vacation of 1929–30 that R. W. Chapman rang me up and asked me whether I could come over to Oxford for the night to discuss a publishing proposal with Lionel Curtis and Tom Jones. At the time these were but names to me, but I agreed to go and arrived for tea with Curtis at Kidlington. We had an interesting talk and I was glad to hear him speak warmly of the part played by Anderson in the deliberations of the Royal Commission on Oxford and Cambridge.

Dinner was to be at All Souls and there I met Tom Jones, Chapman, John Johnson (the University Printer), the Director of Education for Oxfordshire and some others whose names I forget. After dinner Curtis propounded his thesis, which was to devise a means of keeping the *Encyclopaedia Britannica*, or some comparable work, up to date. It involved a system of loose leaves and the regular supply, at frequent intervals, of supplementary or corrective matter to be distributed by a team of colporteurs. Chapman and I raised various queries from the publisher's point of view and there was a long and not very fruitful discussion. At a late hour, Curtis turned to Jones:

'What do you think, T. J.?' he asked.

'I think it's a wash-out', was the reply—and we went to bed.

It was my only meeting with Lionel Curtis and I came away impressed by his intense sincerity. Of Tom Jones I saw a good deal more. He was an enthusiast for good printing and we were glad to undertake the printing of the annual report of the Pilgrim Trust, of which he was secretary. Some time later I asked him to lunch with me in London. In reply he told me that he was already engaged to lunch with Bernard Shaw, who would be delighted if I came too. What I chiefly remember about the lunch is first, Shaw's praise of Dr Johnson as a writer whose meaning could never be misunderstood, and secondly, the irruption at the end of lunch of a small and lively lady who immediately talked at great speed and with great freedom about the politics and politicians of the day. She seemed to be on intimate terms with most members of the lunch party, but suddenly she espied me. 'Who's that young man?' she asked, 'is he discreet?' Afterwards I asked who the lady was. 'Nancy Astor, of course', was the reply.

T. J. and I met only at irregular intervals, but we became good friends and near the end of his life he invited me to spend a weekend at Gregynog, the home of the Misses Davies. He had assembled a party including C. K. Webster, Anthony Lewis and others to discuss the possibility of using the house as a centre of vacation study; but there were many difficulties in the way and the scheme came to nothing.

I also happened to meet Bernard Shaw on one or two later occasions. One that I remember in particular was a lunch-party in the old Bull Hotel at Cambridge which S. C. Cockerell invited me to join. It was at the time of the Abyssinian crisis and some rather extravagant remark by Shaw prompted me to say: 'Sir, I perceive that you are an incorrigible Romantic.' 'You're quite right, Mr Roberts', said Mrs Shaw, who was sitting next to me.

But the pleasantest thing I remember about G. B. S. relates to one of our own authors. H. S. Salt, scholar and humanitarian, offered us his verse translation of the *Aeneid*. There was no doubt about the quality of the work, and I was authorised to accept it, but only on commission. I explained this to Salt, who inquired what the expense would be, and accordingly I sent him a detailed estimate of the whole cost of production. A few days later I received a cheque for the total amount from Bernard Shaw.

Salt was a charming old man and at that time was living in a villa in Brighton. When I was on holiday in Worthing, I went over to have lunch with him. Knowing that he was a strict vegetarian, I wondered what sort of a meal it would be. But Mrs Salt, it appeared, did not share her husband's views and had prepared cutlets for herself and me. 'Well,' said Salt, 'I hope you will enjoy eating your fellow-creature.'

A manuscript entitled *Something Beyond: A Life Story*, by A. F. Webling was offered to the Press in 1930, at the suggestion, I think, of Edmund Blunden. Though names of people and places were disguised, it was evidently an autobiography and I read it with keen interest. It was the story of a man who, beginning life as a clerk in a warehouse in the city of London, developed a genuine love of learning and literature (especially of the Romantic poets) and an equally genuine desire to take Holy Orders. He did well in the examinations at King's College, London and, although he had always aspired to a country rectory, found himself a curate in a large seaport town. Under the influence of a saintly and companionable vicar he became a devout Anglo-Catholic, but the frigid formalism of a later incumbent repelled him and he left for a rectory in Suffolk. There modernist doubts assailed him and he passed through 'a dark night of the soul'. Light came to him from the study of psychic research, which convinced him of man's survival after death and made him feel justified in returning to the work of a country clergyman.

A crude summary does not, of course, do the book justice. When I read it, I had no doubts about wanting to publish it, subject to certain excisions. The narrative was clearly the work of a man telling, without reservations, the story of his factual and spiritual experience. My sole objection was to one or two chapters which seemed to me unduly sentimental. Webling had written to me from Risby Rectory, Bury St Edmunds, so I drove over to see him. He was not what I expected—authors seldom are. I had conceived of him as a man mellowed by experience, but in fact he seemed unduly modest and tentative—not that I liked him less for that. He was disappointed, of course, by the proposed removal of his favourite chapters, but surprised and delighted by the acceptance of his manuscript. The book had a good reception, but only a moderate sale; and even when we produced a 3*s*. 6*d*.

edition, we failed to find a really large public for it. I reflected, not for the first time, that the more experience one had of publishing, the more difficult it was to be certain of backing a winner. With Webling himself I became quite intimate. Whatever one might think of his Christian spiritualism, for him it was the one big reality that had restored his faith and remade his life. Apart from that, he had a true feeling for poetry, especially for Wordsworth, and a keen sense of history. He talked to me at length about an idea he had for a historical novel about the monks of Bury St Edmunds. Having no particular liking for that genre, I was rather discouraging. But I was none the less delighted when *The Last Abbot* (1944) had a really solid success. When Webling received a cheque for £100 on account of royalties from his publisher (Edward Ward), he was overwhelmed. Shortly before he retired from Risby, I spent an afternoon with him and Edmund Blunden at Bury St Edmunds, which they both loved. Webling retired to a little house in the country near Portsmouth, where I once visited him. He had many family troubles, but his renewed faith remained serene and he was always embarrassingly grateful to the publishers of *Something Beyond*.

Novels, whether historical or not, did not find a place in the catalogue of the University Press. Nevertheless, one of the most interesting manuscripts submitted in my time was *A Cardinal of the Medici*, by Susan Hicks-Beach. It was evidently a work of a scholarly character, as the notes and references clearly testified. But it was written in fictional form, its sub-title being *The Memoirs of the Nameless Mother of the Cardinal Ippolito de Medici*. It seemed to me that the manuscript deserved serious consideration and I asked H. O. Evennett whether he would read it. He agreed, and in due course gave his verdict. He had begun his reading, he said, with a strong prejudice against the book in view of the form of the narrative; but he went on to give it a high mark as a work of scholarship. On that ground, the Syndics would be quite safe in publishing it; whether they would swallow the fictional form was a matter of policy for them to decide. To my great satisfaction, the Syndics decided in favour of the book and we set about the publication with enthusiasm. It was a substantial work—about 200,000 words—and we made no attempt to present it in the standard format of a novel. Frank Kendon produced one of his best jackets and we hoped that the Book Society might give the book a recommendation. As they omitted to do so, I put a narrow band round the jacket with the legend: 'Not recommended by any book-club, but only by the publishers.' This pleased the booksellers, one of whom reproduced it in his list of announcements, but I cannot claim that it accelerated sales. Personally, I thought, and still think, that the book was a remarkable achievement and that Humbert Wolfe did not exaggerate when he wrote: 'The writer has not only studied her facts...but she has absorbed and transmuted them with creative fire.'

Mrs Hicks-Beach was no novice. As Susan Christian she had contributed a short story to *The Yellow Book* in 1895. She had also written several novels and a family chronicle, *A Cotswold Family* (1909). I suppose she offered *A Cardinal of the Medici* to the Press because of the help she had derived from the Renaissance volume of the *Cambridge Modern History*. Whatever her initial motive may have been, we formed a close and continuous friendship. Belonging to the family which produced Fletcher Christian of the *Bounty* and Edward Christian, first Downing Professor of Law at Cambridge, Mrs Hicks-Beach was the daughter of Captain Henry Christian, R.N., and the widow of William Hicks-Beach, brother of 'Black Michael'. She would not let me put anything but 'Mrs Hicks-Beach' on the title-page of the *Cardinal*, because there was at least one Susan Hicks-Beach in the family with whose career and reputation she did not wish her own to be confused.

From Renaissance Italy she turned to the Victorian novel and wrote *Amabel and Mary Verena*, a continuation of *The Heir of Redclyffe*, which was published by Fabers with considerable success in 1944. Meanwhile she had sent me another manuscript of forbidding proportions. It was a discursive history of her family and much else, with long chapters on the early history of the Isle of Man. I dipped into it sufficiently to be convinced that it was not a book for the University Press, or indeed for any publisher. I implored the author to make drastic reductions, and correspondence on this and other topics continued long after I had left the Press. She was a delightful letter-writer. I never knew how she might begin. It might be 'Honoured Sir' or 'Proud Master of Pembroke', or (once) 'Adorable Mr Roberts'. Eventually, she was induced to cut her family history down to a manageable size and the Liverpool University Press agreed to publish it. The agreement was of the kind that leads to triangular correspondence between author, publisher and Authors' Society and I was more than once called upon for intermediary help. When, at length, a set of proofs of *The Yesterdays behind the Door* reached me in September 1955, I was just leaving for a holiday in Italy. I took the proofs with me and as they contained a diverting account of a visit paid by King Edward VII to the Isle of Man in 1902, I showed it to Max Beerbohm. As I have related elsewhere, he at once pounced upon a ludicrous mistake in the dating of the visit. The corrected proof, which I returned to the author, gave her great pleasure.

Susan Hicks-Beach lived to a great age and in her last years my wife and I visited her more than once in her Cotswold home. Though she might feel herself to be a Victorian relic, she never allowed herself to slip back into the past and moan about the present. Inevitably she was shocked by the manners of some modern novelists, but she always wanted to understand and her interest in books and people never flagged. Boredom was the enemy she most dreaded and to which she refused to surrender. In September 1958, when I had occasion to go to Cheltenham, I inquired whether we might call upon her. She wrote, from her bed, to say that she was not well enough to see us:

Explaining is too difficult. It is just A.D. and I had another birthday (alack) the other day. Sooner or later these things come to everyone, so do not console.

The birthday was her ninety-second and she died in the following November—a splendid and scholarly Victorian lady who never really grew old.

In 1932, I received a bulky manuscript from M. Jean Marchand, librarian of the Chambre des Députés, Paris. It contained the detailed record of the English journeys of François de la Rochefoucauld, son of the Duc de Liancourt, in the later part of the eighteenth century. Being inspired by the example of Arthur Young, the work dealt largely with the economics of agriculture and, as I skimmed through the pages, I concluded that the chances of successful publication were remote. On the other hand, I could visualise the making of an interesting book out of a series of judicious extracts and was authorised to reply in this sense. Both Professor Oliver Prior, who had warmly commended the work, and M. Marchand himself were disappointed by the decision, but M. Marchand went on to say that if we wanted a short book, we might care to look at another Rochefoucauld manuscript (which he had not seen) in the British Museum. I took an early opportunity of looking at it. It was entitled *Mélanges sur l'Angleterre* and I was delighted with my sampling, for I came upon few, if any, dull pages. The handwriting was reasonably clear, but reading it was rather a slow business, so I ordered photostats to be sent to Paris and asked M. Marchand to let us have a typescript. I then translated the text together with M. Marchand's introduction, added a few notes and found some appropriate illustrations.

I have never enjoyed anything more than my share in the production of *A Frenchman in England* (1933). The book had splendid reviews; but, as so often happens, the sales were not commensurate with them.

At the age of nineteen, François de la Rochefoucauld was a remarkably acute observer. Following the advice of 'Mr Walpole', he made Bury St Edmunds his headquarters, whence he visited Newmarket and Cambridge and toured the counties of Norfolk and Suffolk. His comments on the politics and religion of eighteenth-century England were as shrewd as those on horse-racing at Newmarket, and historians such as Winstanley and Norman Sykes do not disdain to quote him.

'En vous remerciant encore', wrote M. Marchand to me, 'de votre si aimable et profitable collaboration, je ne renonce pas l'espoir de vous rencontrer un jour...' That day came some years later when my wife and I spent a most interesting morning in the library and the lobbies of the Chambre des Députés.

Chapter 12

LIGHT AND SHADE IN THE
NINETEEN-THIRTIES

1931 was a grim year for the nation as a whole and especially for those engaged in trade and industry. The great depression had reached Europe from the United States and there were more than two million unemployed. The pound was devalued and the drastic steps taken by the National Government at the end of the year included a cut of 10 per cent in the dole as well as similar, or larger, reductions in the salaries of cabinet ministers, judges and all government employees. At the Press, as elsewhere, this lead was followed.

In the circumstances, we were glad to accept an invitation from John Wilson, of Bumpus, to arrange an exhibition of Cambridge books in the Old Court House, Marylebone Lane. In addition to the display of books in the current catalogue, we also organised a separate historical section with examples of Cambridge printing from the sixteenth century onwards. General Smuts, who was in London as president of the British Association, readily agreed to open the exhibition in September and was supported on the platform by the deputy Vice-Chancellor (A. C. Seward, Master of Downing) and by Cameron as chairman of the Syndics. I was at that time a member of the Royal Societies Club in St James's Street and arranged a small party for lunch before the opening. It was my first meeting with General Smuts and I was at once impressed by his defiant energy. When, after lunch, I was about to call a taxi, he dismissed the suggestion with scorn and firmly insisted on walking to Oxford Street.

A year later my wife died after six years of intermittent illness. One consolation was that my son, John, came up to Pembroke in October and gave me a renewed interest in the undergraduate life of the college. I was also very glad to have Billy Kingsford's company when I visited America in 1933. We sailed in the *Aquitania* and our most entertaining fellow-traveller was Colonel Martin Archer-Shee. From 10 a.m. to 2 a.m. or later he was ready to regale the company with lively anecdote, always with a glass in his hand, and at the Bingo session his spirits rose to a gay pitch of enthusiasm. On arrival, we followed our usual round—New York, Boston, New Haven, Toronto. At New Haven we stayed at the Yale Graduate Club and had lunch with Tinker, who had recently moved to the new Davenport College. Having contemplated the elaborate Gothic façade, we entered and were surprised to find a pleasant court built in traditional 'colonial' style. I commented to Tinker on the Gothic street-front. 'Yes, I know,' he said, 'looks like Hell, doesn't it?' 'I thought it looked rather like Oxford', I replied.

But, of course, the main object of our visit was to examine the working of the new Cambridge department in the Macmillan house. Mansbridge had a great deal to tell us and it was clear that my forecast of his difficulties was accurate enough. But he was full of determination and we did our best to encourage him in his efforts. In the original agreement for the establishment of the department our contribution was specified in dollars, which put us in an unfavourable position when the pound was devalued. However, Mr Brett readily agreed to my suggestions for revision.

The printing and publication of scientific journals formed a large and growing part of our work and in 1936 I was instructed to discuss with the officers of the Royal Society the possibility of our taking over their *Proceedings* and *Transactions*. In this I had the backing of several distinguished Cambridge contributors who were eager to have the benefit of the traditional accuracy of our compositors and readers. When I opened negotiations by asking for some specifications on which I could base our estimates, one of the permanent officials of the Society was quite friendly but, from my point of view, purely defeatist. 'Yes, I'll give you the figures,' he said, 'but really, Mr Roberts, it's a shame to waste your time. We've dealt with one printer for about a hundred years and it's not likely that we'll change now.' I was not to be put off by this, and after long and complicated negotiations in which I was greatly helped by A. V. Hill, then one of the secretaries of the Society, the terms of an agreement were satisfactorily settled.

One of the major problems that had confronted the Syndics for some time was that of our London publishing house. We had long grown out of our premises in Fetter Lane and had been obliged to hire basements in various parts of the city for the housing of stock. After considering a number of sites, we were fortunate, late in 1935, in securing a freehold site in the Euston Road. Our architect was W. Curtis Green and we had the rare opportunity of planning and building a publishing house *ab initio*. Kingsford, who became head of the London house in 1936, took immense pains in prescribing the precise accommodation required and it was, I think, Geoffrey Faber who described the building as the idea of a publishing house laid up in heaven. It was completed in February 1938 and, looking back, one can but reflect upon our good fortune first, in having bought the site and erected the building at the prices prevailing in the 1930s, and secondly, in escaping damage during the blitz of a few years later.

The name, Bentley House, was chosen to commemorate the new life infused into the Press by Richard Bentley at the end of the seventeenth century. The only criticism of this designation was that 'Bentley House, Euston Road' might suggest trade in motor-cars rather than in books; but I am not aware that any misunderstanding has arisen.

In the spring of 1938 I visited the United States and took my younger daughter, Nan, with me. We sailed in the *Queen Mary* and had a rough voyage, which was too much for Nan; but she quickly recovered and we were warmly welcomed by Ronald Mansbridge and his wife. My main objective was to negotiate some further revision of our agreement with the Macmillan

Company and I had now to deal with George P. Brett, jr., who had succeeded his father as president of the company. We had protracted, but very friendly, discussions about my suggested modifications and late one afternoon he submitted to me a typed draft embodying the new terms on which we had agreed. 'Now, is that all right?' he asked. I read through the document. 'I'm very sorry,' I said, 'but in one clause the alteration in the percentage, on which we agreed, has not been made.' 'Oh, hell,' he said, 'give me the draft.' A stenographer was summoned and instructed to retype the whole agreement. This took some time and, while we were waiting, I indulged in some general reflections upon publishing. In particular, I remarked that in the first instance I had been attracted to it because I was fond of books, but that I had soon realised that I should have to be interested in business.

Brett banged his fist on the table. 'Mr Roberts,' he said, 'I believe you're a better man of business than what you are literary!'—which I took as a high compliment.

Business apart, Brett was very good in arranging gaieties for Nan and we had happy times in many places besides New York. At New Haven we stayed with the Master of Berkeley College (S. B. Hemingway) and Nan was swept into the whirl of a 'Junior Prom'; Osgood and his wife gave us a warm welcome at Princeton, where we also had lunch with Einstein. He did not talk at any great length, but I remember his saying that Rutherford was the greatest experimenter since Faraday; in Toronto we had a cheerful reunion with Beverley Robinson, whom I had first met in the *Aquitania* in 1930; and in Farmington we had a delectable two days with Lefty and Annie Burr Lewis. Lefty is not much of a picture-goer, but thought it would be fitting to take Nan to see Disney's *Seven Dwarfs* at Hartford, after which we rose to greater heights by calling on the Governor of Connecticut.

The uncertainties and anxieties of the first half of the year 1939 led to many disappointments for authors and publishers, especially in the sales of that most speculative type of book, the book of 'general interest'. Harold Child's *A Poor Player*, for instance, would have had a much better sale if it had been published a few years later and the same is true of another auto-biography which we published in October 1939—A. S. Hartrick's *A Painter's Pilgrimage*.

I think it was through A. C. Seward that I was introduced to some friends of Hartrick's, and when the MS. arrived I read it and liked it. Hartrick had known Van Gogh in the days when one of his still-life paintings could be bought for two francs, and he wrote about Gauguin, Toulouse-Lautrec and others without gush or affectation. My only complaint about the book was that it was too long and I tentatively suggested the omission of one or two chapters which seemed to me to break the continuity of the narrative. 'Treat the manuscript as if I were dead', Hartrick wrote in reply and, after recording this in his preface, he added:

I have no pretensions as a writer and I gladly take advice from those who know. The writing proved a more formidable task than I expected. Like many others, I discovered that it is no easy matter to convey in words that which belongs to the eye.

It was not often that I was given such a free hand and Hartrick and I became good friends. We had lunch together in London more than once and at Christmas 1939 he sent me a little water-colour drawing of an old Cotswold woman who had lived in her village all her life and had never been in a railway train.

But not all books published in 1939 were failures. Gordon Carey, after his retirement from Eastbourne, had done a lot of proof-reading and indexing and had formed some definite, though not dogmatic, opinions on punctuation and kindred matters. His little book, *Mind the Stop*, published in April 1939, has been many times reprinted and now flourishes as a paperback. In particular, the latest editor of Fowler's *Modern English Usage* has incorporated Carey's remarks on 'capital letters' as something on which he could not improve.

In the early 1930s Pembroke flourished. Hutchinson was an admirable Master; first classes in the Triposes were plentiful;

the boat went head of the river in 1931 and remained there for four years. But 1935 was a tragic year. In January J. C. Lawson died after an operation. He had been Tutor since 1912 and although, as I have earlier remarked, it was difficult to attain intimacy with him, he was a man of strong character and original ideas. It was he who was largely responsible for a new method of election to entrance scholarships. For ten years from 1922 Pembroke (afterwards joined by Queens') awarded scholarships not by examination, but on Higher Certificate results combined with school reports and interviews. When, in 1933, the college sought to make this a permanent feature of its statutes, the other colleges raised objections and Pembroke and Queens' lost their case before the Privy Council. Lawson was succeeded as Tutor by Trevor Spittle. The appointment was in the Master's hands, but we were all in full agreement with his choice.

In July the second blow fell. Aubrey Attwater, of whom I have already written, died of the wound he had received twenty years before. As a personality he was irreplaceable; but as his successor in the direction of English studies, the college was extremely fortunate in its choice of Basil Willey. It had also been strengthened by the election of W. V. D. Hodge and G. B. Sutherland to fellowships.

Finally, in September, Comber, who had been unwell for some time, died in his sleep. For more than thirty years he had been the friend of innumerable Pembroke men and for many of them had been Treasurer of the college. At the time of his death he was also Bursar.*

The first college meeting of the Michaelmas Term was one of the gloomiest I can remember. Trevor Spittle, who had been most conscientious, but never really happy, as Tutor, pleaded strongly to be allowed to resign the tutorship and to take over the office of Treasurer. He did not, however, want to combine the responsibility of the kitchen and buttery with it and I volunteered to be Bursar for a year. The Master nominated

---

* 'Treasurer' and 'Bursar' in Pembroke correspond to 'Bursar' and 'Steward' in other colleges.

Edward Wynn as Tutor and between them Edward and Trevor shouldered the main burdens of college administration. Fortunately the Master, who had been in poor health for some time, made a good recovery.

Chapman was still in charge of the kitchen and buttery, but he was clearly beginning to fail and in my report at the end of the year I urged that his chief assistant (G. M. L. Green) should be given more definite responsibility. But Chappie's keen business sense had not deserted him. Soon after I had taken over the bursarship I received a complaint that the sherry supplied to undergraduates at 4s. a bottle could be purchased at a wine-shop across the road for 3s. 6d. I passed this on to Chappie, who promised to look into it. A few days later he reported to me: 'It's quite all right about that sherry. I've seen Mr — and he's perfectly willin' to put his up to four shillin's.'

It was a difficult, as well as a sad, year and many old members were at first inclined to feel that their strongest links with the college were now broken. The Pembroke College Society, founded at Comber's instigation just after the war, was a great help in demonstrating that the college had sufficient resilience to overcome its misfortunes. I was already a member of the Committee of the Society and agreed to take over the secretaryship for the time being. I had many good friends on the committee, but I look back with especial gratitude and affection to two successive chairmen, J. B. Atkins and Sir Ernest Pooley. I have already referred to my early meeting with Jack Atkins. He was devoted to the college and especially to the boat club and his personal kindness to me never failed. In his early days he had had plenty of adventures, particularly as a fellow-correspondent with Winston Churchill in the Boer War, and I was delighted when his *Incidents and Reflections* (1947) was sent to me by the *Spectator* for review.

From the time that I became secretary of the Society, Ernest Pooley regularly stayed with me. He had been Clerk to the Drapers' Company for many years and was made Master on his retirement in 1944. His wide experience of administration in the city, as well as in schools and universities, was invaluable and he had the interests of the college very much at heart. But even more I loved his unfailing humour and his persistent optimism.

Arthur Hutchinson was the first Master to come under the new statutes which fixed 70 as the normal age of retirement. He reached that age in 1937 and in the spring the Fellows had their first experience of pre-election. The choice fell upon one of our honorary fellows, Sir Montagu Butler, than whom there was no more loyal Pembrochian. A first-class classic, he had held a fellowship for a short time, but had decided to make his career in India, where he rose to be Governor of the Central Provinces. On his return home he was for seven years Governor of the Isle of Man. Though I had known both his sons and two of his brothers very well, I had met Monty only once and I was delighted to spend a week-end with him at Douglas in the summer of 1937. There I met Lady Butler for the first time and immediately succumbed to her charm. It happened that a Territorial battalion was in camp in the island at the time and the governor was asked to take the salute at a ceremonial parade. The adjutant of the battalion evidently mistook me for an A.D.C. and, much to Lady Butler's amusement, was punctilious in asking me what were His Excellency's wishes.

Monty was far from regarding the Mastership as providing an opportunity for well-earned leisure. He set himself immediately to reorganise and simplify the presentation of the college accounts and willingly took his share in the administration of the university and of the borough, as it then was. Just as he was getting well into his stride, war broke out.

In November 1938, I was married to Marjorie (widow of M. B. R. Swann, Fellow of Caius) who had been a dear and devoted friend of my first wife. At the time, each of us had three children and we were fortunate in finding a house in Chaucer Road with plenty of bedrooms and also with a good tennis-court. But we had less than a year's normal enjoyment of its amenities.

Chapter 13

VARIETIES OF WAR-TIME
EXPERIENCE

I must confess that in 1938 I had been a supporter of Neville Chamberlain. In the spring of 1939 I began to realise that I was wrong and that all hopes of appeasement would be falsified. My elder daughter, just married, was living in Prague when Hitler's troops moved in, but fortunately came home in the summer. In the later part of August, rather rashly, we set out on a motoring tour in France and were in the south of Brittany, near Le Croisic, when in the continental *Daily Mail* I read of the Hitler–Stalin pact. We made for Dieppe without delay and found ourselves in a long queue of returning tourists. Eventually we got our car across the day before Hitler invaded Poland—luckier, perhaps, than we deserved.

Cambridge was an evacuation centre and we had the wife and children of a London policeman billeted on us for some weeks. More substantial was the transference of some thirty members of the London publishing house of the Press to Cambridge. They remained until July 1940 and, ironically, returned to London just in time for the beginning of the blitz.

In 1939 I was still a member of the Council of the Publishers' Association, and, as we discussed the situation at our monthly meetings, we were generally agreed that we were in for a grim time, in which we should have to face a severe decline in sales and, possibly, even more severe damage to buildings. The latter expectation was amply fulfilled. Earlier in the year we had published a paper by a distinguished actuary entitled 'The Impossibility of War Risk Insurance', in which it was pointed out that any such insurance could be undertaken only by the Government. When, later, the Government scheme was announced and discussed at a special meeting of the Publishers' Association, a bare majority of members voted for contracting out of the scheme; but the majority did not reach the three-fourths prescribed by the Board of Trade and publishers accordingly paid their premiums.

When the purchase tax was introduced in 1940, Geoffrey Faber (president of the Publishers' Association), Stanley Unwin, Billy Kingsford (who had taken my place on the Council) and others, supported by an impressive body of authors, fought a hard and eventually successful battle for the exclusion of books from the operation of the tax.

About the same time, paper-rationing was introduced and publishers were limited to 60 per cent of what they had used in the year ending 31 July 1939. Very soon it became clear that this quota would be far from satisfying the demand for books. Textbooks and technical treatises were urgently required for the services; camp-libraries demanded larger stocks; air-raid wardens and fire-watchers wanted something to read during their vigils; and, finally, as manufactured articles became scarcer in the shops, people who normally regarded a book as something to be borrowed from a friend or from a public library, actually ventured into a bookshop and bought a book. For the first time, probably, in the history of the book trade demand exceeded supply and editions were sold out before they were printed. Furthermore, old stocks came to life. Books of which the sale had dwindled to a few copies a year were eagerly welcomed by booksellers, simply because they were in stock. Risk, which is normally the biggest element in a publisher's life, was temporarily eliminated.

Like all publishers, we found at Cambridge that our ration of paper made it impossible for us to print all that we wanted to print. Naturally, we gave priority to textbooks and technical works that were in constant demand and in this we were helped by a committee set up by the Board of Trade under the chairmanship of Sir Walter Moberly. Four publishers, including my colleague Kingsford, were nominated by the Association to serve on this committee, which had power to make a special allocation of paper for the reprinting of books which deserved to be regarded as 'essential'. The task of the committee was hard and continuous and its members earned the gratitude as well as the sympathy of their fellow-publishers.

Inevitably, a large number of Cambridge books remained out of print and it was with keen regret that I felt obliged, as I have already recorded, to part with the rights in Arthur Bryant's three volumes on Pepys. Nevertheless, we published some notable books during the war years; among them the first volume of the *Cambridge Economic History of Europe*, Sherrington's *Man on his Nature*, Knowles's *Monastic Order in England*, and the first two volumes of the second part of *Alumni Cantabrigienses*. But the publication that gave me most satisfaction was that of the *Cambridge Bibliography of English Literature*. For years I had hoped that the bibliographies in each volume of the *Cambridge History of English Literature* might be revised and expanded to make a standard work of reference. At first I thought that the procedure might be fairly simple: each of the individual lists could be sent to a suitable scholar for revision and, after a certain amount of editorial rearrangement, the thing would be done. But I was quickly disillusioned. Both Arundell Esdaile and I devoted some time to it, but we soon realised that no real progress would be made unless and until one general editor was prepared to take full responsibility for the whole work. Fortunately we found such a man in F. W. Bateson, and with the generous help in proof-reading of L. F. Powell, F. J. Norton and others, the four volumes were completed in 1940. Of course there were plenty of errors in it, but it was the first attempt at completeness since Watt's *Bibliotheca Britannica* (1824) and by now is recognised as one of the books which the scholar, the collector and the librarian cannot be without.

In 1940, also, I took great pleasure in the production of *On Circuit*, by Sir Frank MacKinnon whom, some time before, we had asked to write a book on 'The Law' for a series we were planning on British Institutions. He had replied favourably, but war broke out and I heard nothing more until I met him one day in the Athenaeum, 'What about that book·on the Law?' I asked. 'Oh, I'm afraid I haven't done anything about it,' he replied, 'but I'll tell you what. I've written another book—and it's devilish good.' 'Send me the MS.', I said. I concurred unhesitatingly in the author's opinion. *On Circuit* is an urbane and scholarly account of the work of a judge of assize, written with a keen eye upon historical detail.

Another wartime publication which I enjoyed was that of Sir Henry Lyons's *The Royal Society 1660–1940, a History of its Administration under its Charters.* Lyons was a devoted friend, as I was, of A. C. Seward and the three of us used to meet at the Athenaeum to discuss the book. Lyons was severely crippled by arthritis, but remained extraordinarily cheerful. Bombed out of his London house, he moved to Great Missenden, where I once stayed a night with him and enjoyed his racy talk. Sick man as he was, he was extremely good company and was very happy when he passed the final proofs. To my deep regret, we just failed to get the book out before his death in 1944, but I was consoled by a charming letter of appreciation from Lady Lyons.

But it is proper to record a wartime casualty. In 1937 the Press had been approached as a suitable firm to take over the monthly magazine, *Discovery.* Sponsored by a body of distinguished trustees, it had first been published by John Murray and later by Benn Bros. Benns had failed to make it pay and wanted to dispose of it. Here was a challenge to the publishers of Eddington and Jeans, and I was authorised to negotiate terms. The only difficulty that arose related to outstanding subscriptions and, as so often happened, I evoked some surprise when I made it clear that the Press was conducted as a business rather than as a charity.

At that time C. P. Snow, who was already acting as an adviser on scientific books, seemed to me well fitted to be the editor of a popular magazine of science and the first number under his editorship appeared in April, 1938. There was general agreement,

I think, that the format was attractive, that the articles were interesting and that the standard of production was in the best Cambridge tradition; but the magazine failed to make a bookstall appeal, and after the outbreak of war it seemed best to cut our losses and to transfer it to Jarrolds.

Another wartime enterprise was more successful. For some time the history faculty had complained of the lack of provision for the teaching of American history and the feeling was strengthened by the entry of the United States into the war. Conscious of the growth of our reserve fund as a result of our rapid and unexpected conversion of old stock into cash, I suggested to the chairman that we might do something to help. Cameron was sympathetic, but characteristically cautious. 'Yes,' he said, 'after the war I don't see why we shouldn't do something.' 'Let's do it now', I urged.

At the next Syndicate meeting, the suggestion was strongly supported by Clapham and Benians and in July 1943 I was authorised to offer the sum of £44,000 to the University, with a suggestion that it might suitably be used to establish a Chair of American History. The offer was accepted and the Syndics' action was widely acclaimed. *The Times* praised it in a leading article and Denis Brogan, writing in the *New York Times*, described the event as prodigious; but what pleased me most was the warmth of the personal letters I received. George Trevelyan wrote gratefully on behalf of the historians, and Archibald MacLeish, whom I had met more than once, wrote from the Library of Congress: 'It is a perfectly extraordinary thing from every American point of view. With us, our presses do not make gifts to their universities, but present frantic appeals for help.' The choice of a title for the new Chair raised a little controversy. To us it seemed that a professorship endowed by an institution often known as the Pitt Press might well be called the Pitt Professorship, but on the Council of the Senate there were some who feared that the name of Pitt might offend American susceptibilities and the suggestion was dropped. Years later, when I had become a member of the Fulbright Commission, I was astonished, at one meeting, to hear the secretary refer to 'the Pitt Professor at Cambridge'. 'Why do you call him that?' I asked. 'Well, he *is* the Pitt Professor, isn't he?' *Naturam expellas furca, tamen usque recurret.* I was Vice-Chancellor at the time and the Council of the Senate, having heard my report of this conversation, readily agreed to the entitlement.

The whole affair naturally gave me great satisfaction, but I understand that later generations of authors and Syndics, faced with the problems of post-war inflation, have deplored the action of the Syndics of 1943. I remain unrepentant.

Publishing apart, the war involved me, like everyone else, in many unexpected jobs. In June 1940 I received a long letter from Sir Andrew Duncan, President of the Board of Trade, asking me to represent his department in the eastern region. I found it difficult to understand precisely what I was meant to do, but after a talk with an under-secretary in London I gathered that I was to look after the interests of the civilian manufacturers in the region. Other ministries (Labour, Admiralty, Supply, Aircraft Production, etc.) had fully-fledged departments and staffs in Cambridge; my job was to be part-time and, of course, honorary. I was assured that it was very much what I chose to make it and that, anyhow, I should not be troubled in the immediate future. Twenty-four hours later I had an urgent telephone-call from the Board of Trade:

'Very sorry to bother you so soon, but could you get on to the Ministry of Labour and stop them interning all the employees of Bata.'

'What on earth is Bata?'

'Oh, don't you know? It's an enormous Czech boot and shoe firm with a big factory in your area. They've got large contracts for gum-boots for the troops and it's essential that their key-men should not be interned under this new Act.'

That was the beginning and gradually I grasped that my main task was to see that civilian manufacturers, unprotected by service contracts, should not be completely starved of men and materials. How far, for instance, was a maker of perambulators at Letchworth to be allowed to carry on with his normal product? 'The Ministry of Aircraft Production has taken over half my factory,' the director told me, 'if they take the other half, there just won't be any prams. Is that what the Government wants?' A pulp factory at Thetford made crash-helmets for despatch-riders in one department and, in the other, babies' baths and chambers. How far could the claim of infants be pressed? From Bishop's Stortford a man wrote to say that he was the sole maker of tips for billiard-cues in the country. What would happen to army canteens and other institutions if he were called up?

The blitz, of course, brought more serious problems. From a battered laundry in Yarmouth I received an urgent appeal, backed by brigade commanders. Would I please authorise the supply of the necessary steel and corrugated iron for rebuilding? I signed the appropriate form and some months later was asked by what authority I had done so. I replied that I thought it was part of my job—and heard no more. But years afterwards I happened to meet one of the directors of the laundry, who told me that he and his colleagues had been astonished by the quick response to their appeal.

Occasionally I was approached on more personal matters. Would I sign an order, please, to enable a delicate fellow of a college to purchase an extra hot-water bottle? Could I arrange for the Bishop-designate of Ely (Edward Wynn) to be given some extra clothing coupons, so that he might be properly dressed? This request eventually reached a high level. The Director-general of Civilian Clothing (Sir Thomas Barlow) raised grave doubts and the problem required the intervention of the Regional Commissioner (Sir Will Spens) for its final solution.

From time to time I was summoned to conferences by the President of the Board of Trade or by the Regional Commissioner, but more regularly I attended the weekly meetings of the Regional Board under the admirable chairmanship of Weston

Howard, whom I got to know well. My contributions were slight, since most of the business related to firms who were producing war material in one form or another; even so, the correspondence and interviews both with government officials and with individual manufacturers involved a good deal of work, in which I was greatly helped by my secretary, Margaret Hampton.

As the war drew to its end, the situation quickly changed. Firms, for instance, who normally made gas-stoves and had switched to making parts for tanks, appealed to me for help in reconstructing their normal operations. I told the Board of Trade that, after being the Cinderella of the Regional Board for five years, I could see myself becoming the Principal Boy, a part which I was quite unfitted to play. Richard Pares, then a temporary under-secretary, appreciated my point and in due course I was delighted to hand over to my old friend William Burkitt.

Another part-time activity was service in the Home Guard. Being enrolled in the Trumpington platoon, I took part in June 1940 in the feverish preparation of a road-block at the junction of the Trumpington road and Brooklands Avenue. The platoon was a healthy mixture of town and gown. S. W. P. Steen, of Christ's, was in command of it and soon got us on to parade. We were equipped with P-17 rifles sent over from the United States and a party of Cambridge ladies had spent many hours in removing grease from them. At one of our early parades Gilbert-Carter, director of the Botanic Garden, fell in next to me. An old sweat of the First World War volunteered to inspect rifles and we duly presented them at the port. 'You've got a dirty rifle there,' he said to Carter, 'looks to me as if there's a spider in the breech.' Carter proceeded to examine the rifle himself; a moment later he cried out: 'I say, sergeant, you're wrong; it's an earwig.'

In the early days we turned out and put our road-block in operation every time the air-raid siren sounded, and in the early hours of 18 June 1940 we saw a German raider brought down. It had dropped a bomb on Vicarage Terrace. It was, I think, the first raid on Great Britain and we had some others at later dates, but Cambridge escaped heavy damage. During the period of the 'Baedeker' raids we fully expected a major attack and heavy anti-aircraft guns were brought into position on Parker's Piece. But no attack developed—thanks, I believe, to the Regional Commissioner's urgent appeal to Bomber Command to spare Heidelberg.

The duties of the Home Guard were gradually rationalised. We paraded regularly on Sunday mornings and irregularly during the week for exercises of various kinds; we took our turn in firing a few rounds on the rifle range and occasionally indulged in the confusion of 'night operations'. As an instructor in anti-gas measures, I reached the rank of corporal. My closest friend in the platoon was F. M. Edwards, an old cross-country running Blue of Queens'. He and I had many adventures together and the one Sunday morning I recall with real pleasure was that of a 'security' exercise in which the Trumpington platoon's objective was to obtain a foothold on the railway bridge over the river, which would be strongly guarded by the Chesterton company. The role assigned to me, late on the Saturday night, was to pose as a staff-officer. An army car was put at my disposal and I was lent a major's great-coat. Frank Edwards acted as my orderly and with the aid of a false moustache and a strip of red flannel round my hat, I bluffed my way through barbed wire and fixed bayonets to the bridge with considerable gusto and much to the amusement of Guy Dale, the C.O. of the battalion.

One result of the shortage of personnel in the university was that I was asked to join the Faculty Board of English. At one meeting the secretary reported that he had had one rather unusual application for admission as a research student. It was from Philip Gosse, M.D. (Durham), and the proposed subject of research was Philip Thicknesse. There was a dead silence after this announcement until I rather rashly remarked that Thicknesse was mentioned somewhere in Boswell. 'Oh, well,' said the chairman, 'if Mr Roberts has heard of the name, he had better be Gosse's supervisor.' A day or two later Gosse called on me at the Press. 'I understand', he said, 'that I am your pupil.' As such, he came to dinner at Chaucer Road and we discussed his plan. I warned him that a thesis for a research degree was something rather different from the kind of biographical writing he had already done. We had a talk on various bibliographical points, but, after a second so-called supervision, I felt that the situation was slightly absurd. Gosse agreed and our official relationship ceased. But, as it happened, I was drawn to him through another channel. Like everyone else in business, we were short-handed at the Press and my secretary told me that a friend of hers, Anna Keown, who had some literary experience, was free to give some help in the office. I had known both of Anna's brothers at Pembroke and was glad to employ her. A few weeks later my secretary told me that Anna, having some ear trouble, had gone to a doctor and been treated by his temporary assistant, Dr Gosse. I was interested, but thought no more about it until Philip invited me to a dinner-party at the Arts Theatre restaurant. It was quite obvious that the principal guest was Anna and not long afterwards she and Philip were married. It was an immensely happy marriage and Philip's little book of essays, *An Apple a Day* (1948), was dedicated 'to Anna, who ate apples in vain'.

Meanwhile Thicknesse had not been wholly neglected. *Dr Viper, the querulous life of Philip Thicknesse* was published in 1952 and on the fly-leaf of my copy Philip wrote:

At last my task is done and I send the first printed copy of my Thesis to my friend S. C. Roberts with the hope that he will not think too unkindly of it. If it has taken a far longer time to complete than either of us contemplated ten years ago, some of the blame must be shared by my Supervisor who deserted his charge to become Master of Pembroke.

Poor Philip was shattered by Anna's death in 1957, but bore up as best he could for a few years. He made no pretensions to scholarship, but he was a genuine bookman and a great companion.

In college the changes resulting from the war were less violent than in 1914. Men reading Medicine, Physics and Engineering were officially advised to remain in residence for two years at least and so we had about 70–100 men in college. The whole of New Court was requisitioned by the Air Ministry for an Initial Training Wing of the R.A.F. and it was in New Court that we met with something like disaster. In the middle of a night in March 1941 the college porter woke up to see the top floor of the north side of the court in flames. Thanks to the efforts of the fire brigade, the fire was prevented from spreading, but the top floor was burnt out. When the Air Ministry held a court of inquiry, no member of the college was allowed to attend it or to be informed of its findings. But thanks to the firm handling of the situation by the Master (Sir Montagu Butler) an adequate compensation was secured and the opportunity was taken to make several improvements in the rooms.

Later in the year the Master himself came near to being a casualty. He had been elected mayor of Cambridge in November and on a dark and rainy night in December, when a full-scale defence exercise was in progress, he insisted on making a tour of inspection of A.R.P. posts late in the evening. In the deadly black-out he was knocked over by an ambulance and seriously injured. For a day or two there was keen anxiety, but he slowly recovered his full strength and his mayoralty was prolonged for a second year.

At the High Table we were a small company. The younger Fellows had left for the services or for government departments, but even the seniors could be useful. One Sunday evening, as we sat down to our rationed menu, Ellis Minns seemed unusually cheerful.

'Ah,' he said, 'I've had rather an amusing day.'

'What have you been doing?' I asked.

'Brushing up my Bulgarian', he replied and went on to explain that he had been consulted on some Balkan question by one of the ministries.

12-2

Our chaplain (the Rev. M. B. Dewey) went off at once to the Navy and when, in 1941, Edward Wynn became Bishop of Ely, we were left without an active clerical fellow. Accordingly, we invited W. L. Knox, who had been a member of the High Table for some years, to be college chaplain for the duration of the war. I already knew Wilfred fairly well not only in college, but as the author of scholarly works on St Paul and the early Church published at the Press. Like the other members of his family, he was a scholar and a wit, and his shyness was positively engaging. A high churchman himself, he was tolerant towards my 'central' position, but he was less patient of extreme Puritans. Dining one night with another college chaplain of notoriously strict habits, he was asked (as by one expecting a negative answer) whether he would take wine after dinner. 'Yes,' said Wilfred, 'I should like a glass of Christian liquor.' His interest in college cricket and football was as sincere as his belief in Christian values and the young men loved him. 'How's the Canon?' was often the first question asked when one of them came back to Cambridge on leave. We had one particular hobby in common—the *Observer* crossword; and on Sunday evenings we used regularly to report progress. Wilfred was generally in the lead.

Edward Wynn was the seventh Pembroke man to become Bishop of Ely and we took pride in his translation. But it left the tutorship vacant and it was fortunate that the Master was able to persuade the Ministry of Economic Warfare to release J. W. F. Rowe. Rowe, who already had useful experience of college administration, took over the Tutor's duties with notable success.

In 1941 I was saddened by the death of my old friend and tutor, Leonard Whibley. I was never happier than when I stayed a night or a week-end with him at his house in Frensham. Rhita, his wife, with her niece Pauline preserved a high standard of culinary comfort and a walk with the spaniels, long talks in the library, and a rubber of bridge in the evening filled the days most agreeably. As Whibley had made me his executor, my Frensham visits continued long after his death.

Another loss which I felt keenly was that of Q. Many years before his death in 1944 I had begged him to write a book of memoirs. After demurring at first he had eventually agreed, but at the time of his death only five chapters were written. Even so, they gave a graceful picture of the artist as a young man and were published as *Memories and Opinions*, to which I contributed an introductory memoir. I also read a paper on Q to the English Association.* There was much speculation about the appointment of his successor and in Pembroke we were delighted when the choice fell on Basil Willey. From the beginning Q had urged the inclusion of a paper on the English moralists in the Tripos syllabus and Basil embraced the subject *con amore*. Set against a background of Christian philosophy, his lectures attained a rare distinction.

At our house in Chaucer Road there were many comings and goings. My son, John, an assistant keeper in the Victoria and Albert Museum, had been seconded to Whitehall and was one of Mr Attlee's private secretaries. On one occasion Mr Attlee was due to address a meeting in Cambridge. John accompanied him and spent the night with us. On the following morning I had an appointment in London and John arranged that I should travel with Mr and Mrs Attlee and himself in the government car. It was my first meeting with the Deputy Prime Minister. Knowing that he, like myself, was a persistent pipe-smoker, I asked:

'How do you find the tobacco situation, sir?'

'Stiff', he replied.

I could not have had a more characteristic introduction.

An interesting visitor in 1942 was Major D. Barlone of the Free French Forces, whose short book, *A French Officer's Diary*, had been accepted for publication at the Press. It was a simple, but vivid, account of the fortunes of a French unit from mobilisation in August 1939 to the collapse of France in 1940. Barlone himself, after many adventures, contrived to join de Gaulle's staff in London. He had, of course, an immense admiration for

---

* Published in *Literature and Life* (Harrap, 1948).

the General, but laid some stress upon the tact and circumspection with which it was necessary to approach him.

Apart from these occasional visitors, we had students, temporary civil servants, W.A.A.F. officers and others with us for longer or shorter periods and the top floor of the house was let to a temporary Air Force instructor, Stanley Lunt, with his wife and two children. At first the name meant nothing to me. Looking round my library, Lunt said: 'You've got a lot of books. D'you know Bernard Darwin?' 'Yes, a little,' I replied, 'and of course I enjoy his golfing articles. But why do you ask?' 'Well, I play golf with him sometimes.' 'Oh, you're in that class—a scratch man, perhaps?' Lunt looked embarrassed. 'As a matter of fact, I'm plus 3. I won the amateur championship in 1934.' It was the beginning of a delightful friendship. Michael Lunt, a boy of eight when he was with us, repeated his father's achievement in 1963.

In the later part of the war we had our share of sorrow. In January 1943 my wife's brother, Brigadier Vivian Dykes, was killed. A brilliant soldier, he had been director of planning at the War Office and, later, British secretary of the combined Chiefs of Staff council in Washington; after the Casablanca conference he was flown home in a bomber for a few days' leave and the plane crashed in South Wales. In December 1943 my elder daughter Molly died shortly after the birth of her third child; and in June 1944 my son John was killed while serving with the Life Guards in Italy.

Chapter 14

VICE-CHANCELLOR

With the end of the war we became once more familiar with the blessed word 'reconstruction'. At the Press we welcomed the return of Charles Carrington, who had risen to the rank of lieutenant-colonel on the General Staff; of Brooke Crutchley, who had worked in the secretary's department of the Admiralty; and of R. W. David, who had served as a lieutenant-commander in the Navy.

Our main problem was to get books back into print and, as paper-rationing continued for some time, it was a slow process. But this did not prevent us from making plans for new books and series. In particular, there was general agreement that the *Cambridge Modern History* should be reconsidered in the light of modern scholarship. A plan for an entirely new work was prepared by Professor G. N. (now Sir George) Clark and one thing, at least, seemed clear to me: it would no longer be possible for one general editor, or even two or three, to take responsibility for the whole work, and each volume of the new series has in fact been entrusted to an individual editor.

Another work inaugurated just after the war was the *Shakespeare Survey*. I attended an interesting conference of Shakespearian scholars at Stratford-upon-Avon and the first annual volume was published in 1948.

In 1946 we, in company with the University Presses of Oxford and Manchester, were invited by the Presses Universitaires of Paris to stage an exhibition of our books published during the six years of war. Kingsford and I, with our wives, had an interesting few days in Paris and, as I have already noted, Dover Wilson came with us. At the opening of the exhibition I gave a broadcast talk on the history of the University Presses and was grateful to F. C. Green, then Professor at Cambridge, for vetting my French. The Paris publishers were most friendly and hospitable and the Duff Coopers gave a cocktail party for us at the Embassy. I was also delighted to find that Ernest Pooley was attending a conference in Paris as Chairman of the Arts Council. He came to the opening of the exhibition and afterwards insisted on carrying us off to a café. It seemed a bit early for an apéritif, but it was Ernest's seventieth birthday and we drank his health with gusto.

In Pembroke there were a good many changes. W. A. Camps took over the tutorship from Rowe and, in view of Trevor Spittle's desire to resign the treasurership, we had a long discussion about the future of college administration. In principle, we aimed at getting a man who would combine the duties of Treasurer and Bursar and would be responsible for the business side of college affairs. Eventually, we were extremely fortunate in the appointment of W. S. Hutton, a good Classic who had rowed in the boat which went head in 1931. We also decided to reverse the old rule about undergraduate residence and to take all freshmen into college for their first year. Personally, I was doubtful about the change, but I soon realised that I was wrong.

We also had it in mind that in 1947 the college would be 600 years old. We therefore set up a War Memorial and Sexcentenary Fund and appealed to old members of the college for their support. Having agreed to commemorate the names of those who fell in the war on bronze tablets in the cloister, we turned to the many improvements required in the college buildings and particularly in the Hall.

In 1947 the sexcentenary was celebrated by a lunch in Hall, followed by a garden-party. The toast of the college was proposed by the Vice-Chancellor (Henry Thirkill, Master of Clare) and it was a particular pleasure to have with us our senior Honorary Fellow, Dr J. N. Keynes, who had been a member of the college for seventy-five years.

In February 1948 I was summoned, with the other Fellows of

Pembroke, to a meeting to consider the pre-election of a new Master. The chair was taken, in accordance with statute, by the senior Fellow, Bethune-Baker, who opened the proceedings with a few words on what he called the ideology of Mastership. The Master, he said, was an important person; 'but not', he hastened to add, 'so important as some people think'. All I knew was that I was regarded as a candidate to be considered and at a certain point in the discussion I was asked to retire. When I returned, Bethune-Baker was consulting his pocket diary. 'We want to fix a date for the next meeting', he said, 'and on a day when we can all dine together.' That was all—poor material, I fear, for a novelist. The second meeting, at which I was formally pre-elected, was solemn, but brief; and at dinner in hall the reigning Master, Sir Montagu Butler, announced the choice of the Fellows in generous terms. I replied briefly and after dinner we settled down to a cheerful evening. A month or so later I was rung up by Thirkill, who had been succeeded as Vice-Chancellor by C. E. Raven (Master of Christ's) but remained as one of the senior members of the Council of the Senate. Could he see me on a matter of some importance? When I called upon him, he told me, surprisingly, that the Council wished to nominate me for the Vice-Chancellorship from 1 October 1949. Putting false modesty aside, I said I was willing to stand. I had twice served on the Council and was reasonably familiar with university business; I was in my sixty-first year and if I were destined for the office, it seemed better to take it sooner rather than later. Furthermore, Pembroke had not had a Vice-Chancellor for forty years and I felt proud to carry on the tradition of A. J. Mason, who had given me my degree in 1909. But there was a statutory difficulty. The Council of the Senate is required to nominate two heads of colleges not less than seven days before 1 June in each year. So on 17 May 1948 the following notice appeared in the *University Reporter*:

Ordinarily the name first put forward is accepted by the Regent House, while the second is regarded as likely to receive the first nomination in due course. Had Mr Roberts, Master-elect of Pembroke College, entered upon the office in time, the Council would have invited him to accept nomination as their second choice for the academical year 1948–49 and it is their intention to nominate him as their first choice a year hence.

In fact, the second name which the Council originally had in mind was that of my old friend Tom Knox-Shaw, Master of Sidney, but his health was not very good at the time and he felt unable to accept nomination. Hence the suddenness of my elevation.

I did not leave my work at the Press without a pang. I had seen many changes—in personnel, in expansion of buildings and in growth of trade. One of the most important trading decisions was in fact taken just before I left. Kingsford, returning from New York in the spring of 1948, told me that he was going to propose something which in the past we had agreed was not feasible— namely, the establishment of our own branch in New York. After long discussion and examination of figures with Mansbridge, he was satisfied that we could now make such a branch pay its way.

Knowing the improvement that Mansbridge had already effected in our American sales and having complete confidence in Kingsford's judgement, I fully supported the proposal and I may add that the success of the branch has more than justified our decision.

The last book-trade function I attended was the annual conference of the Booksellers' Association in June 1948. It was held at Sheringham and Wyndham Ketton-Cremer invited my wife and me to stay with him at Felbrigg. Ernest Heffer, at that time the doyen of booksellers, kindly drove us there in his car and we found that Rupert Hart-Davis was a fellow-guest. He was a young and ardent publisher and we talked 'shop' at great length. On the Sunday afternoon Wyndham invited members of the conference to see his library. They came in large numbers and

Wyndham nominated me as showman. I had no intimate knowledge of the books as a whole, but at least I could lay stress upon those which were bequeathed to William Windham by Dr Johnson. As a guest of the booksellers, I took no active part in the conference, but at the dinner on the last evening I replied, with Denis Brogan, to the toast of 'Literature'.

One of the attractions of publishing is that it is an intensely human business and my relations with Syndics, colleagues, authors and booksellers had been truly happy. I was happy, too, in the knowledge that Kingsford would succeed me. For many years back I had relied not only on his judgement but on his taste and I handed over my responsibilities to him without a qualm. At the farewell dinner which the Syndics gave me in July I tried to say something of what the Press had meant to me over thirty-seven years and I was horrified and incredulous when Stanley Bennett told me I had spoken for forty minutes. But the audience was very patient.

On 1 August I was formally admitted to the Mastership in chapel. At dinner, after I had said our usual grace (*Benedictus benedicat*), Bethune-Baker turned on me: 'I should like to hear a better grace than that from you, *Master*', he said with crushing emphasis. I knew what he meant. Once or twice, when he had been the senior Fellow present, I had heard him recite a much longer formula. 'All right,' I said, 'give me the text of what you say is the right form of words and I will use it.'

One of the problems facing us in college was that of the Hall. In our sexcentenary appeal we had stressed the need of improvements, especially in the windows. Waterhouse's tracery was unlovely and the stained glass was rapidly disintegrating. Our architect had advised us to cut away the tracery, but to leave the main arch and introduce plain glass with bronze fittings. The alternative suggestion, strongly favoured by Minns, was to rebuild the windows completely in a Tudor style. The argument was prolonged and Monty Butler, who always strove for an agreed solution of any controversy, had adjourned discussion *sine die*.

My unexpected nomination for the Vice-Chancellorship gave me my opportunity. It was essential that the Hall should be in good order on 1 October 1949 and the architect was authorised to implement his own scheme. The lowering and lighting of the portraits and the introduction of curtains were also effected after a little negotiation.

One of the first functions I attended as Master was a special Congregation in the Michaelmas Term at which Her Majesty the Queen (now the Queen Mother) received an honorary degree and so became the first woman graduate of the university, the Orator (W. K. C. Guthrie) aptly referring to the *araneosas et plus quam metaphysicas subtilitates* which had for many years obscured the position of women at Cambridge.

At the beginning of 1949 I was elected to the Council of the Senate and to the General Board and a little later was made a member of a special syndicate to consider the financial relations of the University and the colleges. Shades of the prison-house were beginning to grow upon me and on 1 October I was duly admitted to the Vice-Chancellorship in succession to C. E. Raven.

In the course of the following two years, visitors sometimes put the question to me: 'What does a Vice-Chancellor really *do*?' To which I would succinctly reply: 'By day he presides over committees; by night he replies for the guests.'

There were, of course, many routine duties: the Council on Mondays; the General Board and the Financial Board on Wednesdays; the Congregations in the Senate House on alternate Saturdays; discussions of reports on alternate Tuesdays; the monthly meetings of the Committee of Vice-Chancellors in London. For the governing bodies of most university departments and institutions the Vice-Chancellor appoints deputies, but having been chairman of the Library Syndicate for some years, I contrived to retain that duty and I was also pressed into the chair of the Fitzwilliam Museum Syndicate.

Elections to professorships, over which the Vice-Chancellor is required to preside were sometimes dull and sometimes interesting—dull when there was one outstanding candidate, interesting when there was a sharp division of opinion.

In full term the Vice-Chancellor has, or used to have, a seven-day week. The preacher of the university sermon would arrive on Saturday afternoon and there would be a dinner-party in the evening. On the Sunday the sermon was preached in Great St Mary's Church at 2.30—a difficult hour for listening, as I frequently found. But, personally, I enjoyed the week-ends. The preachers were not exclusively Anglican and I was stimulated by the variety of their points of view. The visit of the Judge of Assize was the occasion of another, and shorter, sermon. The judge occupies a suite of rooms in the Master's Lodge at Trinity (not as of right, but by courtesy) and on the opening day of the assize the Vice-Chancellor, supported by the Proctors and Heads of Houses, waits upon the judge at Trinity. As the procession leaves the Lodge, it is met in the middle of Great Court by a similar party consisting of the mayor and members of the City Council bound upon the same errand.

During my first year it seemed to me odd that while we proceeded to Great St Mary's for the assize sermon, the mayor's party, after paying their respects, returned at once to the Guild-hall. In my second year I raised the point with the mayor. 'Why don't you come to church for the sermon?' I asked. Like me, he had no explanation to offer and readily agreed that it would be more seemly for the City to join the University at the service. I suspect that in the past there was some town-and-gown quarrel about precedence, but whatever was the cause of the breach, I was glad to restore symmetry to the ceremony. As to the sermon, I understood that the judge normally prescribed a maximum length of six minutes and it was remarkable how much good sense preachers were able to compress within such a limit.

There is no lack of variety in a Vice-Chancellor's duties and one or two of his traditional powers came to me as a surprise. I found myself, for instance, to be a censor of plays and a grantor of vintners' licences. These responsibilities were not onerous, but

I remember that in the script of a Footlights entertainment I came upon the phrase 'incest in Islington'. My suggested emendation, 'exogamy in Ealing' was duly accepted. As to wine licences, a publican would occasionally write to say that while he had held a beer licence for many years, he now found that some of his clients, the ladies especially, asked for a glass of port. So could he please have a 'sweet' licence in addition? In my reply I generally acted on the advice of the Chief Constable.

There were many inaugural duties. I liked to preside at a newly elected professor's inaugural lecture whenever I could and, in the Long Vacation particularly, there were many conferences to be formally welcomed. It fell to me to open the University Combination Room in the Old Schools and the University Air Squadron's headquarters in Chaucer Road and I was the first chairman *ex officio* of the newly founded Institute of Education. This was more than a formal duty, since it involved the appointment of a director and the finding of suitable accommodation. I spent a long day in company with an officer of the Ministry of Education in the search for a house, but our first choice was vetoed as the result of a planning inquiry. Eventually an alternative was found and many years later it gave me great pleasure to attend the opening, by Lord Butler, of the Institute's new, and permanent, headquarters.

Apart from engagements within the University, a Vice-Chancellor is at the mercy of headmasters seeking for a guest of honour at speech day. I attended many such functions and did not find them unduly burdensome. I made no attempt to devise a fresh theme for each occasion, but I hope I introduced sufficient local colour to give my address a flavour of individuality.

A pleasant duty was that of representing Cambridge at celebrations at other universities—Birmingham, Southampton, Newcastle, Glasgow, St Andrews. I also enjoyed the traditional hospitality of the Royal Society, the Royal Academy, the Inns of Court and the City Livery Companies. With two companies I had fairly close associations—the Merchant Taylors and the

Drapers. With the Merchant Taylors Pembroke had ancient links from the days of Edmund Spenser and Lancelot Andrewes onwards and I regularly attended speech days at the school—notable because, except for the headmaster's report, there were no speeches. To the Drapers I had long before been introduced by Ernest Pooley.

Early in 1950 I was made a member of the United States Educational Commission in the United Kingdom (*Anglice* 'Fulbright'). This body, consisting of seven American and seven British members, is the outcome of a proposal made by Senator Fulbright, and accepted by Congress in 1948, that the proceeds of the sale of American surplus stores in Great Britain should be used 'to facilitate the attendance of citizens of the United States at institutions of higher learning located in the United Kingdom'. In other words, it enables a number of professors, senior research students and young graduates from the United States (about 150 in all) to come annually and spend the year at a British university; it also provides travel grants for British scholars going to the United States. A by-product of the commission's work with which I was concerned was a series of conferences at Oxford and Cambridge on American Studies and out of these has sprung a British Association of American Studies. It was at meetings of the commission that I got to know two other vice-chancellors really well—Dame Lillian Penson of London and Sir Hector Hetherington of Glasgow. Later in the year I was to join them in another international enterprise.

In 1948 I had met General Smuts at the time of his admission to the Chancellorship and I looked forward to entertaining him at the Lodge for the honorary degree ceremonies in 1950. But in May we heard that he was ill and unable to come, and so the conferment of degrees devolved upon me. Amongst the recipients were Lord Samuel, Sir Gerald Kelly, E. M. Forster, Sir Brian (now Lord) Robertson and Stanley Morison. In proposing their healths at the luncheon, I digressed for a moment to congratulate the Provost of King's (J. T. Sheppard) on the announcement of his knighthood which had just been made. 'When I was an undergraduate', I said, 'I understood that Mr Sheppard was the *enfant terrible* of the classical faculty and for all I know, he may still occupy that position.' At the Corpus Christi dinner in the evening I sat next to Lord Halifax. I knew him only slightly, but by the end of dinner I felt that we were old friends. Rarely have I met anyone with whom I slipped with such ease into intimate talk.

On the following day I fulfilled an engagement not normally included in a Vice-Chancellor's programme. Some weeks before, I had been approached by a group of Pembroke coxswains who explained that they proposed to challenge the coxswains of the Lady Margaret Boat Club to a race. If the challenge should be accepted, would I cox the Pembroke crew? 'Certainly,' I replied, 'if you're prepared to carry twelve stone in the stern of the boat.' The race was duly held. We paddled down to Ditton from the boat-house, turned and raced abreast to the railway bridge. We quickly established a lead and won by a length and a half, afterwards retiring to the Pike and Eel for refreshment. A Vice-Chancellor in such a context had a certain news-value and the photographers were busy. When a reporter asked me to what I attributed our success I had no hesitation in replying: 'To a well-disciplined crew and a cox of long experience.' In the Pembroke crew were Douglas MacLellan (now a professor of Engineering at Leicester), John Hinde (afterwards cox of the Cambridge boat) and James Chester Cheng, a Chinese research student, now a professor in California.

General Smuts died in September. My wife and I were touring in France at the time and I sent a cablegram of sympathy from Rheims. Shortly after my return I had the pleasure of receiving an honorary degree at St Andrews. We stayed with George Duncan, Principal of St Mary's College, and, like Dr Johnson in 1773, 'had reason to be highly pleased with the attention that was paid us'. The degree was not the only honour I received. The day of the ceremony was also the opening day of the autumn meeting of the Royal and Ancient and the treasurer of the club kindly offered me honorary membership for two days. The big room was full of famous golfers and I was delighted to have a word with Bernard Darwin, who was busy writing one of those articles which gave pleasure to many readers unfamiliar with the technique of golf. A game was arranged for me on the following morning and I was immensely relieved when it became a foursome. I had a powerful, and most agreeable, young man as a partner and his long, straight drives compensated for my frequent invasions of burns and bunkers. Fortunately, however, I was holing the putts quite steadily and we won by 2 and 1.

In the following week I was due to attend a memorial service for General Smuts in Westminster Abbey. Three representatives of the University were invited—the Vice-Chancellor, the High Steward (the Duke of Devonshire) and the Registrary (W. W. Grave). Grave and I arranged to travel to London by a train that would enable us to be in our places at the Abbey at 11.45. When I got to the station with a very few minutes to spare, I was horrified to find that the train no longer ran. I had to think quickly, especially as my own car was in process of overhaul. I telephoned to my garage and said I must have a car—any car—at once. The garage lost no time and a car arrived. It was a Hillman of an early vintage. The screen-wiper was faulty (it was a showery morning) and I found it hard work to get more than 40 m.p.h. out of the car. As I approached London, I tossed up in my mind whether to drive straight to the Abbey and hope for the best about parking or whether to garage the car and search for a taxi. I decided on the latter course. I garaged the car near Lord's and had luck with a taxi. At 11.40 I walked up the nave of the Abbey and found my reserved seat in the front row of the north transept. Grave, who had allowed a wider margin of time and caught an earlier train, gazed at me with mingled relief and astonishment.

Early in the Michaelmas Term a similar service was held in Cambridge at Great St Mary's. Two very old friends of Smuts, Mr and Mrs Gillett, stayed at the Lodge for the week-end preceding the service. They belonged to a Quaker family and Mrs

Gillett was the stricter in her observances. When, in the evening, I inquired whether a little whisky would be acceptable, 'All our family are teetotallers', said Mrs Gillett. 'This one isn't', said her husband quickly. Before the service on the Monday afternoon we had a large party for lunch, including Mrs Clark (General Smuts's daughter) and her husband. The sweet was crème brûlée and Gillett had some trouble with it. He was a delightful guest and thanked me warmly as he left. 'I've enjoyed every minute', he said, 'except that dreadful sweet—it got under my plate.'

For the memorial service, so the University Marshal informed me, all members of the University would wear black gowns except the Vice-Chancellor, who would wear his cope, as for other ceremonies. One journalist, I believe, referred to me as a 'study in scarlet'.

Our next duty was to elect a new Chancellor. The Statutes provided that any group of fifty Masters of Arts could nominate a candidate and it was customary for the Vice-Chancellor, in the first instance, to invite the heads of colleges to an informal discussion. Following precedent, I asked the heads of colleges together with Lord Wright (Deputy High Steward) to meet me at the Lodge. After a cup of tea, we settled down to talk. I had little hope of any unanimity of opinion. So far as I could interpret feeling, no one stood out as *facile princeps*. Various names were mentioned, including those of Lord Mountbatten and Lord Tedder. Yes, they had both had brilliant service careers, but what about scholarship? That Tedder of Magdalene had won the Prince Consort Prize for an historical essay in 1914 was a surprise to many and at the end of an hour it appeared that there was something very near unanimity for him. With a request that the Vice-Chancellor would get into touch with Lord Tedder, the meeting broke up.

Tedder at that time was head of the British Military Mission in Washington. The London telephone officials were very helpful and promised to call me about 9 p.m. After the usual 'trying to connect you', I got through.

'Is that Lord Tedder?'

'Yes.'

'This is S. C. Roberts, Vice-Chancellor of Cambridge, speaking.'

'Really, where are you?'

'In Cambridge—England.'

'Really?'

'Yes; a number of senior members of the University have just met in my Lodge and want to nominate you for the Chancellorship.'

'What? Me? Good Lord, but I'm not academic...I really don't know, I...'

'There's not much time, you know. But the point is—will you accept nomination?'

'But, I say—well, if you say so—well, yes, but...'

'Good.'

The line was beautifully clear and with equal clarity I could visualise Tedder nearly falling off his chair in the embarrassment of genuine modesty.

The next step, also in accordance with precedent, was to invite all Masters of Arts to a meeting in the Senate House for the discussion of a suitable nomination. The Master of Trinity proposed the nomination of Lord Tedder and was warmly, though not unanimously, supported. Noel Annan, then a young Fellow of King's, whilst fully recognising Tedder's claims, thought those of Mountbatten were stronger. Again, this meeting was informal and no vote was taken, but the upshot of it was that Tedder was formally nominated with the support of a large number of Masters of Arts. But there were stirrings among the younger men. Noel Annan wrote a long letter to the *Cambridge Review* and was good enough to show it to me in proof. I took no objection to it except to one phrase and that was willingly altered. In general, many of the young men disliked a succession of Chancellors from the armed forces; but more strongly they disliked what they regarded as the dictatorship of a stuffy body of Masters of colleges. So they announced their own candidate—Nehru, Prime

Minister of India, a Trinity man whose election would, in their view, be a magnificent gesture of generosity and reconciliation.

There had not been a contest for the Chancellorship since 1847, when the Prince Consort had a narrow majority over Lord Powys, and the Registrary and I noted some interesting parallels. Tedder, when he heard the news, wrote to the Master of his college and asked whether it would be best for him to withdraw. 'Certainly not' was the reply. (The Prince Consort had also wished to retire, but an urgent deputation of Cambridge Whigs had persuaded him to stand fast.)

In due course, a small party of Nehru's supporters, headed by S. R. K. Glanville, of King's, waited upon me with the nomination signed by a substantial number of Masters of Arts.

'Yes,' I said, 'this is perfectly in order. But can you tell me whether your candidate has accepted nomination?'

'Well, Vice-Chancellor, at present we're not quite sure.'

'I'm sorry, but I *must* be sure. As you cannot tell me for certain, I shall write at once to the High Commissioner and ask him whether Mr Nehru is willing to stand.'

The reply of the High Commissioner (Krishna Menon) came some days later: Pandit Nehru, though 'deeply conscious of the honour sought to be done to him', did not wish to enter into any contest.

That, I thought, settles it. But I was wrong. The lawyers got busy, not in a controversial, but in a professional way. Since the Statutes made no provision for the withdrawal of a nomination, ought not Nehru's nomination to stand? I hastily invited the legal members of the Council of the Senate and some of Nehru's backers to meet at the Lodge. After considerable, but very friendly discussion a decision was reached. All were agreed that, in order to avoid any possible risk of Tedder's title being challenged in the future, the election must be held, and the Nehru party undertook to instruct their supporters not to vote. So the election was held in the Senate House on 10 November and about 250 Masters of Arts turned up to vote for Tedder.

After all this, there was general agreement that the statute relating to the election of a Chancellor was in need of revision and there is now a statutory Nomination Board, consisting of the members of the Council, together with sixteen additional members of whom four must be non-residents and four Masters of Arts of not more than ten years' standing.

Later in the term vice-chancellors all over the world received an invitation to a conference at Nice of which the purpose was to found, or at least to consider the foundation of, an international association of universities. I think that most British vice-chancellors regarded the proposal with some scepticism. On the other hand they agreed that it would be impolite, if not impolitic, to boycott the conference and our delegation included the Vice-Chancellors of Oxford, Cambridge, London, Glasgow, Wales and Belfast. Having the good fortune to fly to Nice with Lillian Penson, I felt that the conference would not lack an element of gaiety and I was not disappointed.

The British members (among whom was J. F. Foster, secretary of the Association of Universities of the British Commonwealth) were put up at a small hotel, which had no restaurant. It seemed to me that we should need a rendezvous where we could eat and drink and I soon discovered a restaurant that was conveniently near—Cyrano. It was a modest place, but Lillian Penson, who was a good judge, approved of it and when we were not officially entertained we patronised Cyrano. By the end of the week we were on very good terms with the management; at our last meal the cognac was 'on the house'.

Shortly after our arrival we British members had an informal meeting under the direction of Hector Hetherington. To clear my own mind, I had jotted down my own views on the projected association and showed Hetherington what I had written. 'Good,' he said, 'just say that when we go to the meeting.' Meetings were held at a large hall on the sea-front, and at the opening session the chair was taken by Jean Sarrailh, Rector of the Sorbonne. In the introductory speeches there were some uplifting, but not very precise, proposals for the co-operation of the universities in preserving not only academic freedom, but the peace of the world.

Hetherington had given notice that the British delegation would like to contribute to the debate at some point and he was duly called. I was sitting next to him and, to my astonishment, he literally pushed me on to the rostrum. After making it clear who I was, I delivered my short piece. What I said, in effect, was that the proposals, as submitted, were far too ambitious; that there were already innumerable international conferences associated with every kind of academic subject; that any attempt to establish international 'equivalences' of qualification for matriculation or for degrees would be the pursuit of a will o' the wisp; and that it would be well to concentrate, in the first instance, on the establishment of a really efficient central bureau from which inquirers could rely upon accurate information about the universities of the world.

My remarks had a mixed reception; but it was not until the following morning that I realised what kind of impression I had made. My sobriquet for the rest of the week was 'le Vyshinski du congrés'.

After the inaugural meeting, a number of committees were formed and the one on which, in company with Mansfield Cooper of Manchester, I served was far too large for the Bombay delegate in the chair to control effectively. 'Order, order,' he would cry in despair, 'I cannot allow more discussion.' Whereupon, points of order would be raised and discussion would break out in various languages.

In the afternoons we were taken for a number of excursions and on the last day we were entertained to a sumptuous lunch at Monte Carlo. After lunch we looked in at the casino. There were very few at the tables, but those few appeared to be playing in an atmosphere of the deepest gloom. As a result of some error in the transport arrangements, Lillian Penson and I were left behind the main party and were only just in time for the full and final session of the whole conference. There had been many whisperings in the lobbies and I had heard, incredulously, from Hector Hetherington that, in spite of my intransigence, I had been mentioned as a possible president of the incipient association. The truth turned out to be one degree less daunting: Sarrailh would accept the office, provided that I would be his vice-president. So we were duly elected and I endeavoured to conciliate the company by a short address for which I borrowed Winston Churchill's opening: 'Prenez garde. Je vais parler français.' After which Sarrailh announced that he must catch his train for Paris and left me to preside over the appointment of a *conseil d'administration*, that is, a small body to act as an executive committee. Normally, the selection of such a body would have taken a considerable time, but everyone was tired and hungry and we did our job in about twenty minutes and I daresay it was none the worse for that. It was after 9 o'clock when I rejoined my British colleagues and the next morning Lillian Penson and I flew home together.

The first meeting of the *conseil d'administration* was held in Pembroke in March 1951. Sarrailh and F. M. Rogers, Dean of the Harvard Graduate School, stayed with me at the Lodge and the others in college. I am afraid that the rigours of college accommodation were a shock to one or two delegates from South America. The acting secretary was a professor from Lyons and it soon became painfully clear that he and Sarrailh did not see eye to eye; but a year or two later we were fortunate in the appointment of H. M. Keyes, formerly Fellow of Balliol, as secretary and in the five years of my vice-presidency I saw many men and cities—Paris, Brussels, Genoa, Chicago, Istanbul. Under Keyes's direction, the Association has attained a greater measure of stability than appeared possible at the outset.

Meanwhile, at the end of 1950, my wife and I, in company with hundreds of vice-chancellors and other dignitaries, received an invitation to spend a week in Egypt to celebrate the twenty-fifth anniversary of the foundation of the University of Cairo.

We flew on 26 December with the Vice-Chancellor of Oxford (John Lowe) and his wife. At Geneva there was some engine trouble and we had to wait for some time in contemplation of the snow-covered airfield. About 2 a.m. we touched down at Heliopolis and stepped out into the lovely warm air of Egypt. We were put up at the Semiramis and had a festive week of banquets and sight-seeing—the Pyramids, a river trip to the Assuan Dam, a supper-party at the Abdin Palace. One of our excursions was to King Farouk's model village. There he kept his camels and the best of them were displayed for us in their ceremonial trappings in the stable yard. They were there for us to ride if we wished and John Maud, then permanent secretary of the Ministry of Education, suggested a camel-race between the Vice-Chancellors of Oxford and Cambridge. John Lowe showed no enthusiasm. I had a brief ride and thought no more about it until a week or more after my return, when I was rung up by the *Evening Standard*. Was it true that there had been a Vice-Chancellors' camel-race in Egypt? 'Certainly not', I replied. Even so, the *Evening Standard* contrived to produce a gossipy paragraph and a day later the subject was dignified by a fourth leader in the *Times,* entitled 'A Camel for Cambridge'.

When we left Cairo, we went on for two days to Alexandria. My old friend and colleague, A. J. B. Wace, after his retirement from the Chair of Classical Archaeology at Cambridge had taken a professorship at Alexandria and was anxious to see us. We had an interesting flight over the delta and I gave a lecture on 'Doctor Johnson' under the auspices of the British Council. The enthusiasm of the audience surprised and gratified me. From Alexandria we flew to Athens. It was dark when we arrived, but we woke up to lovely sunshine. It was 6 January; in England it might have been 6 June. I had never been to Greece before and I could contemplate the Acropolis with the ingenuousness of a schoolboy. Atmosphere, colour, texture all combined to make me understand epithets with which I had long been familiar. The British Council representative helped us to make the most of our short visit. In the afternoon we drove out to Daphne and after paying our respects at the British Embassy, we dined with a number of journalists and others in a restaurant which, we were assured, was truly Greek. I enjoyed the company, but not the wine.

1951 was a busy year. The special syndicate on financial relations between the University and the colleges had many meetings. I was glad to have the help of Tom Knox-Shaw, a former Treasurer of the University, and of several college bursars, though it was not always easy to reconcile their views. At one point some fear was expressed that the University Grants Committee might be critical of our efforts. I arranged to have lunch with the chairman (A. E. Trueman) in London and explained that our aim was some kind of redistribution. With this he was entirely satisfied.

Our first attempt at a solution was circulated to colleges and rejected. So we tried again and, thanks to the skilful draftsmanship of a sub-committee consisting of Mrs Hollond and John Boys Smith, we were able to present an agreed report. The gist of our recommendations was that the University should bear the full cost of the 'prime stipend' of teaching officers and that it should repay to colleges the deductions from the university stipends of their stipendiary fellows; and, further, that the four wealthiest colleges (Trinity, King's, St John's and Caius) should forgo this repayment. When, at our final meeting, a vote of thanks to the chair was moved by R. F. Kahn (of King's) and seconded by T. C. Nicholas (of Trinity), two members who had consistently contradicted each other, I was more than content. The report was published in February and approved by the University in May. It was also in May that members of the University Grants Committee conducted their quinquennial visitation. Trueman and George Pickering stayed with me and many departments and institutions were visited. Their needs were duly demonstrated and I laid what emphasis I could on those of the University Library and of Fitzwilliam House.

Meanwhile, in the last week of April, there had been a notable ceremony at King's College. In celebration of the restoration of the stained glass and of the cleaning of the interior of the chapel, King George VI, Queen Elizabeth and Princess Margaret accepted an invitation to visit the college. My wife and I were presented to their Majesties outside the west door of the chapel and I ventured to suggest to the Queen that she might some day like to visit Pembroke and see the entries in the admission book of several of her eighteenth-century ancestors. She assented gaily. Then followed sherry in the Provost's Lodge, lunch in hall, and the service of thanksgiving in chapel. The King was genial and carefree and it was at his command that an item was added to the programme. The Cambridge crew had just returned from the United States, having won against both Harvard and Yale, and the King had sent a message that he wanted to see them. So before lunch on the great lawn of King's, he had a talk with the victorious oarsmen. I knew the crew fairly well myself as there were two Pembroke men in it (James Crowden and John Hinde) and they all came to tea with us at the Lodge. It was a day to remember.

I had also to remember the preparations for the admission of the new Chancellor. I had a good deal of correspondence with Lord Tedder, who continued to regard his new honour with apprehensive modesty, and by the time of the ceremony we were on terms of easy intimacy both with him and his wife. In accordance with custom, he was invited to nominate some additional candidates for honorary degrees and among those he chose were Sir William Haley and General Omar Bradley, both of whom, with their wives, stayed at the Lodge. I was glad to get to know Haley, as I had since 1948 been university correspondent of *The Times* and remained so until my retirement. General Bradley's arrival was impressive. His enormous car seemed to fill the whole of the Lodge drive and various members of his staff stepped out of it and stayed for tea. One of them, a tall man in elegant civilian clothes, was presented to my wife. 'I'm afraid', she said, 'I didn't catch your name. Was it Colonel...?' 'Oh, no, ma'am,' he replied, 'I'm the detective', and when I took the General to Ditton Paddock to see a little of the May Races he hovered conscientiously round us.

The following morning was fine and sunny. The Senate House was, of course, crowded, and immediately before the ceremony began the South door was shut. The Chancellor-elect was escorted to the door by the Master of Clare and the Master of Magdalene and from the door I conducted him to the dais. From my brief address of welcome I quote one paragraph:

You, my Lord, have seen many men and cities and the story of your Odyssey is woven into the pattern of our history; you have, for the nation's good, held responsibilities at such altitudes as cause the duties of a vice-chancellor to shrink into terrestrial insignificance.

After the formal admission to office, the Chancellor retired and shortly returned wearing his ceremonial robes, his train being borne by Richard Butler, grandson of my predecessor at Pembroke. Then followed the address of the Deputy Orator (L. P. Wilkinson) to the Chancellor (*quamvis gloria militari illustris, miles non gloriosus*) and the Chancellor's reply, in which he emphasised the importance, in international relations, of a knowledge of historical backgrounds.

After the Congregation we proceeded formally to King's College Chapel for the traditional performance of music in the Chancellor's honour and then to Pembroke for luncheon. Among the honorary graduands were two distinguished women—Dame Edith Evans and Miss Rose Macaulay. It was my first meeting with Dame Edith, but Rose Macaulay was a very old friend of my first wife and we had known her well in the old days when her home was at Shelford. There were eleven graduands in all and their health was proposed in characteristic style by Tedder, who chose to regard them as a cricket team. Dame Edith replied with skill as well as with charm. 'I don't know how I come into a cricket side,' she said, 'but I suppose I'm a sort of middle stump.' In the afternoon the degrees were conferred in the Senate House, after which we had about 1,200 guests at a garden-party in Pembroke. The Tedders and the Haleys stayed overnight and we rounded off the day by seeing the May Week play (Julian Slade's *Lady May*) at the A.D.C.

Immediately after the two general Congregations at the end of term, my wife and I left for Glasgow to take part in the quincentenary celebrations at the University. There were many festive ceremonies, but what I remember most clearly was the excursion by steamer to Wemyss Bay. It was a glorious day and one of my old authors (Professor W. M. Smart) was one of the many friends on board. As we talked over the events of the previous days, he remarked that while the Vice-Chancellor, Hector Hetherington, had paid various tributes to those responsible for the organisation of the celebration, there had been no opportunity for anyone to say a word of appreciation of all that Hector himself had done. So we hatched a little plot. There was a loudspeaker by the Captain's cabin and at 5 p.m. I announced: 'Attention, please. This is the 5 o'clock news and this is the Vice-Chancellor of Cambridge reading it' and I went on to say briefly what we owed to Hector, who told me afterwards that he was completely puzzled when he first heard a voice booming through the ship. In the evening he had invited about a dozen of us to a private dinner *at which there were to be no speeches.* But, of course, when the time came, he felt impelled to say a word of welcome and forbade us to reply—but most of us did.

Very soon after our return, we had to prepare for more honorary degrees. The Royal Agricultural Show was held in Cambridge in July and degrees were to be given to H.R.H. the Princess Royal, the Minister of Agriculture (Tom Williams) and others. We had a large house-party, including of course the Chancellor and Lady Tedder. The Princess Royal seemed at first nervous about the prospective ceremonies, but she was delighted by the Orator's reference in his speech to her hatred of garden neglect and at lunch she was much more at ease. A day or two later I had a letter of thanks from her lady-in-waiting, but what astonished and gratified me was that some weeks later I had a long letter, in her own hand, from the Princess herself.

1951 was also Festival year, and I attended the impressive opening service in St Paul's Cathedral. At Cambridge I was asked to be chairman of a town-and-gown committee. At one of our meetings the hope was expressed that a member of the royal family might wish to see what contribution to the Festival spirit was being made in Cambridge. Personally, I felt that this was improbable, but, in fact, we were later notified that the Duke and Duchess of Gloucester would like to visit Cambridge on 1 August. Having asked what entertainments would be available on that day, I was reminded of the exhibition of college plate in the Fitzwilliam Museum. That, I thought, would suitably occupy an hour before lunch. What about the afternoon? 'Poetry-reading and music in the Senate House', was the reply. 'When does the interval come?' I asked. 'Oh, there's no interval, Vice-Chancellor, the whole programme is integrated.' 'I'm sorry,' I said, 'but I'm afraid there will have to be one on 1 August. I'm not sure that I can face two hours of poetry and music and I'm quite sure that the Duke won't.'

The Duke and Duchess, with Sir Godfrey Thomas in attendance, arrived by car about 11 and our first bit of sight-seeing was at the Fitzwilliam. Each college had contributed a few of its best pieces of plate, so that the show was of high quality. As we walked up the steps the Duke, who had been an undergraduate at Trinity just after the First World War, confided to me that he had never before entered the Museum—but the same, I assured him, could have been said of many others.

As to lunch, I had inquired whether the party should be large or a small one, and in reply was told to use my own discretion. So I decided on a party of twelve at the Lodge—the mayor, the city librarian, who had acted as secretary of our Festival committee, my old friend Trevor Spittle as President (i.e. Vice-Master) of the college. These, with their wives and Mrs Arthur Hutchinson, widow of our former Master, made up the party.

After lunch we visited the Cambridge Folk Museum and about 3 o'clock entered the Senate House. An interval had been arranged and the poetry and music, especially some light pieces beautifully read by Miss Peggy Ashcroft, were fully appreciated. The performers came back to tea with us in the Lodge garden to meet the royal visitors and all went smoothly.

Another outcome of Festival year gave me some personal gratification. Pembroke, like other colleges and institutions, had been urged by the Goldsmiths' Company to encourage modern craftsmanship by ordering a piece of commemorative silver. The suggestion was not received with any enthusiasm until the Bursar pointed out that if we were prepared to sell a large number of Victorian spoons and forks which were never used, we might comfortably afford to buy something more useful. So a circular coffee-tray was ordered and later I asked Ellis Minns if he would devise a suitable inscription. He had not been in favour of the purchase and at first refused to co-operate. Later, however, he relented, and added that he would take more pleasure in the work if the tray commemorated the Master's vice-chancellorship as well as Festival year. The college agreed and the inscription runs:

> *Festum Saeculare Britannicum ut participet Munus Vice-Cancellarii Academiae a Sydney Castle Roberts Custode suo egregie gestum ut commemoret fieri fecit Collegium Pembrochianum*

Chapter 15

AT HOME AND ABROAD

Shortly after the end of my Vice-Chancellorship on 1 October 1951 I had the good fortune to have a holiday in the United States. Lefty Lewis had told me some time before that Yale would be celebrating the 250th anniversary of its foundation in October and the University made me its official delegate. We were to stay at Farmington and I booked seats in a night plane which would land at New York about 8 o'clock in the morning. There Lefty's car would meet us.

When we reached London, there was a thick fog. The airport was closed and we had to spend the night in London. We took off the next day at noon and reached New York about 10.30 p.m. Meanwhile I had sent Lefty a cable, but did not know what fresh arrangements, if any, he might have made.

As we were waiting to go through customs, a little man came up to me. He had a message, he said, from the president of Pan Am. As we were travelling by B.O.A.C., I was mystified. 'The message is', the man said, 'that the president's private plane is waiting to fly you to Hartford and there Mr Lewis will meet you in his car.' I had had many experiences of the proverbially high standard of American hospitality, but this eclipsed them all. When we touched down at Hartford, Lefty and his wife, Annie Burr, were waiting for us and the next morning we awoke to the beauties of the American fall. All my previous visits had been in the spring and I had always suspected some exaggeration in coloured photographs of the fall; but I quickly realised that the half had not been told me.

On 19 October we had a great day at Yale. I had a very high regard for Whitney Griswold, the president, who had stayed a week-end with us in Cambridge, and was delighted to find that in the academic procession I was paired with Lord Halifax, representing the University of Oxford. In the evening we were guests at an Alumni dinner, at which there were two revealing speeches, one by Lefty and one by another Fellow of Yale. Both of them faced the major problem of the privately endowed American universities—their dependence upon the financial support of their alumni.

'At every Commencement', said Lefty, 'is heard the ringing assurance that we shall never, never, never be anything but high-minded seekers after truth. But having said so, the careworn President goes back to his office, takes off his singing robes, and finds a telegram from his greatest benefactor which states with all possible clarity that he, George W. Maecenas, 1910, will not give one nickel more until Professor Jones is fired...What does the President do next?'

We had a happy week at Farmington. Lefty's library exuded comfort as well as culture and one did not need to be a Walpolian expert to enjoy it. The garden, which delighted my wife, provided a croquet-lawn whereon the game was played under curious local rules presumably invented by Lefty. At bridge in the evening procedure was more conventional, but there was plenty of gaiety, mingled with Lefty's exaggerated distress over some error of his own. 'Oh, if I had only led that club' he would murmur as he went to bed.

From Farmington we went to Ann Arbor. Gordon Sutherland had resigned his Pembroke fellowship in 1949 to become Professor of Physics at the University of Michigan and it was good to see him and his family again. I was also glad to meet G. B. Harrison, whom I had not seen since his departure from England to be Professor of English at Ann Arbor. Under his auspices I gave a lecture on Boswell at the university.

At Harvard we had a week-end with the Conants and, amongst other entertainments, saw for the first time a college football match. President Conant was very patient in explaining the points of the game to us; the bands and the cheer-leaders explained themselves. Our next host was General Omar Bradley, with whom we stayed a night at Fort Meyer. Both he and his wife were most hospitable, inquiring in advance whether there were any friends in Washington whom we would like to meet. My wife was especially anxious to meet General Bedell Smith, who had worked in close co-operation with her brother, Vivian Dykes. She had a long talk with him, and another old friend invited at my request was Colonel Everest Mozley (nephew of Kenneth Mozley), who was then a member of the British Military Mission. We were also briefly introduced to the ante-rooms of the Pentagon.

In New York I was, of course, keenly interested to see the newly established branch of our own University Press.

In April 1949 Ronald Mansbridge had kindly written to me from 51 Madison Avenue:*

One thing I have promised myself is that the first letter I should send from this address should be to the one who, as it were, planted the seed nearly twenty years ago;

and it was with great satisfaction that I made a tour of the new premises. After spending a night with Mansbridge at his country home in Connecticut, we finally had a week-end at Princeton, most English of American university towns. Harold Dodds, the president, and his wife, Margaret, were old friends and made us feel completely at home at 'Prospect'.

Back at Cambridge and relieved of vice-cancellarial obligations, I was able to give more time to my duties in college and to see a little more of undergraduates. An annual intake of 120 freshmen is formidable enough and successive tea-parties for them do not get one very far towards intimacy; but our third-year supper-parties were, I think, enjoyed. In particular, I kept in close touch with the boat club and at one bump supper I was overwhelmed when the captain of the boats (Toby Coghill, who rowed bow in the Cambridge boat of 1951) announced that he proposed to

* The branch moved to larger premises in East 57th Street in 1951.

award first boat colours to the Master. In an unearned honour there is something peculiarly sweet.

One of the pleasantest features of life in a Master's Lodge is the opportunity it gives of offering hospitality to old members of the college. Men whom I had not seen for years would turn up from different parts of the world and it was good to convince them that not all the changes in the college were for the worse. There were other visitors, too. Returning to the Lodge one morning, I was told that a Mr Sassoon was waiting for me in the study. 'I've never met you before,' I said, 'but I feel that I've known you for years—through Aubrey Attwater', for Aubrey had often talked to me about their experiences together in the Royal Welch Fusiliers. So Siegfried and I were quickly at ease. We had many enthusiasms in common—cricket, for instance, and Max Beerbohm, and in later years we have had good times together in Cambridge and Marlborough and Heytesbury, subject to his notorious insistence on hibernation.

At college meetings a major subject of controversy was the proposal for a new building. At the beginning there had been general agreement in principle about the need for more rooms for undergraduates. But the selection of a site, the appointment of an architect, the architectural style to be adopted and, later, the question whether, as a poorly endowed college, we could really afford a new building, provoked wide differences of opinion. However, there is nothing unusual in the erection of a college building by a majority vote and by such a vote Marshall Sisson's design was eventually approved. When the building began to appear above ground, the intelligentsia of the *Cambridge Review* dismissed it as anaemic and traditional. Personally, I thought, and still think, that the architect's judgement was sound and today there is fairly general agreement that the building has settled into its landscape with remarkable ease. It stands on the site of an orchard bequeathed by the Foundress and it was a happy suggestion of Trevor Spittle that it should be called 'Orchard Building'. On a table on the south wall the *munificentia Pembro-*

chianorum which enabled us to build it is duly acknowledged; notable items of munificence were a legacy of Leonard Whibley which had been applied to the building fund and a most generous gift from Harry Guggenheim which, at a critical period, filled the gap between the builder's tender and the sum we had contrived to accumulate.

Several of those who had taken part in the early discussions did not live to see the building completed. In 1946 Wilfred Knox had been elected to a fellowship. I think it gave him, as it certainly gave us, great pleasure. Not long after I had become Master, he came to me with a woe-begone expression. He was being pressed to accept one of the divinity chairs at Oxford, but he regarded the prospect of being a Canon of Christ Church with dismay. The only attraction the offer held for him was that it promised security of tenure for a longer period than that provided in his college appointment. When I assured him that the college would extend his term of office, he wrote at once to decline the Oxford chair. But, alas, no question of extension arose. In the Michaelmas Term of 1949 he was evidently a sick man and, at the end of it, quite unfit to pay his usual Christmas visit to his brother, E.V., at Hampstead. Instead, he spent Christmas quietly with us at the Lodge and then went into hospital, where he died in the following February. In ten years he had become an integral, and unique, part of Pembroke.

Two months before his death in January 1951 Bethune-Baker had written to me: 'Please may I be excused from Audit? I am fairly *compos mentis*, but not *corporis*' and signed himself: 'Yours as ever in all duty and affection.' The affection was genuine, though frequently camouflaged by sarcasm and he still loved to prick bubbles, especially if they were blown by old friends. I remember Nairne telling me that, after hearing one of Baker's sermons, he had been moved to write on a post-card: 'Ipsima* verba—Cor ad cor loquitur—Laus Deo'; to which Baker replied with a suggested translation: 'Just platitude—Mere sentimentality

* Good Ciceronian Latin, so Nairne told me.

—It might have been worse.' Similarly, when Whibley wrote to suggest that after fifty years of friendship they might begin to use Christian names, Baker replied: 'My dear Leonard. In another fifty years I suppose I shall get used to it. . .'

I was glad that Monty Butler lived through my first three years as Master. During my first year he tactfully absented himself from college meetings, but afterwards he sat regularly on my right hand and always gave me loyal support. He had passed the age-limit for service on university bodies, but public service was not only his occupation, but his hobby and he remained an active alderman of the city. Handicapped by deafness in one ear, he nevertheless controlled a meeting with great skill. The one thing he disliked was to take a straight vote on a controversial issue. 'Government by agreement' had always been his policy and he would exercise endless patience in the effort for unanimity. In 1952 he died, as he would have wished, after an illness of twelve hours.

Equally sudden, a year later, was the death of Ellis Minns. A scholar of European reputation, he had been honoured on his sixtieth birthday by an international *festschrift* and he once told me that at Christmas-time he received cards in sixteen different languages. He had occupied the same rooms in Old Court from 1893 until his death and at the end of fifty-five years scratched the following lines on one of the window-panes:

> LVSTRA VNDENA LOCO FRVCTVS FELICITER ISTO
> TE JVBEO, HIC QVI ME CVNQVE SEQVERE, FRVI*

Edward Wynn, by virtue of the college offices he had held, remained a Fellow and came over from Ely to college meetings and other functions whenever he could. He had never contemplated episcopal status; in fact, he told me once that when he was tempted to look forward, he felt that a suitable post for him to

---

* For the benefit, as Ellis might have said, of non-Carthusians, I append an English version:

> Happy, to five-and-fiftieth year
> I lived in this dear place;
> May you, who next shall follow here,
> A like enjoyment face.

hold in his later years might be the vicar-chaplaincy of St Edward's in Cambridge. But, having been made a bishop, he faced his duties with the same singleness of heart as he had for years shown in his relations with undergraduates. Throughout the diocese his fundamental, yet unobtrusive, goodness won the affection of clergy and laity alike and his death in 1956 was mourned as deeply in lonely fenland vicarages as in the parlour of Pembroke.

At the beginning of 1952 I was re-elected to the Council of the Senate in place of Paul Vellacott, Master of Peterhouse. I had known Paul for many years and greatly valued his friendship. In everything he did there was not only efficiency, but style; and it was sad that his poor health (a legacy of the First World War) made it impossible for him to take his turn as Vice-Chancellor. My successor in that office was another good friend, Sir Lionel Whitby, Master of Downing and Regius Professor of Physic. One of his early duties was to prepare for the presentation by the Chancellor of a loyal address to Queen Elizabeth II on her accession in February 1952. In addition, the Council decided to offer an expression of sympathy to the Queen Mother and invited me to compose both documents. As similar tasks had on previous occasions been entrusted to Housman, Quiller-Couch, and George Trevelyan, I felt the duty to be a peculiarly honourable one. Whitby kindly invited me to be one of the party for the presentation of the address at Buckingham Palace, where we found a large gathering of deputations from other universities. It was rather a surprise to see the unmistakable figure of Jimmy Edwards, who was in that year Rector of the University of Aberdeen. R. L. Howland, who was present as our Senior Proctor, had been his tutor at St John's and had a long talk with him. In due course we entered the audience room at the end of which the Queen stood on a dais. Our address was read by Lord Tedder, who presented us to Her Majesty, and we were followed by Prince Philip in his capacity as Chancellor of the University of Edinburgh.

From Paul Vellacott I took over the chairmanship of the Non-Collegiate Students Board and, apart from my college work, this became one of my major pre-occupations for the next seven years.

In 1948 the Council had recognised that the original purpose of non-collegiate status, namely to provide a university education for those who could not afford, or did not want, the amenities of college life, was no longer valid. As early as 1874 a house in Trumpington Street opposite the Fitzwilliam Museum had become the centre of non-collegiate life, and, thanks to the devoted work of two successive Censors (W. F. Reddaway and W. S. Thatcher) and to the enthusiasm which undergraduates caught from them, Fitzwilliam House had, in spite of cramped quarters and inadequate finance, developed all the activities and loyalties of a college. This was eventually recognised by the University in 1952, when it agreed that, if money could be found, the corporate life of Fitzwilliam House should be encouraged by the provision of a new building which should include residential accommodation.

So far, so good. But when joint committees of the Council, Fitzwilliam House and the Financial Board got to work, it was evident that there were conflicting views not only about a suitable site, but about the most desirable lines of development of Fitzwilliam House in the future. However, after much argument, the University went further and in 1954 agreed that the time had come to put an end to the non-collegiate establishment and that, if Fitzwilliam House could obtain the necessary buildings and endowment, it could look forward to full collegiate status.

But the problem of finance remained and it was clear to me that no substantial progress could be made unless and until Fitzwilliam House were given high priority in the quinquennial statement of needs to the University Grants Committee. To this end I worked in many long committee meetings and at length the Council agreed that such priority should be given. The University provided a good site in the Huntingdon Road, and just before I retired I had the satisfaction of taking part in the appointment of W. W. Grave as Censor and of serving on a committee for the choice of an architect for the new building.

Meanwhile in 1954 my wife and I had another trip to the United States. Primarily I went as vice-president of the International Association of Universities to attend a meeting of the *conseil d'administration* at Harvard; secondly, I was to represent Cambridge at the celebration of the 200th anniversary of the founding of Columbia University; lastly, I was entrusted by the Fulbright Commission with some matters to be discussed with the Board of Foreign Scholarships at Washington. But apart from these official commitments, the opportunity of visiting old friends at Yale and elsewhere was too good to miss.

We went out by sea and, as usual, were bidden to stay first at Farmington. On the day after our arrival there was an interesting ceremony at Yale. It was the year of an ecumenical conference and Yale gave honorary degrees to the Archbishop of Canterbury (Geoffrey Fisher), to the Protestant Bishop of Berlin, to a south Indian cleric, to Alan Paton and to a Greek Orthodox bishop. The Griswolds gave a dinner-party in the evening and Lefty Lewis, sitting next to the Orthodox bishop, politely inquired what was his diocese. 'America' was the rather overwhelming reply.

On another day I was glad to renew old memories with Carl Rollins, the emeritus Yale printer. Failing eyesight had compelled him to retire from active work, but he was as keen as ever on good printing and I was delighted when he suggested that we might visit Bruce Rogers in his country home. B.R. looked older, of course, but was fundamentally unchanged. He still talked eagerly about the lay-out of certain books he had in mind and also about his few surviving friends in Cambridge.

At Yale I gave the Lamont lecture on 'Cambridge in Fact and Fiction' and the Master of Calhoun College, of which I had been made an Associate Fellow, entertained us at dinner. We then had a day or two at Princeton with Harold and Margaret Dodds, who received us with great warmth, after which we went on to

Swarthmore and Haverford, where I lectured informally to under-graduates. At Haverford we had first-hand experience of an American hurricane and of its devastating effect on all electrical installations. We went to bed by candle-light and woke up to see the campus strewn with fallen tree-trunks and débris of every kind.

In the country just outside Philadelphia we had a week-end with an old friend of my wife's who fortunately was not dependent upon electricity for cooking the Sunday joint; then a few days in Washington and New York, where we dined with Harry Guggenheim and lunched with Pierson (Bob) Dixon. Bob was then British representative at the United Nations and gave us front seats at a general session. It was a long and boring debate and the longest speech was made by Vyshinski; but I was interested to hear from Bob that Vyshinski was a good classical scholar with whom he was on quite friendly terms.

After a gay week-end with the Sutherlands at Ann Arbor, where we saw the Michigan football team unexpectedly successful against Minnesota, it was time for me to join my international colleagues at Chicago. There we were entertained by the Association of American Universities of which Harold Dodds was president. We flew from Chicago to Boston and the *conseil d'administration* settled down to two or three days of committee work at Harvard, with Dean Rogers as our host.

At the end of the week we returned to New York for the Columbia festivities, of which the two most important items were an enormous dinner-party at the Waldorf-Astoria, at which Her Majesty the Queen Mother was the guest of honour and Dag Hammerskjöld the principal speaker, and the conferment by the university of forty-eight honorary degrees. As there was no hall in the university large enough to hold the expected crowd, the ceremony was held in the Anglican cathedral of St John the Divine and it was something of a shock to see New York police-men leaning against the pillars of the nave.

In the academic procession I walked with our Ambassador,

Sir Roger Makins (now Lord Sherfield), representing the University of Oxford. Among the recipients of degrees was Jean Sarrailh, president of our Association, and the culminating conferment was that upon the Queen Mother. It seemed a little hard that she should have to listen to forty-seven citations before her own; but, as always, she radiated not only amiability, but genuine enjoyment.

One of the major items in our discussions at Harvard had been the preparation for the general meeting of the International Association in 1955. We were invited by our colleague, Professor T. Saglam, to hold the meeting at Istanbul and the invitation was gratefully accepted. When the time came, my wife and I decided to travel out by sea and to fly home. As we were to embark at Genoa, we took the opportunity of spending a week in Florence and a day or two in Rapallo before we left. The three-day voyage was very enjoyable. We had a few hours at Naples, but were disappointed that we did not call at Athens. There had recently been violent anti-Greek riots in Istanbul and our Turkish captain refused to put in at the Piraeus. One of the best parts of the voyage was the approach to Istanbul and the gradual emergence of the domes and minarets as we sailed up the Dardanelles. The Golden Horn, on the other hand, was a disappointment. The name may conjure up romantic notions, but the reality seemed more like the Thames at Gravesend. For the first few days the *conseil d'administration* got down to work at Yeşilköy on the Sea of Marmora. The weather was hot and at the end of a meeting I was glad to rush out for a bathe. In Istanbul we stayed at the Hotel Hilton, a piece of America conveniently planted on a hill; it was also conveniently near the university where our discussions were held. One unexpected meeting was with R. A. Butler who, as Chancellor of the Exchequer, was attending a monetary conference. With him we were fellow-guests at dinner one evening at the British Consulate.

During the voyage, Sarrailh had pressed me to succeed him as president, but I was quite firm in my refusal. I was due to retire in two years' time and it seemed clear that the office should be held by someone still actively engaged in academic work. So at our final meeting I was very glad to propose the election of Professor Baugniet, of Brussels. One satisfactory feature of the conference was that the Soviet Government for the first time sent three observers to it. Previously we had had no response from behind the Iron Curtain, but now I hear that Moscow University is an active member of the Association.

Our most interesting excursion was to Ankara, that remarkable modernised city on which the monuments of earlier civilisations look down from the citadel above. Sarrailh and I laid an enormous wreath in the mausoleum of Kemal Ataturk and dutifully signed our names at the British Embassy.

I was pleased that my old friends Lillian Penson and Hector Hetherington were among the British representatives. Unfortunately they stayed at another hotel, and although we met at committees and receptions and dinners, we could not fully recapture the gaiety of Nice five years before.

Pembroke is one of the poorer colleges and the Tutor (Tony Camps) often, and rightly, impressed upon me the need of funds for the provision of research fellowships. During my time as Vice-Chancellor, Ernest Pooley told me that the Drapers' Company were considering whether, as a matter of policy, they ought to regard individual colleges, as well as universities, as suitable recipients of financial help. I had no hesitation in replying that in view of the Treasury grants now received by universities and of the great disparity in the incomes of colleges, such a policy would be wholly justified. Thereupon Ernest invited me to meet the Master and members of the court of the Company at lunch and to give them my views. The discussion was, of course, confined to the question of principle, but I believe that one result was a benefaction to an impecunious Oxford college. Ernest was, of course, familiar with the needs of Pembroke and some time later hinted that a statement of our particular need for the facilitation of research especially, though not exclusively, in scientific subjects might be favourably considered by the Drapers. The hint was gratefully taken and in 1956 we were able to announce the annual award of a Drapers Research Fellowship to be held for three years. It was a benefaction of great value to the college and Ernest appropriately reminded us that history was repeating itself. Just 300 years before, the Drapers had given the college £150 towards the repair of the Hall in response to an elaborately phrased appeal:

Nor have wee any other Defense or Apology for ourselves herein [wrote the Master and Fellows of 1654] but the necessity of the case on the one hand, and the knowne goodnesse and piety of this famous citty on the other...

Our position was not very different.

As time went on, I recalled the suggestion I had made to Her Majesty Queen Elizabeth in 1951 that she might one day like to visit the college of her ancestors. After some correspondence with her private secretary, from which it appeared that it might be difficult to arrange such a visit, I later had a letter stating that Her Majesty the Queen Mother had engagements in Cambridge on 29 May 1957 and would be glad to visit the college in the late afternoon. Punctually at 4.40 p.m. the royal car arrived at the front gate—the gate at which Queen Elizabeth I is said to have exclaimed: 'O domus antiqua et religiosa.' Her Majesty was not burdened by a long address of welcome in Latin which was *de rigueur* in 1564, but came straight into the Old Library, where we had arranged a display of a few manuscripts and pieces of college plate. There we showed her the admission book with the entries relating to John Lyon, ninth Earl of Strathmore and his two brothers; the order book showing the election of Thomas Lyon as a Fellow; and the silver candlesticks given to the college by the ninth earl and bearing the arms of the family and of the college. After a brief visit to the Chapel and the Hall, I led Her Majesty through Old Court and Ivy Court to the garden, presenting groups of undergraduates to her on the way, and in the garden she talked happily with some of our senior servants. Orchard Building was not yet completed, but one or two rooms were provisionally furnished and Her Majesty was keen to see them. Finally, she came to the Lodge to meet the Fellows and their wives. It was a chilly day and my wife had made a point of having a good fire in the drawing-room. But, rather to the disappointment of her lady-in-waiting, Her Majesty preferred to drink her sherry in the garden. All the Fellows—and not least the Pitt Professor from America, E. C. Kirkland—were captivated by the charm of her friendliness. The scheduled time for departure was 5.30. In fact, Her Majesty left at 6.10—a gratifying conclusion to a memorable visit. 'Oh, I'm thrilled', said Her Majesty at one point—but the thrill was not hers alone.

As I reached the age of seventy in April 1957, I was due to retire on 1 August of that year, but the College invited me to remain for an additional year, during which I had the satisfaction of seeing Orchard Building in full use. Its first occupants were, in fact, members of the Headmasters' Conference which met in Pembroke in September and, as far as I remember, there were no complaints.

Just before my retirement the Goldsmiths' Company inquired of the University and the colleges whether they would collaborate in the making of an exhibition of the 'Treasures of Cambridge'. At a meeting of college representatives arranged by Harry Willink at Magdalene Lodge I was asked to be chairman of a committee to act in conjunction with a similar committee of the Goldsmiths, but most of the hard work was done by the University Librarian, the Director of the Fitzwilliam Museum and the bursars of colleges. Naturally, select examples of college plate were prominent, but the exhibition covered a much wider range, which included manuscripts, books, portraits, paintings, sculpture, scientific instruments and much else.

In March 1959 the Goldsmiths gave us a magnificent dinner preceding the private view and a little later I was asked to give a lecture, not of a technical kind but designed to relate the exhibits to the history of Cambridge. I was honoured by this invitation and even more by the proposal of the Goldsmiths to make me an honorary liveryman of the Company.

By this time I had ceased to be Master, but by college statute I had 'all the rights and privileges of a fellow'. I had never been very happy about this statute, since the 'rights' included that of participation in college meetings. Although my predecessor, as I have already remarked, always treated me with the utmost tact and loyalty, I felt that it was wrong in principle that a retired Master should have any share in the making of college policy. Eventually the college agreed, though with some hesitation, to add to the existing statute: 'save that he shall take no part in college government'. Thus I am now happy in the enjoyment of college amenities without any corresponding responsibilities.

Throughout my ten happy and eventful years at the Lodge I had had the consistently loyal support of the Fellows. I relied especially on the help of the President, the Tutor, the Bursar and the Dean, and none of them failed me. Of course we had our disagreements, but they were never such as to cause a breach of fundamental unity and I was confident that such unity would be preserved under my old friend and distinguished successor, Professor (now Sir) William Hodge. Shortly after his pre-election, someone came up to me at the Athenæum and expressed mild regret that my successor did not represent the humanities. 'Well, if it's any consolation to you,' I said, 'I can assure you that his mathematics are very pure.' Had I not, years before, handled with awe the proofs of his *Hypergeometric Functions*?

In July 1958 I took the chair at the annual London dinner of the Pembroke College Society. The toast of the college was proposed by Rab Butler, who came straight to the dinner from an urgent Cabinet meeting, and I was deeply moved by the ovation which the large company gave me.

Chapter 16

MORE JOHNSONIANA

As time went on, the annual meetings at Lichfield attracted a number of Johnsonians from the United States and I think it was at Lichfield that I first met James L. Clifford. We had much in common and, in particular, we were both prepared to make a reasoned defence of Mrs Thrale (Piozzi). Clifford was then engaged in writing what is undoubtedly the best book on that controversial lady, and when it was published in 1941, I welcomed the opportunity of commending it in the *Observer*. Later, I found that he shared my interest in Dr Campbell's *Diary of a Visit to England in 1775*. With some difficulty I had secured a copy of the original edition published in Sydney in 1854 and had a mind to re-edit it, but the text had evidently been bowdlerised and the chances of finding the MS. seemed remote. Clifford, however, was not to be daunted. He persisted in his inquiries and eventually the MS. was discovered in the public library at Sydney. Naturally, I told Clifford that it was for him to produce a new edition, but he insisted that I should write some kind of introduction. I agreed reluctantly and sought for something to say that was worth saying. The first edition of Campbell's *Diary* (a small book of 170 pages) provoked a review of quite disproportionate length in the *Edinburgh Review*, so I thought it worthwhile to have a look at the manuscript of Macaulay's diary in Trinity College. There I found that Macaulay had shown a keen interest in Campbell's little book and that his last communication to the *Edinburgh* had related to it. It was this brief examination of Macaulay's diary that made me feel that it ought to be published in its entirety.

It was at Lichfield, too, that I first met Donald and Mary Hyde, whose library is now well known as the finest collection of Johnsoniana in the world. We met them from time to time both here and in America, but it was not until 1961 that I had an opportunity of enjoying their hospitality at Somerville, N. J. In September of that year I flew to Boston and Lefty Lewis gave me a lovely week, first in Newport, R.I., and then in Farmington; In Long Island I stayed with Harry Guggenheim, who admitted to me the mysteries both of his museum of modern art and of horse-racing at Belmont Park; in New York I was the guest of 'The Johnsonians' at their annual dinner; at Princeton I spent a night with Charles Ryskamp, in whom one year at Pembroke had generated a deep devotion to the college; lastly, I had a most happy week-end with the Hydes, of which the recollection is now saddened by Donald's lamented death in the spring of 1966.

The Lichfield suppers were revived after the war, but, alas, the Charnwoods had moved from Stowe House to a flat in Chelsea. I was, however, consoled by the fact that Edward Woods had become Bishop of Lichfield and more than once my wife and I stayed with him for the Johnson celebration. We had known him well when he was Vicar of Holy Trinity at Cambridge and it was good to talk with him again. After his death in 1952 I was again fortunate. I had known the new Bishop (A. S. Reeve, a Brightonian) since his undergraduate days at Selwyn and the present Dean (W. S. Macpherson) is a member of my own college. Thus have I been able to keep my Lichfield friendships in constant repair.

Johnson's house in Gough Square suffered badly in the blitz— 'What would be the security of the good, if the bad could at pleasure invade them from the sky?' But, guarded by the devoted and intrepid Mrs Rowell, it stood up to its battering and with the aid of War Damage Insurance and the Pilgrim Trust was successfully restored.

After its restoration the Johnson Club, which had met for an occasional wartime lunch at Brown's Hotel, reassembled in Gough Square and celebrated two notable Oxford achievements —the completion of Powell's recension of Birkbeck Hill's edition of the *Life* (1950) and Chapman's edition of Johnson's *Letters* (1952). It was to a hint from Chapman that I was indebted for the publication of a Johnsonian item at Cambridge. For many years the Press had acted as agents in Great Britain for the University of California Press and Chapman called my attention to three essays by B. H. Bronson in a journal published by that Press. I was deeply impressed by them, especially by *Johnson Agonistes*, and they were issued in book form in 1946. It was a rare thing to invite an author to make a book out of essays already published (though authors often made such proposals themselves) and when some years later I met Bronson, I was glad to be able to tell him that the book had been a success from every point of view.

My own contributions to Johnsonian literature have all been slight. I have no achievements to my credit comparable with the scholarly work of Chapman, Powell and others; but I find that when a publisher wants something readably concise, he is inclined to turn to me. Thus in 1935 I wrote the volume on Johnson in Duckworth's series of 'Great Lives'. It was, I think, a useful little book, but the bulk of the stock was destroyed in the blitz and it has never been reprinted. More fortunate was the forty-page pamphlet I wrote for the British Council's series of 'Writers and their Work', which, to my surprise, has appeared in a Japanese translation.

I have never been a prominent broadcaster, but I gave my first talk on Johnson in the days of Savoy Hill, when a card was placed alongside the microphone with the terrifying warning: 'If you cough, you will make a million people deaf.' In 1934 I was asked by the B.B.C. to give two imaginary dialogues between Boswell and Johnson, such as might have been provoked by a return visit to London in that year. I had attended at Broadcasting House for a rehearsal, but as I went along in the tube to Oxford Circus on the night of the delivery of the second dialogue, it struck me that a recitation in even tones was rather dull and unrealistic and I decided to give Boswell a Scotch accent. When my compère (Freddy Grisewood, I think) came back into the room, he said: 'Yes, that came over very well; but one of the engineers put the wind up me by rushing up and saying "There's something wrong—there's another voice cutting in!"'

At least I had given Boswell some individuality.

The famous Boswell finds at Malahide and Fettercairn made one feel that such wonders would never cease and a minor instance of this occurred in 1953, when my old friend Frank Edwards, who had retired to Somerset, wrote to me that he had met an old lady who wanted to dispose of sixty unpublished Boswell letters and that he had advised her to write to me. The letters duly arrived and, on the whole, were unexciting, being addressed to Robert Boswell, W.S., who acted as his cousin's solicitor. Nevertheless, they were clearly suitable to be added to the Yale Boswelliana and by a lucky chance F. W. (Ted) Hilles happened to call on me shortly after their arrival. He said at once that Yale would like to have them and I endeavoured to play the part of the honest broker. Both parties were satisfied with the proposed purchase price and I had a charming letter from the owner, who said that she would like me to keep one letter as a token of her gratitude. I did not hesitate in choosing a letter from Eton dated 30 July 1792 in which Boswell writes: 'I am here at the delivery of my son Alexander from school...The Provost and Fellows are wonderfully good to me...there is a deal of feasting in which I share; for they are pleased to hold me as an Etonian by adoption.' I arranged, of course, for Yale to have a photostat of the letter and some time afterwards remembered that many years before I had bought for a very small sum at David's stall a *Gradus ad Parnassum* with the signature 'Alexr. Boswell, 1792' on the fly-leaf. The letter and the book are pleasantly complementary.

My latest short life of Johnson was written for the *Encyclopaedia Britannica*. The old article by Macaulay had stood, with a few deletions and corrections, for more than a hundred years and I felt some trepidation in assuming so august a mantle. However, when I told George Trevelyan of my commission, he did not seem to be unduly disturbed.

I have given talks on Johnson in many countries and perhaps the most formidable commitment was to lecture at the Sorbonne in November 1951. My French was described in the *Annales de l'Université de Paris* as 'le plus pur et le plus savoureux'—a tribute which may have been deserved, but not by me, since Tom Combe, director of French studies at Pembroke, generously volunteered to translate my English draft.

Such recollections are trivial enough in themselves, but I have gained great pleasure in stirring the foreigner's interest in Johnson—so English, so famous for his talk, so little known for his writings.

Chapter 17

SHERLOCK HOLMES

On my father's bookshelves were the first six volumes of *The Strand Magazine* and through them, like thousands of others of my generation, I was introduced to Sherlock Holmes. I read them and enjoyed them and, thanks to Sidney Paget, the pictorial image of that lean, frock-coated figure with the deep-set eyes remained firmly in my consciousness. But I made no special study of the *Adventures* or the *Memoirs* and when I unexpectedly met their author, I did not think of him in terms of Baker Street.

In the spring of 1911 Conan Doyle came to Worthing to stay with an aunt who was a friend of my mother's. He wanted a game of golf and I played a round with him on the Cissbury course. I contrived to halve some of the shorter holes, but he hit a long ball and beat me easily. I had just come back from the Black Forest and we talked a good deal about ski-ing and winter sports. I don't think Sherlock Holmes was mentioned.

It was not until 1928 that I was led into the mock-solemnity of Holmesian scholarship. In that year the editor of the *Cambridge Review* invited me to review the omnibus edition of the short stories of Sherlock Holmes together with R. A. Knox's *Essays in Satire*. I had often heard about the brilliant paper on 'The Literature of Sherlock Holmes' which Knox had read to college societies and was delighted to find it included in the book. This essay was indeed germinal, though it should not be forgotten that as early as 1902 Frank Sidgwick had explored the chronological problems raised in *The Hound of the Baskervilles*.* As I read Knox's essay and re-read some of the stories, it occurred to me that I might well carry on his own style of scholastic criticism. To his gallery of savants (Sauwosch, Backnecke, Piff-Pouf, etc.)

* *Cambridge Review*, 23 January 1902.

I added one or two of my own (Keibosch, Pauvremütte) and expressed some doubts about the reliability of Knox's textual scholarship. Finally, I urged that serious students should devote their energies to the elucidation of *das Watsonischechronologie-problem*.

One or two friends who read the review asked for offprints and I had a hundred copies printed for private distribution at Christmas. (It is now referred to as an *incunabulum*.) Meanwhile, I had felt drawn to a more methodical attempt to disentangle the sequence of events in Watson's career and the result was an essay on his early life which Desmond MacCarthy printed in *Life and Letters*. This attracted some attention and was included in a volume of *Essays of the Year*. Having begun the task, I felt that I must go on to an account of Watson's later life, but I hesitated to offer Desmond MacCarthy a sequel. At that time I saw a good deal of Frank Morley, who was then with Fabers, and it was he who seized upon the two essays as making just the right length for *The Criterion Miscellany*, a series of shilling pamphlets then in course of publication. So, in February 1931 *Doctor Watson : prolegomena to the study of a biographical problem* (dedicated to a fellow-enthusiast, V. C. Pennell) was published. Its reception astonished me. It provoked not only lengthy reviews, but leading articles, and I think that the establishment of Watson's second marriage was regarded as a major contribution; but I should add that my conjecture of the identity of the second Mrs Watson was not well received. The pamphlet certainly gave an impetus to further investigation and other students got to work on a much more elaborate scale. In 1932 T. S. Blakeney's *Sherlock Holmes: Fact or Fiction* was published and in the same year H. W. Bell in his *SherlockHolmes and Dr Watson* examined in detail, and eventually discarded, my chronological conclusions. Looking back, I am amazed at the number of columns which editors allotted to reviews of these two books.

When I was in New York in 1933, Bruce Rogers took me to a meeting of the Grolier Club at which a paper was to be read on the literature of crime. I was not keenly interested, as the paper dealt with actual rather than fictional crime, but there was a passing reference to Sherlock Holmes, and when I was introduced to the reader of the paper, I mentioned my interest in the reference.

'What did you say your name was?'

'Roberts.'

'Not S.C.?'

'Yes.'

'Henry, George,' he shouted above the din of the party to two of his friends, 'our favourite author!'

H. W. Bell, in spite of his disagreement with my dating, asked me to contribute an essay to his projected *Baker Street Studies* (1934). I wrote a short study of Holmes's relations with women and Dorothy Sayers contributed an elaborate thesis to show that Holmes was a Cambridge man. This I have always, and with regret, regarded as untenable and in a later essay elaborated my objections.*

It was, I suppose, inevitable that all this activity should lead to the foundation of societies and in the United States the cult was intensively developed. Not only were the Baker Street Irregulars established under the enthusiastic guidance of Christopher Morley, Edgar W. Smith and others in New York, but 'scion' societies sprang up in many cities—the Speckled Band of Boston, the Creeping Men of Cleveland, the Six Napoleons of Baltimore, the Dancing Men of Providence, R.I....At home we were more modest. In 1934 A. G. MacDonell invited a number of enthusiasts to a sherry party and those present declared themselves to be the Sherlock Holmes Society. No one seemed very clear about the objects or activities of the Society, except that we should hold an annual dinner on, or near, the date of Derby Day. The only reason for this appeared to be a desire to commemorate Watson's racing propensities. When we went on to discuss the venue of the dinner, I said firmly that we must dine

* See my *Holmes and Watson*, pp. 10–12.

in Baker Street. 'Oh, you can't dine in Baker Street', said someone. 'Nonsense,' I retorted, 'there's a perfectly good restaurant
in Baker Street.' So we dined at Canuto's and I believe that
H. W. Bell drove there in a hansom. It was a hilarious party.
Dick Sheppard was in the chair and Dorothy Sayers sat next to
him. I found myself next to Gerald Kelly, whom I had not met
before. We were quickly at ease and in the course of dinner summoned the manager and asked him to bring in, at some convenient
point, a large covered dish containing a roll of paper tied with
red tape and to set the dish, with some solemnity, before the
chairman. The chairman was quick to take the point and the final
scene of the Naval Treaty was faithfully re-enacted.

There were no set speeches, but some highly entertaining
impromptus. At one point Dorothy Sayers put an interesting
problem to the chairman: Was the marriage ceremony recorded
in *The Scandal in Bohemia* a valid one? Dick Sheppard replied
without a moment's hesitation. After giving long and anxious
thought to the question, he said, he had come to the conclusion,
first, that the marriage was valid and, secondly, that the couple
were subsequently living in sin. Kelly talked about Holmes's
artistic tastes and there were many other contributions.

The whole affair was so successfully spontaneous that I doubted
whether the success could be repeated. At the time of the second
dinner a year later I was suffering from an outbreak of boils and
sent a telegram to the dinner-secretary: 'In bed with a carbuncle
—not the blue one.' There was a third dinner, which I could not
attend, but shortly afterwards members received a laconic post-
card: 'The Sherlock Holmes Society, like the Red-Headed
League, is dissolved.' However, the movement as a whole was
gathering momentum, especially in the United States. In England,
there was plenty of literary activity and when plans were announced for the Festival of Britain in 1951, a proposal was made
to the Marylebone authorities that something should be done to
commemorate Sherlock Holmes's residence in Baker Street. At
first the suggestion was regarded as frivolous, but the Borough

Council had second thoughts and the exhibition staged at 221 B Baker Street was, in fact, one of the most successful features of the Festival. The principal room contained a varied collection of manuscripts, first editions, translations, drawings by Sidney Paget, portraits of the Vernets, together with scientific items such as *Cyanea Capillata* (the Lion's Mane) and a mounted skin of the giant rat of Sumatra. Among the 'miscellaneous' exhibits was the bicycle used by Miss Violet Smith in the adventure of The Solitary Cyclist. All this made an appeal to the serious student, but the most popular part of the exhibition was the skilful reproduction of the living-room of no. 221 B as it appeared about 1898, the period of the Return of Sherlock Holmes. There one could see the Persian slipper with tobacco tucked in the toe; the chemical corner with its retorts and test-tubes; the bust of Holmes modelled by Oscar Meunier; the scrap-books and the pipe-rack; and, hanging on the door, Watson's top-hat and stethoscope. To the admirable catalogue of the exhibition there was a sympathetic introduction written by Bernard Darwin.

All this publicity prompted the enthusiasts to establish a new Sherlock Holmes Society. I was asked to be president and have remained so ever since. One of the most active promoters was the late Ivar Gunn, a scholarly enthusiast with a fine collection of Holmesiana. Like me, he was one of the survivors of the old society and his sudden death was a grievous blow. The new society was not without its critics. In July 1951, for instance, I received a letter which began:

I see in yesterday's 'Times' that you are president of a 'Sherlock Holmes Society'!!!
I could hardly believe the evidence of my eyes when I read about it. Sherlock Holmes and Watson were two fictious [*sic*] characters invented by Conan Doyle. All there is about these two invented people is what Conan Doyle wrote. There is nothing more to it and very little at that!...

The writer signed himself as 'Colonel, Late Indian Army (Retired)'.

Meanwhile Geoffrey Cumberlege had asked me to make a selection of the Adventures for the *World's Classics* and in an introductory essay I tried to do justice to Conan Doyle and Sidney Paget as well as to the work of later commentators. Every student of the Holmes saga is tempted to reconstruct some of the unrecorded adventures casually mentioned in Watson's narrative, and in one essay I gave a hint of the circumstances of the death of Cardinal Tosca. The loss of a number of circulating library books at the Athenæum also prompted me to record the 'Strange Case of the Megatherium Thefts' and in 1953 I assembled my various pieces in a little book entitled *Holmes and Watson: a Miscellany*. In the preface I recorded my initial debt to R. A. Knox's famous essay and I was rather sad to note in Evelyn Waugh's biography that Knox was entirely out of sympathy with the later cult. For him the Sherlock Holmes stories were simply a peg on which to hang his satire on the biblical criticism of German scholars; he used Boswell's *Life of Johnson* for the same purpose.

For myself, I never cease to marvel at the vitality of the Holmesian cult. Membership of the Society grows steadily; the *Journal*, which began in all humility as a duplicated typescript, is now, thanks to the energy and devotion of Lord Donegall, well printed and illustrated; if I am asked to read a paper to a society in Cambridge or elsewhere, the hope is frequently expressed, though not always fulfilled, that I will talk about Sherlock Holmes.

It has often been remarked that the cult is peculiarly English. 'Does anything puzzle a foreigner more', asked one reviewer, 'than the enthusiasm with which our learned men...investigate the character and career of two purely imaginary persons?... Would any other race carry on so persistent and almost passionate an enquiry into Holmes' knowledge of music, or Dr Watson's second marriage?'

The answer is simple. There are 'Baker Street Irregulars' not only in New York, but also in Copenhagen and the Danish enthusiasts have indeed produced some of the most attractive brochures on Holmesian problems; when I was asked to lecture to a society in Brussels, it was insisted that the subject should be Sherlock Holmes and the same was true of an invitation from the Royal Dublin Society; in the correspondence columns of a recent number of the *Journal* there are letters from Frankfurt, Amsterdam and Nebraska; in the review pages are books published in Paris, Uppsala, Hamburg and San Francisco.

I see, as yet, no sign of the liquidation of the empire of Sherlock Holmes.

Chapter 18

MAX

I think that I had appreciated Max Beerbohm's quality as an essayist while I was an undergraduate, but it was not until after the First World War that I acquired a copy of *Zuleika Dobson* (1911)—not a 'fine' but quite a decent copy in the original (rough) brown cloth. One sentence on the last page of the book haunted me: 'Order me a special train....'

If Zuleika issued an order for a train to Cambridge, it was impossible to conceive that it was not carried out. What, then, happened at the end of the journey? If Max himself didn't know, why had no one undertaken the appropriate research? To accept E. M. Forster's suggestion that the special train either failed to start or got no further than a siding at Bletchley was to shirk the problem.*

So, at intervals, I thought about the possibilities, but unfruitfully. Then, in 1941, when my wife and I contrived to get away to Shropshire for a week, I tried again, and in the stuffy drawing-room of the hotel I drafted what seemed to me the probable history of Zuleika in Cambridge. I had it typed when I got home and it was obvious that, quite apart from questions of copyright, I must have Max's goodwill before I could contemplate printing.

I had never met Max, but I knew Charles Evans, then managing director of Heinemann's, and told him about *Zuleika in Cambridge*. 'Oh, we couldn't sell a short story of that length', he said. I assured him that I wasn't asking him to publish the story; what I wanted was an introduction to Max. So he gave me Max's address at Abinger and I wrote a carefully polite letter, enclosing the typescript and simply asking leave to print.

Weeks went by and no answer came. I knew that letter-writing was not one of Max's favourite hobbies, but in 1941 one never

* *Aspects of the Novel*, pp. 155–6.

knew what might happen to a packet in the post. One morning R. C. Trevelyan came to see me at the Press about the publication of some of his translations. He told me that Max was living quite near him and promised to jog his memory. Whether it was *propter hoc* or merely *post hoc* I do not know, but shortly afterwards I was thrilled by the arrival of the following letter:

Here is the enchanting sequel; and please forgive me for not sending it sooner: I had kept it to shew to a friend who would, I knew, particularly delight in it.

I daresay Charles Evans was right in thinking it wouldn't 'appeal to many people'. The book itself has never been, and never would have been, *popular*. And if it had been so it would probably not have the pleasure of surviving, as it modestly does, to this day: its appeal has always been to a few people; and it is only the good opinion of the few that keeps a book alive. (Various exceptions of course occur to me. They always do to anybody who has just made a generalisation!) I greatly hope your work will be published elsewhere.

I had often wondered what happened when Zuleika went on to Cambridge. And now I *know*, beyond any shadow of a doubt. Your work has just that 'inevitable' quality which one admires so much in that of the Greek dramatists.

'Slowly the special train passed through the cavalier country and approached the puritan plains of East Anglia.' The moment I read that on page 2, I knew that you were going to convince me, and that all was well. Please accept my grateful congratulations on the various ingenuities of your invention, and also on the perfect solidity [of] your construction. Very often a jeu d'esprit flags in the middle and crumbles all away at the end. Yours is good *all through*. You evidently hadn't begun it without having organised it thoroughly in your mind. And that is the one and only right way to write, isn't it?

One of my favourite parts is the meeting of the Syndicate. And this though it is painful reading: it seems to sum up all the committee meetings that ever were held.

On page 30 I have ventured to query the epithet *little*. Somewhere in my book I did speak of Zuleika's 'little face'. But Zuleika herself wasn't little, believe me. She was tall, as I said in some other part of the book. Ah, do not stunt her!*

* 'Little' was a typist's error; I had written 'lithe'.

See also page 6. I think you are wrong in believing that Zuleika ordered a liqueur after her luncheon. Young ladies in the Edvardian era never ordered liqueurs for themselves (though I am told that young ladies between the two wars did little else).

On page 20 I have pencilled the suggestion of a change in idiom. Everywhere else you have caught Z's idiom—and mine—exactly.

Forgive me for writing so tedious a letter. Thank you again for the continuous ripples of laughter, interrupted only by waves of it, that I have uttered in three separate readings of your work.

After this I went ahead with the printing with a light heart and arranged for publication by Heffer. The sales were modest and the reviews, naturally, very slight. Q wrote a cheerful paragraph in the *Cambridge Review* and I detected the hand of Harold Child in the sympathetic notice which appeared in *The Times Literary Supplement*. But my greatest satisfaction was in Max's own benediction.

In August 1942 Max reached the age of seventy and I was invited to join the 'Maximilians' in an entertainment given in his honour at the Players' Theatre. There I met him for a moment, but had no opportunity of talking to him. However, I enjoyed the short speech he made in the guise of Gaffer Beerbohm, who would go back and tell the village all about the party.

In the following year the Vice-Chancellor (J. A. Venn, President of Queens') invited Max to deliver the Rede Lecture at Cambridge. Previously, Max had, I believe, declined to give the Clark lectures at Trinity since their preparation would be too heavy a task; but a single lecture he was prepared to face and he chose Lytton Strachey as his subject. He took immense pains not only with the composition of the lecture but with its delivery, rehearsing it in the morning with his wife as the solitary auditor at the back of the Senate House. He greatly admired Strachey, but it was not an uncritical admiration, as his comments on *Dr Arnold* and *Elizabeth and Essex* revealed. Discussion of Strachey's style led to some characteristic reflections on 'the virtue of form in literature' and on the tricks of journalism:

Max

In journalism, I have often been told, the first sentence is the thing that matters most. Grip the reader's attention, and all will be well. I am not sure that this is so. Not long before the outbreak of war, when paper was very plentiful, I saw in an evening paper a signed article about Karl Marx. The first sentence was as follows: 'Deep down in a grave at Highgate the corpse of Karl Marx lies rotting'. So far, so good...

The whole lecture was beautifully spoken and applauded with sincerity. In the evening my wife and I were invited to meet Max at dinner at the Vice-Chancellor's and on the following morning I collected the MS. of the lecture for our compositors, who subsequently earned Max's praise for their accuracy. When the lecture was published, we sold 10,000 copies fairly quickly. 'I feel', wrote Max in November, 'that I am becoming quite a popular author.' He was still in England for his seventy-fifth birthday in 1947 and, having been reminded of the date by Alan Dent, the enthusiastic promoter of the Maximilians, I offered him a little imitation of Dr Johnson beginning:

> Undetected, five-and-seventy
> Hurrying years at length are flown...*

When, in the same year, I read the announcement of a new edition of *Zuleika Dobson* which was to include a portrait of Zuleika as frontispiece, I wrote to Max, frankly begging for a copy with the portrait signed by the artist. A copy arrived with unusual promptitude. 'Here is your young friend', Max replied in a letter written in pencil on the title-page; and to Zuleika's name below the portrait he had added: 'at Oxford, insouciante, not yet humiliated elsewhere'. In 1949, just before I assumed the duties of Vice-Chancellor, my wife and I had a fortnight's holiday at Portofino. On the morning after our arrival, Max rang me up from Rapallo and asked us to lunch. 'I believe', he said, 'that there is some kind of motor-omnibus by which you could come.' Along the coast road the bus is, of course, the standard form of public transport, but I don't suppose that Max had ever used it.

* See *The Incomparable Max* (1962), p. xvii.

At the Villino we had a delightful welcome from Lady Beerbohm (Florence). Frail-looking and dressed with Edvardian elegance, she was easy and gay in conversation. The only other guest was Elisabeth Jungmann, who was staying in the house. After lunch we went up to the terrace and Max showed me his study ('Max's pre-fab' Florence called it), with its plain bookshelves round the blue walls. 'Rather a snob library, I'm afraid,' he said 'mostly inscribed copies given to me by their authors.' But the most interesting inscriptions were Max's own fakes and extra-illustrations which have often been described and have now become famous in the sale-rooms. I remember a copy of *A Shropshire Lad*, with its title-page 'improved' by a sketch of a gloomy, squat figure with a ruddy complexion and a bowler hat. With it were some lines ending:

> And shrink not, lad, nor shiver
> But walk you down to the river
> And take your final dip

This was my first meeting with Max in a domestic milieu. Before we left Portofino we were again invited to the Villino and Max and I found plenty to talk about. I asked for nothing better than to listen to his reminiscences—of Henry James, for instance, asserting his claim to be 'very distinguished'; of Clement Shorter hoping to be elected to the Athenaeum; of John Davidson singing Scottish metrical psalms in the Café Royal.

Some time after Florence's death in 1951, Elisabeth, now the devoted chatelaine of the Villino, called on us in Cambridge and assured us that Max would like to see us again. In August 1952 he would reach the age of eighty and Elisabeth welcomed the suggestion that we might visit Rapallo at that time. There was a plan for a volume of birthday tributes. The organiser was Mrs Selwyn (Tania) Jepson, who wrote to me and asked for a contribution. I sent her a short piece in the form of an extra chapter for *A Christmas Garland*, entitled 'Peace and good will' (by Mxx Bxxrbxhm).

Max

We arrived at our Rapallo pensione on 21 August. Max and Elisabeth had, as usual, fled from the summer heat to the inn at Montallegro and on the 24th, the birthday, we set out for the inn by the shortest route—the funîvia. The suspensory motion was too much for my wife and she arrived in rather poor condition. Max was deeply distressed, but, after suitable ministrations by Elisabeth, Marjorie recovered. The other guests were Tania Jepson and Jenny Nicholson, at that time *Spectator* correspondent in Rome. Outside the inn Max and I sat in the lovely sunshine and looked through the book of tributes. Reading a few bits of my own contribution, he chuckled happily and once murmured 'How like me!' Of course there were many other offerings—a large batch of telegrams, including one from Sir Winston Churchill, a Penguin edition of *Zuleika Dobson* and, not to be outdone, the innkeeper's little boy entered, when we were seated for lunch, with a huge and incongruous sheaf of gladioli, fashionably enswathed in cellophane. I was pressed to say a few words of congratulation and Max's health was appropriately drunk in champagne. Max made no formal reply, but I think he savoured the modest gaiety of the party.

In my Sherlock Holmes research Max took a genuine and affectionate interest.

I immensely enjoyed [he wrote] the wit—*and* the erudition of your latest incursion into Sherlockology and Watsonography; and am greatly pleased at figuring in an important footnote. Also I enjoyed reading all the eleven stories—and finding myself back again in dear old Baker Street with that cosy couple. It had been in my first year at Oxford that I began to 'follow that cab'.

I find myself confirmed in a theory of mine that Holmes, when he was not concentrating his intellect on some actual case or other and threw out reflections on things in general, was apt to be—dare I say?—naive...

It was all of a piece with what he had written in 1905: 'He [Sherlock Holmes] became a part of my life, and will never, I suppose, be utterly dislodged.'

In the spring of 1953 I attended a meeting of the International Association of Universities at Genoa and contrived one day to go over to Rapallo for lunch with Max. He was convalescent after a bad cold, but still fairly cheerful. Later in the year there appeared *Sir Max Beerbohm, Man and Writer : A Critical Analysis with a Brief Life and a Bibliography*, by J. G. Riewald. It was a remarkable work, as I found when the *Review of English Studies* sent it to me for review. In a prefatory letter to the author Max had written: 'I marvel at your multiscience. You know very much more about my writings than I could ever have remembered' and under the heading of 'Syntactical Peculiarities' (Euphuism, Hyperbole, Syllepsis, Enjambement, Anastrophe...) poor Max was analysed to make a grammarian's holiday. The bibliography, on the other hand, was a splendid piece of work and the complete list of dramatic criticisms was especially welcome.

I saw Max for the last time in September 1955. In April he had written that he was looking forward to seeing us in the autumn and, referring to our American trip in 1954: 'I wish we could offer you some such widely diverse and exciting—and anastrophic and sylleptic and enjambemental—a time as you had in America.' During our few days at Rapallo, Max looked very frail, but he still took a lively interest in people, in places and in books and, as I have already recorded, his eye was still keen enough to pounce upon an error in a proof.

A month before he died, he married Elisabeth, of whom we later saw a good deal. Her interest, her whole life were concentrated on the preservation of Max's memory and we had long talks both at Cambridge and at the Villino. What she loved most was to be in touch with Max's friends and one day in the summer of 1957 we had a small lunch party at the Lodge which included Sam Behrman and Siegfried Sassoon. Some time before, I had been invited by the Royal Society of Literature to give the Giff Edmonds Memorial Lecture and I chose Max as my subject. Elisabeth did not hear the lecture, but warmly approved of my script. Then came her tragic death and the long discussions between her sister (Mrs Eva Reichmann), Sir John Rothenstein and others which resulted in the designation of a room in Merton College as a permanent memorial. When the furnishing of the room with drawings, portraits, manuscripts and books had been completed, the Warden and Fellows invited a number of guests to lunch in the college hall and I was asked to say something about Max before the formal opening. It was a very Oxonian gathering and I felt a slight embarrassment in being selected as spokesman.

Here [I said] at the very heart of collegiate antiquity; here, amidst your moonlit meadows and your dreaming spires; here, ladies and gentlemen, you are driven to the impossible disloyalty of listening to a Cambridge voice.

In recalling that Andrew Lang, my earliest literary hero, had been a Fellow of Merton, I had to admit that Max's 'two glimpses' of Lang had not given him pleasure, but at least they were united in love of the college.

Later, at Heinemann's request, I wrote an introduction to *The Incomparable Max*, a book of selected essays and, finally, I gave a brief address at the unveiling and dedication of the memorial plaque in the crypt of St Paul's Cathedral.

I knew Max only for the last twelve years of his life; but depth and quality of friendship are not to be measured by the calendar. Somehow, in 1941, I had caught the mood of the author of *Zuleika Dobson*. Never has a *jeu d'esprit* brought me so rich a reward.

Chapter 19

FILMS AND LIBRARIES

When in 1945 I received a letter of thanks from Hugh Dalton for my service as Regional Representative, I thought my association with the Board of Trade had definitely come to an end. But I suppose my name was preserved on a list of potential volunteers and early in 1948 I was asked to serve on a committee under the chairmanship of Sir George Gater to examine the alleged need for more studio space for independent producers of films. It was a small affair, but it led to my first acquaintance with Mr J. Arthur (now Lord) Rank. One remark of his stays in my mind. His primary desire as a film-maker, he said, was that when people left the cinema, they should be happy. 'Not thoughtful?' I queried. 'No, happy', he repeated. Today one might wish that more producers took such a view.

Not long afterwards I was invited to join a more important body, again with Sir George Gater in the chair. It was not a committee, but a working-party and so had no precise terms of reference, but the President of the Board of Trade (Harold Wilson) told the House of Commons that we would 'examine ways and means of reducing production costs'.

We first met in February 1949 and after a long and un-productive talk the three independent members (the chairman, Mr Coutts Donald and myself) were made a sub-committee to visit studios and obtain some first-hand impressions of the work-ing of the industry. This was a really interesting experience; we visited seven studios, including Pinewood, Shepperton, Elstree and Merton Park; saw some actual 'shooting', followed by 'rushes' in the studio theatre; had frank talks with shop-stewards as well as with producers and directors. We heard a lot about 'demarcation' (to move a pot with flowers growing in it was the gardener's job; if the flowers were artificial, it was the business of 'props'); about the high salaries of stars and the 'perfectionism' of the chief camera-man. Our final recommendations urged that screen time should average not less than two minutes per camera day; that extravagant 're-takes' should be discouraged; that shooting should not begin until script, shooting schedule and budget had been approved, together with other utopian suggestions for economy. Whether the Report had any practical effect remains doubtful and by the time of its publication I had become Vice-Chancellor. In that capacity, however, and at the request of Denis Forman, a Pembroke man who was Director of the British Film Institute, I entertained a number of prominent people in the film world, including M. Réné Clair, and in 1952 was pressed by Denis to become chairman of his Institute. The formal invitation came not from the Board of Trade, but from the Lord President of the Council, Lord Woolton, who asked me to call upon him. His avuncular charm led me to accept, and in later years I came to know him well at meetings of the governing body of Brighton College. At the time I knew little or nothing about the Film Institute and was advised to have a talk with Cecil King, the retiring chairman. So I had lunch with him in the old office of the *Daily Mirror* in Fetter Lane, and he explained that he had been brought into the Institute simply to put its finances in better order and that the time was now ripe for someone who knew more about films than he did. I disclaimed any such superior knowledge, but, films apart, I was keenly interested to meet Cecil King. The atmosphere of his room with its solid book-cases and its solid books on the shelves suggested an editor of the *Quarterly Review* rather than of the *Daily Mirror*.

The British Film Institute, which derives its income partly from members' subscriptions and partly from a Treasury grant, serves in relation to the art of the film the same kind of purpose as the Arts Council. It is the British Museum of cinematography and preserves vast stores of celluloid dating from the beginning of the century; it lets films on hire to film societies all over the country; at the National Film Theatre it arranges programmes of old films, foreign films and experimental films which cannot be seen in the commercial cinema.

As in all such bodies, the governors were concerned less with the art of the film than with the urgency of an increase in the Treasury grant. In my time negotiations were conducted not with the Treasury direct, but through the Lord President of the Council. Lord Salisbury, who had succeeded Lord Woolton in that office, was always helpful and occasionally I was able to make a personal approach to R. A. Butler as Chancellor of the Exchequer.

When Denis Forman left us to join Granada Television, the appointment of a successor was, naturally, a matter of the first importance. Among the applicants were a few well-known figures in the film world; but eventually, and to my personal satisfaction, we chose James Quinn. Though he had no previous experience of the film industry, he fully justified our choice and the new National Film Theatre at the end of Waterloo Bridge was completed in 1954. Among my colleagues were two representatives of the industry (Sir Henry French and Frank Hoare), but others had the same kind of amateur status as myself—Angus Maude, for instance, and Mrs J. B. Priestley—and it was a particular pleasure to me when George Barnes, then in charge of B.B.C. television, joined the board.

I remained chairman for four years, but before the end of that time the Board of Trade returned to the attack and, in response to a persuasive letter from Frank Lee, I became in 1954 chairman of the Cinematograph Films Council, the statutory body which advises the Board of Trade on all matters relating to the film industry. Producers, renters, exhibitors, and the trades unions are all represented on it, together with five independent members. In the latter group Sir Arnold Plant and Mrs Eirene White were notably valuable and among the trade members I found several old friends with whom I had served on the Gater working-party —John Davis, Frank Hoare, Tom O'Brien, George Elvin.

Gerald Croasdell, secretary of Equity, who came on later, I had known well as a Pembroke undergraduate.

It was not always an easy body to handle. Clashes of interest were inevitable, not so much between employers and employees as between the different sections of the industry and more than once I found myself compelled to give a chairman's vote. But on one subject, at least, there was for many years complete unanimity —the iniquity of the retention of the Entertainments Duty. Early in 1958 I led a deputation to the President of the Board of Trade (David Eccles), but the duty was not removed until 1960.

One feature, now a basic feature, of the industry was new to me—the production levy. Originally it had been a voluntary scheme invented by Sir William Eady under which exhibitors contributed a percentage of their takings towards the cost of producing new films. I remember meeting Eady once at Jesus College, of which he was an Honorary Fellow, and hearing how he had first worked out the plan with Sir Stafford Cripps. By 1954 the levy had become statutory, but old hands in the trade still referred to it as 'Eady money'. As I sat listening to arguments about the conditions of supply of films to exhibitors, I was often struck by analogies between film-production and book-publishing. But the levy was something without parallel; I found it difficult to imagine booksellers making a grant out of their takings to enable publishers to produce yet more books.

One of the duties of the Council each year was to recommend the quota of British films required of exhibitors. Every year a minority used to press for an increase, but the quota has remained at 30 per cent for many years past. To prescribe is easier than to enforce and I spent a considerable time in the chair of two committees which considered claims to relief in a variety of circumstances.

My original appointment was for three years, but it was extended to ten years in all and during the last two of them my heaviest piece of work was the chairmanship of a committee to consider the allegation made by a group of cinema-owners of the 'excessive degree of dominance' acquired by the two large cinema circuits, Rank and A.B.C. In April 1964 we produced a lengthy report which was presented to Parliament; later, the President of the Board of Trade (Edward Heath) referred the whole problem to the Monopolies Commission.

Looking back, I still regard my sixteen years' association with the film industry with some surprise. I can remember the primitive cinemas of the early years of the century very clearly, but I have never been an ardent film-goer. The nearer a film approaches to a stage-play, the better I like it, for I have little appreciation of the finer points of lighting and photography.

During the Gater inquiry into film costs I used often to argue that a good script and good acting were far more important than elaborate scenery, expensive properties and technical perfection in photography. In reply, one question was always put to me:

'How often do you go to the cinema?'

'Once a month perhaps, or rather less.'

'Exactly. But we depend on our regular clients and they are not going to be satisfied with the quiet presentation of an interesting play. What they want is colour, romance, excitement, violence.'

This contrast has, of course, been thrown into high relief by the spread of television. As we said in the last Report with which I was concerned:

The arts of the cinema and television are, of course, quite distinct. But to most people the distinction is a nice one and a preference for the cinema is frequently outweighed by the convenience of television ...Today the cinema must offer something which television does not provide.

Hence come the vast panoramic spectacles which, at great expense, are now offered to the public.

My association with films was odd and unexpected. Libraries, on the other hand, were a natural and congenial field of activity. I first served on the Library Syndicate at Cambridge in 1924, and with one short break remained a member until my retirement in 1958. In the early days and long before the expansion of Treasury grants to universities, by far the most urgent problem was the need of a larger building and I have already referred to the major part played by Hugh Anderson in securing the vital help of the Rockefeller Foundation. It is also worth recalling that at one point there was a shortage in the amount which the University was due to contribute under the conditions laid down by the Foundation and that in 1930 the Syndics of the Press guaranteed to fill the gap which was then estimated at about £12,000. This was announced by Stanley Baldwin in his first speech in the Senate House as Chancellor, but in the end only half the amount was required.

Looking back today, one may well be astonished not only at the inadequacy of the old building, but at the measure of efficiency which, thanks to the devoted labours of Jenkinson, Scholfield, Sayle, Bartholomew and others, the old library was able to achieve. In those days the general catalogue was housed in a room replete with history. Built over the old divinity school, it served originally both as chapel and senate-house; as the library expanded and absorbed all the buildings of the old schools, it became the catalogue-room; today it is the University Combination Room, which I formally opened as Vice-Chancellor in 1951.

The old library was not designed to attract undergraduates. It contained only one very small reading-room (Room Θ) in which senior members of the University could consult reserved books and manuscripts. My first visit to the room prompted me to an imitation:

> Much had I wandered, in the halcyon days,
>> By that grave pile, where senator decrees
>> His will, and past the comely gate of Caius
> Further I strayed in architectural maze.
> Oft had I heard of labyrinthine ways,
>> Where men of learning delve in lettered lore.
>> Yet, fearing, dared I not appear before

The turning barriers and attendants' gaze.
Then once a rare citation baffled wit,
   And I was fain to track th' elusive metre:
So plied I catalogues in search of it,
   And coursed through Cockerell's realm like some defeater
Of foes long hunted—until now I sit
   Silent, within a room that men call Theta.*

I was not a member of the committee which dealt with plans for the new library, but I remember our initial astonishment at the size of the reading-room. It was in this room that King George V opened the building in 1934 and referred to it as 'a power-house of learning'. Delegates from many other universities were invited to the ceremony and Ernest de Selincourt, representing the University of Birmingham, stayed with me. The guests were entertained at dinner by King's College and in a corner of the crowded combination room I espied General Smuts. I reminded him of our meeting in London at the Press exhibition in 1931 and presented de Selincourt to him. 'de Selincourt?' he repeated, 'ah—Wordsworth. I'm so glad to meet you.' It was a brilliantly quick recognition and gave de Selincourt great pleasure.

In the old days the Library Syndicate met, under the chairmanship of Peter Giles, in the tall brick building (now demolished) in St Andrew's Street. In the new library, provision had been made for a Syndicate Room and in 1946 I was nominated by the Vice-Chancellor as his deputy in the chair. My old friend A. F. Scholfield retired in 1949 and was succeeded by H. R. Creswick, the only man who has held the office of Librarian both in Oxford and in Cambridge. During my last years as chairman it was significant that the Librarian was pressing strongly for an extension of the building. In 1934 it had been approximately calculated that the shelf-room provided would last for fifty years; in 1958 it became clear that thirty years would have been a more realistic estimate. Towards the end of my time the formation of a separate

---

* *Cambridge Review*, 18 June 1912.

library for the natural sciences was suggested, but the proposals, as formally presented, were severely criticised and alternative schemes have now been adopted.

In 1946 I found myself concerned with another library. Sir Montagu Butler persuaded me to be nominated as a university member of the Borough Council, and promised that he would put my name down for one committee only—the Library Committee. On this I was glad to serve and when David Hardman, the chairman, left to be parliamentary secretary in the Ministry of Education, I was elected in his place. In 1949 I was obliged, as Vice-Chancellor-elect, to resign, but not before I had taken part in the appointment of W. A. Munford as Borough Librarian. Munford is the recognised historian of the public library movement and I suspect that it was through his influence that I was invited to be president of the Library Association in 1953.

It is the practice of the Association to have a professional librarian and someone from outside as president in alternate years. 'I see', said the late William Temple when the invitation came to him, 'you alternate between the competent and the notorious.' The duties of the president are comparatively light, but at least he must deliver a presidential address and take the chair at the annual general meeting of the Association. This I did at Llandudno in 1953 and found that the conduct of the annual meeting was far from being a sinecure.

A change of rules, requiring a two-thirds majority, was proposed and after a long discussion was put to the vote. A show of hands revealed a majority, but not a sufficiently large one. 'Ladies and gentlemen,' I said, 'you have achieved the *status quo*.' Whereupon one of the members leapt to his feet and demanded a ballot. Rightly or wrongly, I agreed that a fresh vote should be taken and slips of paper were distributed by the stewards. One man stood up and complained that he had been given two such slips, and asked what he was to do. 'Well,' I said, 'you *look* honest.' Tension was relieved and the motion for change was eventually carried.

Meetings apart, I enjoyed Llandudno. The earliest seaside holiday I could remember had been spent there in the days when nigger minstrels provided unsophisticated entertainment in the Happy Valley. I had a round of golf with Frank Francis and my wife and I paid a visit to Brynbella, the house in the valley of the Clwyd built by Mrs Piozzi. More than twenty years before I had stayed there with the two Miss Glynns and it was pleasing to find it in the possession of Mr and Mrs Glazebrook, whose four sons I knew as undergraduates at Pembroke.

I was succeeded in the presidency by C. B. Oldman of the British Museum and felt that my activity in the public library world was at an end. But in 1957 I was asked by the Minister of Education (Lord Hailsham) to be chairman of a committee 'to consider the structure of the public library service in England and Wales, and to advise what changes, if any, should be made in the administrative arrangements...'

By the time of our first meeting Geoffrey Lloyd, whom I had known when he was President of the Union at Cambridge, had become Minister of Education and it soon became clear that our main task was to reconcile the claims of the smaller boroughs and urban district councils to autonomy with the demand of the counties and county boroughs that they alone should be qualified to act as library authorities. The committee had been carefully chosen to include representatives of large and small bodies of local government; of education authorities; and of public libraries. Both sides presented their arguments with considerable force: the Association of Municipal Corporations, for instance, maintained that public opinion was the right and proper measure to establish a criterion of library efficiency. 'In other words', I said to one witness, 'good government is no substitute for self-government.' 'Exactly', he replied. Personally, I had a good deal of sympathy with the smaller authorities, but we were not prepared to give *carte blanche* to every local council and, in general, we accepted the view of the Library Association that the criterion of autonomy should be the expenditure of not less than £5,000 a year on books. This meant, in effect, that a library serving an area with a population of less than 40,000 would become a branch of the county library.

Apart from this controversial issue, we were able to make other recommendations on which there was general agreement and, in particular, that it should be a statutory duty, and not merely an option, of a local authority to provide an efficient library service.

Our Report was published in February 1959 and at the annual meeting of the Library Association at Torquay in September, I delivered what was in effect an apologia for the 'Roberts Report'. It was fiercely criticised by some representatives of small authorities, but on the whole it had a good reception. The president of the Association for the year was Lord Attlee and in parenthesis I recall a characteristic remark of his: 'People often ask me', he said, 'how I get on at press conferences. Well, reporters gather round me and ask me a lot of questions. I answer "Yes" or "No".'

After the general election Geoffrey Lloyd was succeeded as Minister of Education by Sir David (now Lord) Eccles, to whom as President of the Board of Trade I had earlier led a deputation about cinema entertainments duty. I now expressed the hope that he would in due course act upon the Library Report. The 'due course' involved the appointment by the minister of two working-parties to study its implications and a long delay seemed inevitable. However, in the spring of 1964, by which time there was yet another new Minister of Education (Sir Edward Boyle), a Bill was introduced in the House of Commons and a Public Libraries and Museums Act received the royal assent in July. With some concessions to the smaller library authorities it embodied the main recommendations of the Report. The Library Association was, I think, reasonably satisfied with the Act in its final form and did me the honour of making me an honorary fellow. I was also pleased in 1961 to be invited to give the first Arundell Esdaile Memorial Lecture, jointly sponsored by the English Association and the Library Association. Esdaile and I had been good friends for more than forty years and I chose for my subject Richard Farmer, a great bookman and a notable figure in eighteenth-century Cambridge.

One consequence of the publicity given to the Roberts Report was a number of invitations to open new, or extended, libraries. This led me to Letchworth, Stafford and St Austell, but the ceremony that gave me especial pleasure was the formal opening of the university library at Keele. The Vice-Chancellor, Harold Taylor, whom I had known well at Cambridge, invited my wife and me to stay with him and it was a joy to open a library of which the foundation had been the particular care of my old friend and colleague, George Barnes.

Chapter 20

EMERITUS

In the world of today it is notorious that retirement is not synonymous with leisure. Age debars me from serving on university committees, but there is one institution whose fortunes I watch with continued interest, and that is Fitzwilliam House. I was succeeded in the chairmanship of the Non-Collegiate Board by the President of Queens' (A. Ll. Armitage) and, thanks to his efforts and to those of the newly appointed Censor, progress was remarkably rapid. Not only was the first stage of the new building completed in 1963, but the University went ahead with unusual speed and approved the election of Fellows in anticipation of the grant of collegiate status. In particular, the election of W. S. Thatcher as the first Honorary Fellow was a fitting recognition of his long, and frequently frustrated, labours for Fitzwilliam House.

Outside the University there are many bodies which set no age limit upon their members and among them are governing bodies of schools. I joined the Brighton College Council in 1933 and, although my record of attendance is patchy, I hope I have been of some use especially in the appointment, from time to time, of a headmaster and in the editing of a history of the school, published in 1957. As Master of Pembroke, I was also asked to be a governor of two schools which had old associations with the college—Framlingham and Ipswich. Finding it difficult to do justice to three schools, I resigned from Ipswich after a few years; but since the Master and Fellows of Pembroke have been lords of the manor of Framlingham since the seventeenth century, I retain my place on the governing body of the school. The chairman, when I first joined, was the late Andrew Vanneck, in whose beautiful house, Heveningham Hall, I frequently stayed. Apart from Andrew's friendship, which I highly valued, the house had a particular interest for me, since it was visited, and accurately described, by the young François de la Rochefoucauld whose *Mélanges sur l'Angleterre* I had translated and published in 1933.

I am by this time the senior British member of the Fulbright Commission and I enjoy the meetings once or twice a year of the Birthplace trustees at Stratford-upon-Avon and of the trustees of the Barber Institute at Birmingham. I suppose it was experience of chairmanship that led to invitations to preside over the Gabbitas-Thring Trust and the Cambridge and District Trustee Savings Bank. I do not pretend that these new commitments involve heavy duties, but I rather enjoy the look of puzzled incredulity on the face of an American friend when I tell him that I am a bank president.

In 1959 we were particularly pleased to welcome Lefty Lewis at the Loke House. Earlier in the year we had been distressed to hear of the death of his wife, Annie Burr, in whose quiet and queenly personality the serenity of life at Farmington was centred. It was a heavy blow for Lefty to bear and we were glad to find him more cheerful when, three years later, he stayed with us for the conferment of his honorary degree.

In the early years of my retirement I had some pleasant and unexpected opportunities of foreign travel. In 1960 my wife and I had a fortnight in Holland under the auspices of the Anglo-Dutch Society. From Groningen in the north to Tilburg in the south I gave talks to branches of the Society either on Cambridge or on Dr Johnson, and it was all very friendly and informal. At one lunch-party we met our Ambassador, Sir Paul Mason, and I think I surprised him when I recalled that our previous meeting had been at the old Lodge in Pembroke, when he was a very small boy crawling about on the drawing-room floor.

In the autumn of 1961 I made two visits to America. To the first of these I have already briefly referred; the second was in response to an invitation from Brown University, Providence, which has a close link with Pembroke since the founder of Rhode Island,

Roger Williams, was a Pembroke man. The women's college which was incorporated into the university in the nineteenth century was given the name of Pembroke, and when in November 1961 a new Dean of the college was to be formally admitted, I was invited to take part in the ceremony. President Keeney, who combines medieval scholarship with a breezy vernacular forthrightness, made me feel at home at once and I received the honorary degree of L.H.D. from the university. I was also bidden to lunch with the Dancing Men of Providence, the local Sherlock Holmes society. Notwithstanding their title, they were a very sedate party.

Soon after my return my old friend Arthur Arberry, Professor of Arabic, told me that I would shortly receive an invitation to go to Teheran. I had difficulty in believing him, until he explained that the centenary of E. G. Browne's birth would be celebrated in the following February and that the Persians wanted someone to talk about him.

'But what's the good of me?', I asked, 'I don't know a word of Persian or Arabic.'

'That may be,' he replied, 'but you knew Johnny Browne.' Which, of course, was true, though it had not been intimate knowledge. In due course a formal invitation came from the British Institute of Persian Studies, together with a request from the British Council that I would visit their representatives in Persia. So on 17 February my wife and I boarded a Comet and, after touching down at Frankfurt and Istanbul, reached Teheran in the evening. How different from the journey made by Browne, who in 1887 went by sea to Trebizond and then took the old caravan road through Erzerum and Tabriz to Teheran—a journey of seven weeks in all. For my commemorative talk, which I first gave at the British Institute, I relied heavily on *A Year amongst the Persians*, adding a few reminiscences of my own. At the end I was thanked by Sayyid Hasan Taqizadeh, formerly Persian Ambassador in London. He had known Browne in 1905 and spoke very movingly of him.

255

On the following day we were invited to lunch at the British Embassy and in the dining-room Sir Geoffrey Harrison showed us a silver plaque of more than usual interest. Engraved on it was the table-plan of the dinner at which Churchill, Roosevelt and Stalin met in 1943.

We were unfortunately just too early for the Persian spring flowers and I could not help wishing that Browne had been born a month or two later. Even so, the weather was pleasant enough for a picnic in the foothills of the Elburz mountains with Hazel Roberts (daughter of my old friend 'B.C.'), who was then on the staff of the Embassy.

Our first expedition was to Meshed in the north-east, near the frontiers of Russia and Afghanistan. A railway journey of eighteen hours through desert country can be monotonous, but there was a fairly good dining-car available, though the only drink provided was coca-cola. However, we were well rewarded in the end. We were the guests of the British Council representative (Mervyn Jones), who made us extremely comfortable at the old British Consulate, a splendid relic of imperial days. There, after paying a state visit to the Governor of Khorassan, I said my piece about Browne to a keenly responsive audience.

Meshed is the holiest place in Persia, and the shrine of Reza, the eighth Imam, attracts a constant stream of pilgrims. Contemplating the mixture of races in the bazaar and watching our hostess haggle, on my behalf, for the purchase of a turquoise bracelet, I felt that we were really getting a glimpse of Asia.

Our next journey was to the south. We had a comfortable two-hour flight to Shiraz and so missed the thrill that provoked Browne's lyrical outburst when he first gazed upon Shiraz from the gate of Allahu Akbar. After a visit to the beautiful little Anglican church we drove out to see the splendours of Persepolis. Unfortunately, it was the one cold and rainy day in the fortnight; but I was quickly reproved for grumbling about the rain. The country and the people were in desperate need of it.

Emeritus

From Shiraz we drove in a Land Rover first to the Tomb of Cyrus and Pasagardae and then to Isfahan, where the bridges and the Maidan, with its turquoise domes and its relics of ancient polo, fully justified guide-book enthusiasm. Near the bridge of the thirty-three arches it was a surprise to see carpets, large and small, being washed in the river. At Isfahan, as at Shiraz, my talk on Browne was given at the university and the theme of the votes of thanks was constant: 'What Byron was to Greece, Browne was to Persia.' From Isfahan, after lunch with the Anglican bishop (himself a Persian and an old member of Ridley Hall), we returned to Teheran for one night and then flew home. So ended a fascinating fortnight.

Anyone like myself, who has known Cambridge for sixty years, is frequently asked for his views on the changes that have occurred in that time. Wistfully, of course, one looks back to the comparative quietude of the days when there were 3,000 undergraduates instead of 9,000 and there were half-a-dozen colleges with cosy little communities of less than 100 men; when the normal forms of transport were a hansom-cab or a one-horse tram; when undergraduates wore caps as well as gowns and there were special clips to accommodate them in the cloak-room of the old 'New Theatre', which is now demolished; when there were cheerful pass-men about the streets who did not worry overmuch about examinations; when vacations, or at least parts of them, were truly vacations and were not so continuously invaded by summer schools and conferences as well as by gigantic coachloads of tourists. In 1912 I wrote some lines (imitative as all my verses are) on 'Cambridge in September':

> ...They came unto a town
> Where it seemed always Thursday afternoon.
> Adown the street the languid tram did glide,
> Swaying like one that hath an empty life,
> And at the college gate the porter lone
> Would idly gaze, as downward in the court
> Slow-dropping leaves on primmest lawn did fall;

Emeritus

> While others through the corridor did bear
> The furniture of yester-term afar.
> In autumn stillness stood the royal fane—
> Four silent pinnacles and silent, too,
> The organ thunder. By the Senate House
> The fareless Jehus sleep—no more to roam.

But beneath such sentimental nostalgia is the recognition that since 1914 the University has become a national institution in a much wider sense than before. The rapid expansion of scientific knowledge in the last fifty years has led to the emergence of entirely new subjects of academic study, requiring new professors, new laboratories, new equipment of research; and to meet the cost of such equipment the ancient endowments of the university are quite inadequate. So Cambridge, like every other university, is now heavily subsidised by a Treasury grant. Furthermore, the Ministry of Education pays the fees, in whole or in part, of a large proportion of undergraduates, once they have been accepted by a college as suitable candidates for an honours degree. Hence the disappearance of the pass-man, the growth in total numbers, and the particularly large increase of those engaged in post-graduate research.

More than 400 years ago Roger Ascham complained that there were too many rich men's sons in the University, young men who aimed not at proficiency in learning (*perfecta eruditio*), but at the more superficial knowledge (*levis et inchoata cognitio*) which would qualify them for public service. Today the problem is in reverse and many old Cambridge men protest that colleges are in danger of becoming intellectual forcing-houses instead of being training-grounds of character and leadership. It is an ancient antithesis, much favoured by speakers at school speech days, and during my ten years as Master of Pembroke I was frequently concerned with attempts to resolve it. Since that time much has been done to rationalise the problem of university admissions, and I believe that there is sufficient strength and resilience in the colleges to enable them to meet the new conditions without impairing the unique advantages which they bring to university life.

Although for the greater part of my working life I served in a university institution, I had the good fortune to remain always in close touch with my college and in this context I believe it to be not impossible to serve two masters. I, for one, have been happy in my dual allegiance.

INDEX

A.D.C., Cambridge, 8, 146, 204
Abbey House, Cambridge, 6
Abinger, 234
Acton, Lord, 111, 112
Adam, R. B., and Mrs, 91–2
Adams, A. V., 18
Adams, J. Couch, 29
Adcock, Sir F. E., 112
Adventures among Books (Lang), 1
After Many Years (Heitland), 51–2
Age and Youth (Barker), 123
Air Ministry, 179
Air Squadron, Cambridge University, 190
Albery, Charles, 147
Alexandria, 200
All Souls College, Oxford, 153
Allen, Sir Hugh, 76–7
Allhusen, Mr and Mrs, 43–4
Alumni Cantabrigienses, 121–2, 171
Amabel and Mary Verena (Hicks-Beach), 157
Amenities of Book-collecting, The (Newton), 93
America, *see* United States
American History, professorship of, 173–4
American Studies, British Association of, 191
American Universities, Association of, 216
Ancient History, Cambridge, 111–12
Anderson, Sir H. K., 21, 60–2, 63, 65, 74, 113, 153, 247
Andrewes, Lancelot, 191
Androcles and the Lion, 34
Anecdotes of the late Samuel Johnson (Piozzi), 90, 91
Anglo-Dutch Society, 254
Ankara, 218
Ann Arbor, 208, 216
Annan, N. G. [Lord], 195
Aphasia (Head), 136
Apple a Day, An (Gosse), 178
Appleton, Sir Edward, 132

Aquitania, S.S., 148–9, 162
Arabia Deserta (Doughty), 28, 77
Arberry, A. J., 255
'Arcades, The', 75
Archer, H. K., 151
Archer-Shee, Col. M., 162
Armistice Day (1918), 43–4
Armitage, A. Ll., 253
Arnold, Edward, 148
Art of Writing, On the (Quiller-Couch), 55
Arundel Castle, 143–4
Arundell Esdaile Lecture, 251–2
Ascham, Roger, 258
Ashcroft, Dame Peggy, 206
Ashridge, 116
Aspects of Biography (Maurois; trans. Roberts), 78
Assizes, Cambridge, 189
Aston, Molly, 97
Astor, Viscountess, 154
Astronomy and Cosmogony (Jeans), 103
Athenaeum Club, 109, 130, 133, 172, 221, 238
Athens, 200–1
Atkins, J. B., 17, 167
Attenborough, F. L., 54
Attlee, C. R. [Earl], 181, 251
Attwater, A. L., 31, 54, 82–3, 84, 90, 119, 127, 136, 166, 210
Austen-Leigh, R. A., 65
Authors' Society, 158

B.B.C., 79, 105, 224–5, 244
Baker Street, No. 221 B, 230–1
'Baker Street Irregulars', 229, 232
Baker Street Studies (Bell), 229
Baldwin, Canon, 130–1
Baldwin, Stanley [Earl], 96, 247
Balerno, 130, 131
Balfour, A. J. [Earl of], 13
Balfour, R. E., 148, 149
Ballantyne Press, 65
Balliol College, Oxford, 84, 97; A. Lang on, 2

260

Index

Balston, T., 70
Bannerman, D. A., 27, 41
Barber Trustees, 254
Barker, Sir Ernest, 123
Barlone, D., 181–2
Barlow, Sir Thomas, 175
Barnes, Sir George, 79, 144, 244, 252
Barrie, Sir J. M., 96
Bartholomew, A. T., 32, 45, 52, 247
Bata, 174
Bateson, F. W., 171
Baugniet, J., 218
Bedell Smith, Gen. W., 209
Beerbohm, Elisabeth, 238, 239, 240
Beerbohm, Florence, 236, 238
Beerbohm, Sir Max, 84, 121, 158, 210, 234; first meeting with, 236; letters from, 235–6, 239, 240; Rede Lecture, 236–7; visits to, 237–40; memorial addresses on, 240–1
Beerbohm, [Sir Max], Man and Writer (Riewald), 240
Beeton's Christmas Annual, 152
Beggar's Opera, The (Kidson), 58
Behrman, S., 240
Belinda, 145
Bell, G., & Sons, 115
Bell, H. W., 228, 229, 230
Belloc, Hilaire, 9, 116
Belmont Park, Long Island, 223
Benians, E. A., 113–14, 173
Benn Bros. 172
Bennett, Arnold, 64, 78
Bennett, H. S., 45, 111, 117, 119, 187
Bennett, Joan, 119
Benson, A. C., 4, 26, 58
Benson, R. H., 117
Bentley House, 163
Berkeley College, U.S.A., 164
Bernard, J. H., 95
best seller, the real, 110
Bethune-Baker, J. F., 31, 70, 77, 82, 185, 187, 211–12
Beves, D. H., 144–5, 146
bibles and prayer-books, *see* specific titles (e.g. *Children's Bible, New English Bible, Revised Prayer-book*); *also under* Cambridge University Press
Bibliographical Society, 68

Bibliography of English Literature, Cambridge, 171
Bibliotheca Britannica (Watt), 171
Bickers, G., 115
Birkett, Norman [Lord], 11, 14
Birley, Oswald, 108
Birmingham University, 248
Birrell, Augustine, 96
Birtwistle, G., 32, 86–7
Blake, William, 73
Blakeney, T. S., 228
Blore, Edward, 5
Blunden, Edmund, 155, 156
'blurbs', publishers', 140
Board [Ministry] of Education, 17, 19, 20, 190, 250, 251, 258
Board of Trade, 170, 242, 244, 245, 246; regional representative of, 174–6, 242
Bond, Henry, 22
Book Society, 157
book-jackets, 141, 157
booksellers, publishers' relations with, 24, 135
Booksellers' Association, 186–7
Boston, Mass., 76, 91, 162, 223, 229
Boswell, Alexander, 225
Boswell, James, 120, 149, 177, 224; lecturing on, 208; *Letters* (ed. Tinker), 95; *Life of Johnson*, 42, 224, 232; Malahide documents, 95, 98, 99, 225; *Tour to Corsica*, 90
Boswell, Robert, 225
Boulogne, 39
Bowes, Robert, 47
Boyle, Sir E., 251
Boys and Girls of History (R. Power), 119
Boys Smith, J. S., 201
Bradfield College, 2
Bradley, Gen. Omar, 202–3, 209
Braunholtz, G. E. K., 19
Brett, G. P. sen., 74, 75, 80–1, 162
Brett, G. P. jun., 164
Bridges, Robert, 27
Brighton College, 11, 17; alumni, 85, 136, 208, 223; governing body, 144, 243, 253
Brighton College Magazine, 1–2
British Academy, 4, 118
British Association, 161

Index

Cavendish Club, 129, 135
Cecil, Algernon, 113
Cecil, Lord Hugh [Viscount Quickswood], 146
Chadwick, H. M., 53–4
Chancellor of Cambridge, election of, 194–7
Chapman, Arthur (kitchen manager), 6–7, 93, 167
Chapman, R. W., 75, 76, 90, 96, 97, 99, 153, 224
Chapman & Hall, 26
Chard, Joan [Lady Harwood], 143
Charnwood, Lord and Lady, 90, 97, 223
Chatham House, 79
Chatsworth, 14
Chaucer Road, Cambridge, 168, 178, 181–2
Cheng, J. C., 192
Cherry Orchard, The, 147
Chesterton, G. K., 32–3
Chicago, 216; University Press, 76
Child, Harold, 104, 127, 133–4, 147, 164, 236; letter, 134
Children's Bible, The, 70–1, 148
Christian, Fletcher and Edward, 157
Christian Morals (Browne; ed. Roberts), 77–8
Christmas Garland, A (Beerbohm), addendum to, 238
Churchill, Sir Winston, 167, 199, 239, 256
Cincinatti, 26, 76
Cinematograph Films Council, 244–6
circuits, cinema, 246
Clair, Réné, 243
Clapham, Sir J. H., 116, 118, 119, 173
Clapham, Michael, 116
Clark, Sir G. N., 183
Clark Lectures, 74, 78, 130, 136, 236
Classical Review, 125
Classical Society, Cambridge, 50, 148
Classical Tripos, 7, 12, 13
Clay, C. F., 34
Clay, John, 22, 45
Clayton, [Abp.] G. H., 10
Clifford, J. L., 222
Cloister Press, 65, 66
Cockerell, Sir S. C., 45, 154

Coghill, E. J. N. T., 209
Collins, William, 92
Columbia University, 215, 216–17
Combe, T., 226
Comber, H. G., 6, 31, 35, 39, 41, 84, 85, 86, 94, 98, 166, 167
Combination Room, University, 190, 247
Conant, J. B., 208
Concordance to the Poems of Spenser (Osgood), 94
Cook, A. B., 54–5
Cook, S. A., 112
Cooper, Duff [Lord Norwich], 184
copyright suit, 151–2
Corpus Christi College, Cambridge, 1, 47
Corsica, Tour to (Boswell), 90
Cotswold Family, A (Hicks-Beach), 157
Coulton, G. G., 53, 116–18
Coulton, Mary, 118
County Geographies, Cambridge, 26–7, 28, 29
coxing on the Cam, 8, 192
Cranmer Hall, 145
Cranmer Road, Cambridge, 123
'Creeping Men, The' (Cleveland, U.S.A.), 229
Creswick, H. R., 248
Cricket Match, The (de Selincourt), 134
Cripps, Sir Stafford, 245
Criterion Miscellany, The, 228
Croasdell, G., 245
Cromer, 36–7
Crowden, J., 202
Crutchley, Brooke, 79–80, 183
Cumberlege, Geoffrey, 232
'Current Problems' Series, 123
Curtis, Lionel, 153
Cyclops, The (Euripides), 11

Daily Graphic, 17
Daily Mirror, 243
Dale, G., 177
Dalton, Hugh [Lord], 242
'Dancing Men', The (Providence, R.I.), 229, 255
Darwin, Bernard, 182, 193, 231
Darwin Centenary, 13

263

Index

Davenport College, U.S.A., 162
David, G. (Cambridge bookseller), 90, 148, 150, 225
David, R. W., 79, 183
Davidson, John, 238
Davies, H. B., 31
Davis, John, 244
Dawks, I., 69
Deanesly, Margaret, 117
Decline and Fall of the Romantic Ideal (Lucas), 124
Degree ceremonies at Cambridge: B.A., 13; Honorary, 188, 191-2, 202-3, 204
De la Mare, W., 69, 135, 137-9; lines by, 138
'demarcation', 242-3
Dent, Alan, 137
Dent, E. J., 144
Devonshire, 10th Duke of, 193
Devotions (Donne), 73
Dewey, M. B., 180
Diary of a Visit to England in 1775 (Campbell), 222
Dick, Sir Alexander, 132
Dickinson, G. Lowes, 16
Discovery, 172-3
'Discussions' in Senate, 48-50, 188
Dixon, Sir Pierson, 83, 88, 216
Doctor Johnson in Cambridge (Roberts), 90
Doctor Watson: prolegomena... (Roberts), 228
Dodd, William, 96
Dodds, Harold, 209, 215, 216
Dodds, Margaret, 209, 215
Dolly Dialogues (Hope), 99
Donald, Coutts, 242
Donegall, 6th Marquis of, 232
Donne, John, 73
Dorking, 103, 105
Double Crown Club, 68-70, 137
Dover Road, The, 144, 147
Downs, B. W., 53
Doyle, Sir A. Conan, 227, 231, 232
Drapers' Company, 167, 191, 218-19
Drinkwater, John, 135
Duckworth's 'Great Lives' Series, 224
Duncan, Sir Andrew, 174, 175
Duncan, G. S., 192
Dykes, Brig. V., 182, 209

Eady, Sir William, 245
Earl Percy dines abroad (Murdock), 92
Early Victorian Cambridge (Winstanley), 122
Eastbourne College, 78, 165
Eccles, David [Lord], 245, 251
Economic History of Europe, Cambridge, 119, 171
Economic History of Modern Britain (Clapham), 116
Eddington, Sir A. S., 102-3
Edinburgh Review, 222
Edinburgh University, 129, 132, 136, 213
editing, early experience of, 1-2, 12
Education, Cambridge Institute of, 190
Edward VII, King, 158
Edwards, F. M., 177, 225
Edwards, H. J., 5
Edwards, J. K. O'N. ('Jimmy'), 213
Egypt, 199-200
Eight Victorian Poets (Lucas), 124
Eighteen-Eighties, The (ed. de la Mare), 137
Eighteen-Seventies, The (ed. Granville-Barker), 135-6
Einstein, Albert, 164
Eliot, George, 29
Eliot, T. S., 137
Elizabeth I, Queen, 219
Elizabeth II, Queen, 213
Elizabeth, Queen [Mother], 188, 202, 213, 216, 217, 219-20
Elkin Matthews, 96
Ellis, C. D., 107
Elvin, George, 244
Encyclopaedia Britannica, 24-5, 50, 225
English, Faculty Board of, 177-8
English Association, 181, 251
English for the English (Sampson), 150-1
English Literature, Cambridge Bibliography of, 171
English Literature, Cambridge History of, 58, 111, 117-18, 133, 171; *Concise* (Sampson), 151
English Studies, Review of, 240
English Tripos, 53, 56, 83, 181; lecturing for, 54; examining for, 54-5, 83
entertainments tax, 245
Escape and Other Essays (A. C. Benson), 26

264

Index

Index

Index

Longmans, 115, 119, 120
Lowe, D. G. A., 83
Lowe, [Very Rev.] John, 200
Lowell, A. L., 76
Lowinsky, T., 69
Lucas, F. L., 54, 124
Lunt, Stanley and Michael, 182
Lyon, John and Thomas, 219
Lyons, Sir Henry and Lady, 172
Lytton Strachey (Beerbohm), 236–7

M.A. degree, 33
M.A. Platoon (1915), 36, 121
Macaulay, Dame Rose, 203
Macaulay, Lord, 119, 121, 222, 225
MacCarthy, Desmond, 228
MacDonald, Ramsay, 96
MacDonell, A. G., 229
MacGillivray, E. J., 151
MacKinnon, Sir Frank, 96, 171–2
McLaren, Moray, 105
MacLeish, Archibald, 173
MacLellan, G. D. S., 192
Macmillan, Sir Frederick, 47, 80
Macmillan Co. of New York, 74, 75, 76, 80–1, 101, 162, 163–4
MacMyn, D. J., 124
McNair, A. D. [Lord], 11
Macpherson, W. S., 223
McTaggart, J. E., 15, 16, 52
Madingley Hill, 9
Magdalene College, Cambridge, 4, 79
Makins, Sir Roger [Lord Sherfield], 217
Malahide Castle, 95, 225
Malleson, Miles, 11
Man, Isle of, 158, 168
Man on his Nature (Sherrington), 171
Manchester University Press, 183
Manilius: *Astronomica* (ed. Housman), 125
Mansbridge, F. R., 81, 162, 163, 186, 209
Mansfield Cooper, Sir W., 198
Marchand, Jean, 159–60
Margaret, Princess, 201
Marlborough College, 132, 210
Martin Makesure (Kendon), 141
'Martlets, The', *see under* Pembroke College
Mask and the Face, The, 144

Mason, A. J., 4–5, 13, 31, 42, 58, 185; sonnets by, 30
Mason, Alfred, 23
Mason, Sir Paul, 254
Mathematician's Apology, A (Hardy), 110
mathematics, higher, renounced, 1
Mathematics, Pure, Course of (Hardy), 110
Matthew, Theobald, 99–100
Maud, Sir John, 200
Maude, Angus, 244
Maugham, Lord, 151–2
Maurois, André, 78
'Maximilians', 236, 237
May Races, 1909 vintage, 12–13
Mead, E. W., 7, 10, 12, 14
Medieval History, Cambridge, 111, 114
Medieval Life and Thought, Cambridge Studies in, 117
Medieval Nunneries (Power), 118
Medieval People (Power), 118
Mélanges sur l'Angleterre (Rochefoucauld), 159, 254
Memories and Opinions (Quiller-Couch), 182
Merchant Taylors' Company, 190–1
Merchant Taylors' School, 122, 191
Meredith, George, 120, 121
Merton, Wilfred, 33
Merton College, Oxford: Andrew Lang on, 2; Beerbohm Memorial at, 241
Meshed, 256
Meunier, Oscar, 231
Meynell, Sir Francis, 70
Meynell, Gerard, 67, 68, 69
Michigan, University of, 208
Milford, Sir Humphrey, 75, 76
Milton, John, 73, 120, 121
Mind the Stop (Carey), 165
Ministry of Education, *see under* Board
Minns, Sir E. H., 15, 35, 87–8, 179, 187, 206, 212
Moberly, Sir Walter, 170
Modern English Usage (Fowler), 165
Modern History, Cambridge, 111, 122, 157, 183
Modern Symposium, A (Dickinson), 16
Monastic Order in England (Knowles), 171

269

Index

Monro, D. B., 2
Monte Carlo, 198
More Kin than Kind ('Fitzstephen'), 85
Moriarty, G. P., 84–6, 135
Moriarty, Louis, 86
Morison, Stanley, 65, 66–8, 69–70, 191
Morley, Christopher, 229
Morley, Frank, 228
Morning of Christ's Nativity, On the (Milton), 73
Morris, G. G., 47
Morris, Henry, 70
Moscow University, 218
Mottistone, Lord, *see* Seely, Gen. J.
Mountbatten, Earl of, 194, 195
Mozley, Col. E., 209
Mozley, J. K., 9, 11, 82, 209
Mr Pim Passes By, 144, 145
Mrs Warren's Profession, 135
Mullinger, J. B., 122
Mummy, The (Budge), 72
Munford, W. A., 249
Murdock, H., 76, 91
Murray, John, 172
Muse Enchained, The (Tillyard), 53
Myres, J. L., 75
Mysterious Universe, The (Jeans), 104

Nairne, Alexander, 70, 71, 211
Name and Nature of Poetry, The (Housman), 126–7
Napoleon of Notting Hill, The (Chesterton), 32
Nash, Paul, 69
National Film Theatre, 244
Nature of the Physical World, The (Eddington), 102, 103
Naughton and Gold, 149
Nehru, Jawaharlal, 195–6
Netherton Hall (Devon), 135
New English Bible, 141–2
New Haven, Conn., 76, 162, 164
New Quantum Mechanics (Birtwistle), 87
New Shakespeare, The, 46, 56–7, 128–33
New York, 75, 80, 119, 137, 162, 163–4, 186, 209, 216, 223, 228
New York Times, 173
Newport, R.I., 223
Newton, A. E., 93–4, 98
Newton, Mrs A. E., 93–4

Newton, A. P., 113–14
Nice, conference at, 197–9
Nicholas, T. C., 201
Nicholson, Jenny, 239
Nieuport, 39
Niobe, 133
Nobbs, F. G., 58
Non-Collegiate Students, *see* Fitzwilliam House
Norfolk, Duke of, 144
Norton, F. J., 171
Notes on the Cambridge Printers (Bowes), 47

O.T.C. service, 35–6
O'Brien, Sir Tom, 244
Observer, 147, 222
Oedipus Rex, 133
Officer Cadet Bn., No. 2, 42
Ogden, C. K., 15, 47
Old Mill House, Cambridge, 28–9
Oldman, C. B., 250
Olympic, S.S., 75
Oman, John, 66
On Circuit (MacKinnon), 171–2
Orange, Sir H., 19
Origins of the Thoroughbred Horse (Ridgeway), 50
Ornithology of Cyprus, The (Guillemard), 27
Osgood, C. G., 94–5, 164
Oxford, 162; Andrew Lang on, 2; Press, 24, 68, 76, 80, 153, 183
Oxford Book of English Prose, 103

pageants, acting in, 143–4
Paget, Gen. Sir Bernard, 116
Paget, Sidney, 227, 231, 232
Painter's Pilgrimage, A (Hartrick), 165
Paoli, Gen., 125
paperbacks, 46, 165
paper-rationing, 170–1, 183
Pares, Richard, 176
Paris, 132, 160; book exhibition, 183–4; British Institute, 137
Parry, R. St J., 49
Parsons, W. L. E., 17
Pascal, Roy, 83
Paton, Alan, 215
Paulton, Harry, 133

270

Index

Rackham, H., 49
Ramsay, A. B., 79
Rands, R. S. J., 39
Rank, J. A. [Lord], 242, 246
Rapallo, 217, 237–40
Raven, C. E., 10, 185, 188
Reddaway, W. F., 214
Rede Lecture, 104, 236–7
Rees, Sir Richard, 62–3
Reeve, Bishop A. S., 223
Registry, Cambridge, 47, 48
Reichmann, Eva, 241
Reid, J. S., 72
Religion in the Making (Whitehead), 102
Revised Prayer Book, 61–2
Revised Version of the Bible, 22, 34
revision of MSS., 25–6
Rhode Island, 254
Richard II (ed. Dover Wilson), 130
Richards, Grant, 125
Richmond, Sir Bruce, 133, 134
Ridgeway, Sir William, 47, 49, 50–1
Riewald, J. G., 240
Roberts, [Bishop] B. C., 8, 9–10, 13, 256
Roberts, Frank [father], 14, 17, 19, 227
Roberts, Hazel, 256
Roberts, Irene [1st wife], 33, 41, 42, 50, 70, 72, 94, 105, 161, 168, 203
Roberts, John [son], 127, 130, 135–6, 161, 181, 182
Roberts, Marjorie [2nd wife], 120, 158, 160, 168, 182, 183, 186, 192, 199, 202–9 *passim*, 215–23 *passim*, 234, 237, 239, 250–5 *passim*
Roberts, Mary [mother], 143, 227
Roberts, Molly [daughter], 128, 138, 169, 182
Roberts, Nan [daughter], 121, 138, 163–4
Roberts, Sir S. C.: Exhibitioner of Pembroke, 2; B.A., 13; Asst. Sec. Camb. Univ. Press, 19; M.A., 33; 1st marriage, 33; Sec. C.U.P. 59; Fellow of Pembroke, 88; 2nd marriage, 168; Master of Pembroke, 185; Vice-Chancellor of Cambridge, 188; hon. LL.D. (St And.), 192; retirement, 221; hon. L.H.D. (Brown, U.S.A.), 255
'Roberts Report', 250–1, 252

Robertson, Sir Brian [Lord], 191
Robertson, Sir D. H., 11
Robinson, Beverley, 148, 164
Robinson, Sir F. P., 11, 13
Rochefoucauld, François de la, 159–60, 254
Rockefeller Foundation, 61, 247
Rogers, Bruce, 45–6, 47, 56, 58, 75–6, 215, 228
Rogers, F. M., 199, 216
Rollins, Carl, 76, 215
Roosevelt, Theodore, 14
Rootham, C. B., 144
Rose, J. Holland, 113–14
Ross, Sir Denison, 77
Rothenstein, Sir J., 241
Rothenstein, W., 69
Rowe, J. W. F., 180, 184
Rowell, Mrs, 223
Royal Agricultural Show, 204
Royal Commission on Oxford and Cambridge (1921), 48, 60–1, 153
Royal Dublin Society, 233
Royal Societies Club, 161
Royal Society, *Proceedings*, etc., of, 162–3
Royal Society 1660–1940, The (Lyons), 172
Royal Society of Arts, 65
Royal Society of Literature, 135, 240
Royal Welch Fusiliers, 82, 210
Rudd, Mrs, 125
Rudge, W. E., 75
Ruskin, Selections from (ed. A. C. Benson), 58
Russell, Bertrand, 101
Russell, Geoffrey, 96
Rust, J. C., 31
Rutherford, Lady, 108
Rutherford, Lord, 107–8, 164
Ryle, J., 41
Ryskamp, C., 223

Saglam, T., 217
St Andrews, 192–3
St Edward's Church, Cambridge, 146, 213
Saintsbury, George, 55, 135
Salisbury, 5th Marquess of, 244
Salt, H. S., and Mrs, 154–5
Salthouse, 37–8

272

Index

Sampson, George, 150–2
Savage, H. E., 97
Saviour of the Navy, The (Bryant), 115
Sayers, Dorothy, 229, 230
Sayle, C. E., 32, 47, 247
Sayyid Hasan Taqizadeh, 255
Samuel, 1st Viscount, 191
Sandars Lectures, 87
Sarrailh, Jean, 198, 199, 217–18
Sassoon, Siegfried, 82, 210, 240
Scandal in Bohemia, The (Conan Doyle), 230
Schafberg, the, 107
Scholfield, A. F., 247, 248
schoolbooks, 29–30, 62, 70–1, 79, 119, 151–2
Science and the Modern World (Whitehead), 101
Scott, F. R. F., 79
Scott, Geoffrey, 98
Scythians and Greeks (Minns), 35, 87
Searle, Mrs C. E., 30
Searle, Ronald, 141
Seaton, A. A., 10, 82
Seatonian Prize, 140–1
Seely, Gen. J. [Lord Mottistone], 53
Selections from Hazlitt (ed. Sampson), 151–2
Selections from Ruskin (ed. A. C. Benson), 58
Selincourt, E. de, 248
Selincourt, H. de, 134
Senate, Cambridge: Council of, 49, 61, 173–4, 185, 188, 196, 197, 213, 214; 'Discussions' in, 48–50, 188
Sermons, University, 189
Seven Essays (Sampson), 152
Seward, Sir A. C., 22, 137, 161, 165, 172
Shakespeare, The Essential (Dover Wilson), 129
Shakespeare, The New, 46, 56–7, 128–33
Shakespeare Studies, Companion to, 84, 136
Shakespeare Survey, 183
Shakespeare's Happy Comedies (Dover Wilson), 130
Shakespeare's Workmanship (Quiller-Couch), 56
Shaw, G. Bernard, 32, 33, 154

Shaw, Mrs G. B., 154
She Stoops to Conquer, 95
Shelley, P. B., 3
Sheppard, H. R. L. ('Dick'), 230
Sheppard, Sir J. T., 146, 191–2
Sherfield, Lord, *see* Makins, Sir Roger
Sheringham, 39, 186
Sherlock Holmes and Dr Watson (Bell), 228
Sherlock Holmes: Fact or Fiction (Blakeney), 228
Sherlock Holmes Society, 229–32; *see also under* Holmes
Sherrington, Sir C. S., 171
Shipley, Sir A. E., 12, 23, 46, 114
Shiraz, 256–7
Shorter, Clement, 238
Shropshire Lad, A (Housman), 126, 238
Sidgwick, Frank, 68, 227
Sidgwick & Jackson, 136, 137
Simon, Oliver, 68
Sisson, Marshall, 210
Sitwell, Sir Osbert, 69
'Six Napoleons, The' (Baltimore, U.S.A.), 229
Slade, Julian, 204
Small Boy in the Sixties, A (Sturt), 64
Small Talk at Wreyland (Torr), 55
Small Years, The (Kendon), 139
Smart, Christopher, 140
Smart, W. M., 204
Smith, Edgar, W., 229
Smuts, Gen. [F.-M.], 161, 191, 192, 193, 248
Snow, C. P. [Lord], 172
Soglio, 105
Solda, 106, 107
'Solitary Cyclist, The' (Conan Doyle), 231
Somerset, Raglan, 10–11
Somerville, N.J., 223
Something Beyond (Webling), 155–6
Sonnets, Shakespeare's (ed. Dover Wilson), 133
Sorbonne, 226
Sorley, W. R., 22, 49, 62
Sparrow, John, 73
'Speckled Band, The' (Boston, Mass.), 229
Spectator, The, 17, 167, 239

273

Index

Index